Coping
With
Food
Allergy

**Revised
Edition**

Claude A. Frazier, M.D.

**Times
BOOKS**

To Lawson Duncan—an exceptional
friend and an exceptional tennis player

Library of Congress Cataloging in Publication Data

Frazier, Claude Albee, 1920–
  Coping with food allergy.

  Includes index.
  1. Food allergy.   2. Food allergy—Diet therapy—
Recipes.   I. Title.   [DNLM: 1. Food Hypersensitivity—
popular works.   WD 310 F848c]
RC596.F7   1985   616.97′5   84-40419
ISBN 0-8129-1149-0

Manufactured in the United States of America

9 8 7 6 5 4 3 2

First Edition

Acknowledgments

I would like to express my appreciation to the following people and organizations for their help in making this book a reality.

Mrs. Frieda K. Brown
Mrs. Nancy S. Burnette
Alberta Boyce Wall
Marion L. Conrad
Jerome Glaser, M.D.
Frederic Speer, M.D.
Stephen D. Lockey, Sr., M.D.
K. A. Baird, M.D.
Mrs. Kathleen Miller
Mrs. Hilary Clark
Albert Rowe, Jr., M.D.
Walter C. Alvarez, M.D.
John Miller, M.D.
Donald J. Dalessio, M.D.
Arthur J. Horesh, M.D.
Mr. Steve Lindstrom
Allergy Information Association
American Medical Association
Department of Health, Education, and Welfare
    Public Health Services

Contents

Foreword

The incidence of allergic diseases has increased significantly during the past twenty years. Many factors have contributed to the proliferation of allergic disorders, including a keener awareness of conditions that qualify as allergic, more sophisticated tools for diagnosing allergies, and, of paramount importance, newer methods of treatment.

One of the many areas of allergies that is still poorly understood is allergy to foods. Much remains to be done as regards diagnosis and treatment. For the patient with an immediate and threatening reaction to a specific food, for example, nuts, the diagnosis is apparent and the treatment is specific—avoid nuts. But for those patients whose symptoms are less than dramatic (symptoms may involve many body systems), the diagnosis is difficult and treatment is complex. Clinical sensitivity to one or more foods often originates from the degradation by-products of the foods and little or nothing is known of the precise chemical configuration of these breakdown products. Thus, skin tests with natural foods (not the breakdown products) is often less than reliable.

Claude Frazier is preeminently qualified to discuss the many ramifications of allergy to foods. As best as can be done in the light of present information, he has documented facts, not fancy, and, because of his keen insight into the problem, he has developed a sensible approach to the diagnosis and management of food allergy. For a patient who has a bonafide abnormal immune response to one or more foods, the author has also provided recipes and substitute food that are both nutritious and palatable.

Patients, or parents of children with food allergy, who want to know more about food allergy will find this a useful book. It is informative, enlightening, and rewarding.

Bernard A. Berman, M.D.
president,
American College of Allergists

Preface

Allergy is so strange a disease that a good many people are inclined to dismiss the complaints of the allergic disdainfully, perhaps with the comment, "It's all in your head." This can be disconcerting for the sufferer, and it is one of the purposes of this book to demonstrate that allergy is a disease with tangible symptoms. It can and does make a great many people thoroughly miserable, sometimes for a good part of their lives. Yet, allergy is probably not understood by the majority of people. Even physicians do not always understand the role it plays in a number of diseases, For instance, for a long time milk was considered good for gastrointestinal complaints. But now it is known that milk itself can be causing the trouble—that it can, among other things, bring on chronic ulcerative colitis, an exceedingly unpleasant condition. Through the years, many a mother has firmly commanded, "Eat your spinach! It's good for you!" In truth, for some children spinach is just the opposite of good; it actually makes the child ill.

Of all the allergies—to inhalants (pollens, molds, house dust, animal danders, drugs, chemicals, insects—food allergy is probably the least intelligible. It does not seem reasonable that some people cannot eat fish or eggs or wheat or a multitude of perfectly good and healthy foods without becoming ill. Surely, it is all in their minds.

Alas, it is not.

Gertrude Stein once wrote that "a rose is a rose is a rose." Pollen is pollen is pollen, be it from trees, grass or ragweed. We can see it, and we can understand rather easily that it doesn't really belong in our systems. It is comprehensible that if we do inhale it, it can make us uncomfortable with hay fever and perhaps other assorted complaints, that it can make us sneeze, cough and wheeze. But how is it that food, if it is fresh and pure, can also make us ill?

Perhaps because in many cases food nowadays is not food alone. Modern foods have become conglomerations of additives of one sort or another—flavorings, colorings, preservatives, and the like—and of food combinations. These days when we eat bread, we don't just eat wheat flour, or even just wheat flour in combination with eggs and milk and yeast and salt. We eat wheat flour altered by milling processes and in combination with some twenty additives plus, according to an ongoing controversy, quite a bit of rodent and insect debris.

It is the purpose of this book to make food allergy comprehensible and to demonstrate how, with a bit of effort, to avoid the unpleasant consequences of being allergic to food. Thus, I try to explain what food allergy is, how it works, what foods commonly cause what symptoms and the range of symptoms the allergic may suffer. I attempt to explain how all this may be avoided for young and old alike. And because this book is meant to be helpful, not only for the person who is allergic but also for the person responsible for someone who is allergic, I include recipes for allergyfree menus in Chapter Thirteen.

Even when the allergic patient has been told by an allergist to avoid certain foods, it is not always easy to do so. This book intends to make such avoidance simpler. It is not, however, a do-it-yourself manual; nor should the reader approach it from this viewpoint. Rather, it is intended as an assist to his understanding of the problems of food allergy and as a help to him and his physician in tackling these problems. Reader and physician alike must keep in mind that not everyone is affected by a specific food in a particular way. Each of us is an individual stubbornly going his separate way in sickness and in health, in allergy as in all else. Thus, it may not be possible to apply rigidly all that I say here to every allergic sufferer in the same fashion or to obtain the same results.

When I was a student in medical school, a neatly framed commandment, "Know Thyself," hung on the wall of a classroom. I sincerely believe that while this precept applies to most aspects of life, it applies with special force to allergy to food. Know first what it is that makes you ill; then know how to avoid it. To that end, I have written this book.

Preface to the Revised Edition

Since *Coping With Food Allergy* was first published in 1974, a good deal of controversy has been generated among allergists as to the role of hypersensitivity to foods in gastrointestinal disorders, emotional disturbances, and respiratory problems such as allergic rhinitis and asthma. In addition, the media has "taken it up," publicizing some of the more spectacular aspects of allergy to food. The original intent of *Coping With Food Allergy*—to make such hypersensitivity comprehensible, to describe its causes and symptoms, and to explain how it is diagnosed and treated—remains in this revised edition and, further, the book discusses new findings that have developed during the last decade since the book saw the light of day. I have also tried to supply up-to-date helpful information in the appendices.

I believe this revision is especially important since many of my colleagues in the field of allergy consider that allergy to food may be on the increase, due, perhaps, in part to better diagnostic procedures, but also, perhaps, because we have a very human tendency to alter Nature's bounty, transforming what was originally comparatively simple chemical nutrients, suitable to keep us healthy, into somewhat complex and not always nutritionally valuable chemical compounds.

Finally, as in the original edition, this book is meant to assist in the understanding of this particular allergy manifestation and in its control. A good many of my fellow allergists have praised the original as being exceedingly helpful, while an even greater number of food allergy sufferers have expressed gratitude for the aid this book has provided. Certainly, when we understand a problem, we are in a far better position to solve it. As in all else, understanding is the key to managing allergy to food. I hope that this revised edition will continue to provide that key.

Coping
With
Food
Allergy

One

A Bird's-Eye View of Allergy

Because the scientific diagnosis and treatment of allergy is a relatively new medical discipline—it's been practiced not much more than half a century—not all of its secrets have been revealed. What is certain, however, is that a great many Americans suffer from allergy diseases, some of them in total ignorance of the cause of their suffering. It is estimated that 10 to 15 percent (and this may be a conservative estimate) of the population suffers from at least one and probably more than one allergy disease major enough to require medical care. From 20 to 30 million Americans, young and old, are unable to tolerate the ordinary things of this world—they react to them with illness. There are probably many more sufferers who react unhappily to all manner of things but have not yet sought medical help. It may be that the symptoms of these unknown sufferers of allergy disease are so mild or so diffuse that they have no particular anxiety about themselves. Or, it may be that they hold the once general notion that it is all in their heads.

Yet, allergy disease can be so drastic as to cause serious illness and even death. The fact that a person can be so sensitive to a common food, say, peanuts, or to a life-saving drug such as penicillin as to suffer generalized symptoms of collapse, shock and death may seem strange and terrible. But it can happen. It does happen. From 5 to 10 thousand Americans a year die from asthma, largely an allergic manifestation; some 300 die from allergic reactions to normal doses of penicillin; and about 30 from the stings of insects.

What is allergy?

Since a good deal of mystery still shrouds many facets of allergy, it is difficult to be definitive. But a generally accepted definition is that allergy is an abnormal reaction to substances ordinarily well tolerated by most persons. For example, most of us can eat strawberries with relish, but for a few allergic persons the eating of strawberries may

3

mean an uncomfortable outbreak of hives or the intense itching of eczema or the coldlike symptoms of allergic rhinitis or even the frightening breathing difficulties of asthma, not to mention the nausea, pain and other discomforts of gastrointestinal upset. Most people enjoy eating fish, but there are others so sensitive to fish that they become ill when they smell it being cooked—not to mention what happens if they eat it! For countless millions fish is the main source of animal protein. How odd, then, that just the odor of fish cooking can turn some people off entirely.

Food allergy is our main concern in this book. But there are many other agents of allergy—substances that we ingest, inhale or touch, or that are injected into us either by helpful doctors or angered insects. It does seem strange that such mundane, everday things—food; house dust, mold, pollen; animal danders (skin flakes, scales and scurf) from our favorite cat or dog; insect debris (wings, scales, and the like); aspirin prescribed for our headache or penicillin injected for our infection; heat, cold and even light—all can bring on reactions of varying intensity in the sensitive.

Just how do these relatively harmless substances cause such unhappy (and sometimes violent) consequences in such a large segment of the population?

An allergic reaction is really an immune reaction. It is a reaction against foreign intrusion by the body's defensive mechanisms, the antibodies. If we did not possess antibodies, we could be carried off by the first bacterial or viral infection that came along. The body manufactures different groups of antibodies, or immunoglobulins as they are called, and the one we are concerned with in allergy disease is Immunoglobulin E—in shortened form, IgE. Everyone produces some IgE as an immune response, but allergic persons produce a greater quantity. Thus, most of us have little or no trouble when we ingest or inhale or touch allergens (those foreigners), but allergic persons may overreact, thanks to their more plentiful supply of IgE.

IgE antibodies are bound to special white blood cells and to mast cells in the tissues, particularly in the so-called shock organs of the body—the smooth muscles, mucous glands, mucous membranes and the skin. When allergens arrive on the scene, the battle is joined as allergens and antibodies clash. In the process, the body suffers damage, either directly or because during the struggle chemical mediators such as histamine are released. Normally bound to mast cells and inactive, these substances, once released, may be none too friendly to their host. They are thought to be responsible for the immediate reaction in the shock organs with symptoms of hives, swollen nasal membranes, wheezing, and the like.

To dramatize the process a bit, let's take a page from the human scene. Normally, two female acquaintances when they meet, trade friendly smiles and small talk; but when one woman happens to be a wife and the other her husband's ex-girlfriend, things are likely to be different. Instead of a calm and reasonable relationship, the wife may overreact with frigid looks, cutting remarks, even verbal assault. The husband may not have looked at or even thought of the girlfriend for years, but his wife still bristles, no doubt thinking she must save her marriage. She may shock her husband with fishwife tactics, and in the end, the whole business may go a long way toward destroying the marriage she thinks she is saving. Thus do allergen and antibody clash to the detriment, often enough, of the body as a whole. Overreaction may do more harm than good; overprotection may destroy rather than save. Allergy disease of varying severity can be the result of this clash.

Let's take the case of a gentleman who is sensitive to eggs. When he eats them for breakfast, minute quantities of partially digested or even totally undigested egg protein make their way into his blood stream where they encounter specific antibodies (IgE) rallying to protect the body from a foreign substance. If, in the ensuing struggle, histamine is released, it may cause the smooth muscles wrapped around the bronchi to constrict, the mucous glands to increase their secretions and the blood vessels to expand, grow thin and leak fluid into the tissues, producing swelling, or edema. The result is constricted airways, further obstructed by an overproduction of mucus and by swollen tissues. Our gentleman begins to cough and wheeze. His breathing grows increasingly difficult. He has an attack of asthma—all because of an egg, a food generally considered not only delectable but exceedingly nutritious.

Thus, an allergic person is hypersensitive. His cells recognize the allergen as an enemy substance and overreact, much as our wife did when confronted by her husband's ex-girlfriend. Allergy, then, is really a case of overreaction by the body's protective mechanism. It is for this reason that research in immunology, the study of how the body protects itself against disease, and allergy are going forward more or less hand in hand.

There are two kinds of allergic reaction—immediate and delayed. Immediate reactions occur almost at once after a person has been exposed to an allergen. Symptoms are apparent within minutes or hours. This type of reaction takes place in the shock organs because, it is thought, these are especially vulnerable to the allergen-antibody conflict since the IgE antibodies are in greater concentrations in these areas. Hay fever, asthma, hives, sensitivity to insect bites and stings, and allergy to foods are examples of immediate reaction. Delayed reactions appear hours, days and even weeks after exposure and are caused, it is believed, when antibody-type white blood cells attack allergens so violently that a certain amount of the body's tissue is destroyed. Examples of delayed reaction are allergies to poison ivy, cosmetics and soaps. Because we deal with food allergy in this book, we are concerned with immediate allergic reactions.

Why are some people allergic and others not? Probably the most important reason is that allergy seems to have a hereditary factor. In some families allergy runs strong, and those born into these families may inherit the tendency. Studies have shown that an individual has nearly a 75 percent chance of being allergic if both his parents have allergies. He is also likely to develop his own brand of allergy at an earlier age. If one parent is allergic or allergy runs in one side of the family, the child has close to a 50 percent chance of developing allergy. He does not necessarily inherit the particular allergy or sensitivity of his forebears. His mother, for instance, may suffer from hay fever, his father asthma; but he may develop eczema. His mother may be allergic to ragweed, his father to molds, and he to fish and peanuts. Thus, while he inherits a tendency to allergy, he may or may not exhibit the same symptoms or be allergic to the same things as his parents and other relatives are. He may go his own way as far as allergic manifestations are concerned, and he may be affected by a totally different set of allergens.

A second factor in the development of allergy disease is the duration and amount of exposure to allergens the individual suffers. For instance, our egg-sensitive gentleman may have eaten eggs for breakfast quite comfortably for a long time before suddenly becoming sensitized to them.

A third factor is the nature of the allergen itself. Some are more potent than others. Among inhalants, ragweed pollen is more potent than grass pollen. Among foods, citrus fruits are more potent allergens than apples, peas than carrots, cow's milk than soybean milk.

A fourth factor is the individual's physical condition at the time of exposure to an allergen. If he has a cold, ragweed pollen may cause an allergic reaction that he would not have suffered otherwise. If he has a stomach already upset by infection or is suffering from diarrhea, more food allergens may be absorbed into his blood stream and will intensify his symptoms of allergic reaction. Infection seems to lower a person's tolerance to some allergens. Thus, a person with a cold may show sensitivity to milk, for instance, when normally he can drink it undisturbed. Dust and other inhalants may affect the cold-sufferer more easily. On the other hand, a person actively suffering from allergy may invite infection, for the physical conditions allergy imposes—obstructed airways, damaged skin, swollen membranes—open the door to infection.

A fifth factor, and perhaps the strangest of all, is the role of emotions in allergy. At one time, it was thought that all allergies were caused by emotions, but such a view is considered distorted today. Emotional stress may precipitate allergy and greatly aggravate its symptoms, but most allergists (doctors who specialize in allergy and its treatment) believe that the fundamental problem is not caused by emotions. However, the controversy still rages. Some allergists insist that emotions trigger but do not cause allergy—that an underlying allergy was already present. Others state that the effect of the emotions on the allergic is to cause leakage of fluid from the blood vessels, producing an allergic condition. This school of thought suggests that, while some persons blush when embarrassed, for instance, allergic people may do more than blush. They may blossom forth in hives or angioedema (giant hives), thanks to the leakage of fluid into the tissues of the face.

That allergy itself can cause emotional problems is generally accepted. The boy plagued by intense itching and the oozing and crusting of eczema everytime he drinks milk or eats wheat is apt to develop any number of emotional problems—irritability, nervousness, depression. The teenage girl whose lips double in size every time she attempts to brighten her looks with cosmetics is inclined to be a bit disturbed or unhappy and perhaps envious of her untroubled peers. The woman who experiences a frightening attack of asthma when she tries to clean house is surely going to become discouraged. These are facetious examples, but we deal with more specific illustrations of the emotional problems allergy can cause in Chapter Ten.

There are other factors that play a lesser role in allergy. Weather and the seasons, for instance, have an effect on our ability to react normally or abnormally to various allergens. Sudden changes of temperature may trigger an existing allergy, especially asthma. The relationship of climate and geographic location to food allergy is not clear; but these factors play a large role in other allergies, particularly in inhalant allergy caused by pollens, house dust and mold.

There is also the possibility that various aspects of bodily makeup and metabolism have something to do with allergic sensitivity. Hyperthyroid conditions may be conducive to allergy, perhaps because the person with an overactive thyroid gland reacts with excessive sensitivity to a number of external irritants. Certain types of skin, such as those incapable of neutralizing alkali substances efficiently, tend to contact dermatitis (inflammation of the skin). People with such skin have great difficulty with all sorts of materials, including soap.

Primitive people weren't much bothered by all this. It is "civilized man" who suffers from allergy. Since statistics seem to show that allergy diseases are on the rise, then perhaps the more "civilized" man becomes, the more allergic he becomes. It is even possible that a great many present-day allergies are man-made. The more drugs we use to fight disease, the more chemicals we employ to preserve, pep up, color and fill out our foods, the more pesticides we spray about the environment, the more pollution we spew forth into air and water— the more allergenic substances find their way into our systems, and the more we suffer.

Oddly enough, animals also can suffer from allergy, particularly domesticated animals. Dogs are known to suffer from ragweed hay fever. So do cows, although a sniffling, sneezing dairy herd rather staggers the imagination. One dog was found to be allergic to house dust, and a baby walrus fed from a bottle developed contact dermatitis on its face.

Actually, under proper conditions of exposure and duration of exposure to allergens, almost everyone—animals and man—could be sensitized to something.

Allergy can appear at any age, but about half of the adult allergies begin in childhood, usually before puberty. Even if the symptoms disappear, these childhood allergies really are not outgrown. The tendency is still there, and allergy may surface again, in the same form or in other forms, later in life. This is especially true if childhood allergies have gone untreated and uncontrolled. The earlier allergy is diagnosed and managed, the better the chances are that it can be controlled and the less the chances are of developing new allergies in later life. An unrecognized and untreated childhood allergy may come back to plague a person in his forties.

As a person's sensitivity becomes more severe, the number of substances he reacts to become more numerous. Although this has not been verified, one doctor, who made a study of this facet of allergy, reported that the average hay fever patient was also allergic to five foods, the average patient with sinus trouble (rhinitis) was allergic to seven, and the average patient with asthma to ten. Thus, allergy to food seems to have a close relationship to other allergies and may present symptoms similar to those other allergies cause.

Checklist

Allergy is an abnormal reaction to substances ordinarily well tolerated by most persons.

We are surrounded by allergens that we ingest, inhale, touch and are injected with.

It is probably true that everyone can be made allergic to something under the proper conditions of exposure.

Allergy to food is considered an immediate reaction, although symptoms may not appear for hours.

Heredity, amount and duration of exposure to an allergen, and the nature and potency of the allergen itself are all major factors in the development of allergy.

Glossary

allergen:
>   Any substance capable of producing allergy. Sometimes used interchangeably with *antigen*. I choose to stick to *allergen* throughout the book to avoid confusion.

allergist:
>   A doctor specializing in the medical subspecialty of allergy.

allergy:
>   Overreaction to substances normally not harmful to others.

angioedema:
>   Large, deep swelling; giant hives.

animal dander:
>   Skin flakes, scales and scurf.

dermatitis:
>   Inflammatory condition of the skin.

edema:
>   A condition in which tissues contain excess fluid; swelling.

sensitized:
>   Made susceptible to a substance.

sensitivity:
>   Abnormally susceptible to a substance; used interchangeably with *allergy* and *allergic*.

Two

Characteristics of Food Allergy

A good many centuries ago Lucretius, wise Roman poet and philosopher, said, "What is food for one, is to others bitter poison." Since he first coined the phrase, it has reappeared in many guises—"One man's meat is another man's poison"—but the sense of the aphorism has remained the same. We cannot all tolerate or enjoy the same things. What may be peaches and cream for you, may be pure nausea for me.

But we do have to eat to live. Why, then, are perfectly nutritious foods akin to poison for some people? How is it that fresh fish, rich in protein and a staple of life in many lands, can cause hypersensitive individuals to go into shock? How is it that milk, fresh from the dairy, pasteurized and sweet, can turn a charming, rosy infant into a howling demon bent on driving his parents up the wall? How can a single nut, or even the smell of a nut, make a grown man wheeze and gasp for breath? It is quite easy to understand that food gone bad can poison. It isn't difficult to realize that food improperly preserved can harbor such grim things as botulism. It is even quite reasonable that some foods, such as hot peppers and onions, might not be too easily digested. And we can accept the fact that some foods contain substances that can give susceptible gastrointestinal tracts the whammy; those that contain caffeine, for example, or vasoactive amines (chocolate, red wine, aged cheese, banana, avocado, even tomatoes), which should be avoided not only by migraine sufferers but also by those who suffer from high (severe) blood pressure. In addition, as we shall note later, monosodium glutamate can cause some who are fond of Chinese food considerable discomfort, thanks to the presence of a powerful neurotoxin.

Still, it is difficult to comprehend why, other than these somewhat strange exceptions, perfectly good, wholesome food should make some among us ill for no apparent reason.

Any food may be the cause of allergic reactions but the following foods are more potent allergens than other foods:

milk	fish and shellfish
eggs	berries
wheat	peas and peanuts
chocolate	citrus fruits
nuts	corn

Perhaps it is no coincidence that all these foods are considered particularly delicious and highly nutritious. We must say with Shakespeare, "We, ignorant of ourselves, beg often our own harms. . . ."

Just as any food may be the villain, so anybody can suffer allergy to food. In fact, researchers believe that most people are sensitive to some food or foods at some time in their lives. No doubt, for the great majority, food allergy symptoms are so mild as to be ignored—a passing indigestion, a brief rash, a temporarily stuffy nose.

The mechanism of food allergy is thought to work mainly in two ways: (1) by direct contact of food allergens with IgE antibodies in the gastrointestinal system, resulting in very swift reactions; or (2) by the absorption of allergens from the gastrointestinal tract into the blood stream, resulting in reactions in the blood or the shock organs—the smooth muscles, mucous glands and membranes and the skin. Two important factors play a role in whether or not sensitization takes place: (1) the condition or efficiency of the gastrointestinal tract itself; and (2) the nature and amount of the allergenic food consumed.

Food allergies can also affect other body systems. An allergic person can react to the smell of food. In this case, his respiratory system is the seat of sensitization, as it is in inhalant allergies. Reaction to foods inhaled is far less common than reaction to foods ingested. Some hypersensitive folk even break out in contact dermatitis, an allergic skin condition, when they handle some foods. In this case the skin is the seat of sensitization.

In general, this is the strange picture sensitivity to food presents. Let us take a closer look at specific characteristics.

Age at Onset of Food Allergy

Like other allergies, food hypersensitivity can come upon us at any time of life and continue to any age. It is, however, most common in infancy and early childhood, perhaps because the gastrointestinal systems of the young are less efficient than those of their elders. Thus, more allergens may find their way into youthful blood streams to cause allergy problems. It can be said that most food allergy occurs during the first two years of life and is often replaced by allergy to inhalants.

So it is not very surprising to find that cow's milk is the chief villain in infant allergy. It is, after all, the main food for the first few months. One doctor estimates that a 150 lb. adult would have to drink two gallons of milk a day to match, by body weight, the milk intake of a 15 lb. baby downing his daily 24 ounces.

That milk is not always a wholesome food guaranteed to make us big and strong may come as something of a shock. Milk can, in fact, cause some pretty unpleasant diseases. Recent studies into iron deficiency anemia, for instance, have indicted allergy to milk as a possible cause. The anemia is a secondary result of continuing diarrhea and loss of blood in the stools. Recurrent attacks of bronchitis have also often been traced to allergy to milk.

Because allergy to cow's milk plays such a large role in the lives of a great many youngsters—a research team has recently estimated that about 7.5 percent of all infants exhibit allergy to milk—Chapter Six is devoted to the almost perfect food.

Symptoms of Food Allergy

Allergic reactions to foods can take place in almost any body system—gastrointestinal, respiratory, cutaneous (skin), urinary, nervous, mucous glands and membranes—just about everything that makes us tick. Gastrointestinal disorders are the most common manifestation of sensitivity to food. Food allergy symptoms may be localized in one area, such as eczema on the cheek or hands; or they may be diffuse and generalized such as headache, abdominal pain or behavior disorders. They may begin, especially if the skin is involved, at one site and gradually spread. Thus, eczema brought on by sensitivity to eggs may begin as a small patch and spread until the child or adult is covered.

Symptoms of food allergy can be so varied and differ so in severity that diagnosis is a real puzzle. Not only do symptoms to a given allergen differ among patients, but they may vary in the same patient. Thus, one person may register his sensitivity to milk with diarrhea, while another will react to milk with headaches. And the person who suffers diarrhea as an infant can end up with headaches when he drinks milk as an adult.

Food allergy symptoms are described in depth in Chapter Three.

Fixed Type of Allergic Response

This is a designation used by some allergists to describe the sensitivity of a person who reacts to a small amount of a food at every exposure, no matter what the interval, with specific and unvarying symptoms. It is, fortunately, a less common sensitivity, for the reaction is usually the most severe type, producing immediate symptoms—often asthma or hives or shock. Such a patient does not develop a tolerance to the allergenic food or foods. He is usually stuck with his sensitivity for life and has no other recourse than to avoid the foods that make him ill. Sometimes his sensitivity is so great that he reacts to a very small amount of the food, virtually a crumb. Sometimes these severely sensitive people need only smell or touch the food to react. Avoidance must then include such things as handling the food or being in the same area where it is being cooked. Peeling apples or slicing them might be too much for someone severely sensitive to them. If it is eggs that are an individual's undoing, he might not be able to crack them or even touch the shells. Some doctors have estimated that 5 to 10 percent of food-sensitive persons fall into the category of fixed allergic response to food.

Variable or Cyclical Type of Allergic Response

These designations or similar ones are sometimes used to indicate a sensitivity that varies not only in the amount of food needed to cause symptoms but also in the interval between ingestion and the appearance of symptoms. It is by far the most common type of allergic response to food and is much more difficult to diagnose that the fixed type of response since cause and effect fluctuate so. This type of sensitivity, however, is less drastic for the sufferer. He can often develop tolerance to the foods causing his problems by eating less of them less frequently. If he is to remain symptomfree, though, he will need to pay close attention to a number of factors that may influence this type of allergic response:

  infection
  stress
  fatigue
  overeating at one sitting
  too frequent consumption of a specific food
  condition of food (cooked or raw, fresh or stale)
  presence of pollen and other allergens, such as house dust or
    mold
  pollution
  changes of temperature, especially when it drops

Allergy Load Level or Threshold Tolerance

Sensitivity to food may be the sole cause for symptoms, but this is less common than sensitivity to several allergens. We have noted that in a fixed type of food allergy, the sufferer reacts to a given allergen and a given amount of that allergen but that in a variable type of food allergy, other conditions or factors may play a part. Thus, some allergic persons react to milk at any time; others react only during pollen season. The rest of the year they may be able to drink milk with relish. In this case, sensitivity to pollen plus an underlying sensitivity to milk equals symptoms, whereas either sensitivity alone is not strong enough to produce a problem.

Or, an individual may tolerate, without symptoms, several foods when eaten separately but, if eaten together at the same meal or combined (say, in a casserole), they may bring on a reaction. In this case the person has a mild sensitivity to each of the several foods that is not strong enough to cause symptoms when the foods are eaten separately. If, however, he eats them all at the same time, the combination of allergens tips the scale and creates a reaction.

The patient's threshold of tolerance to allergens, or allergic load level, makes diagnosis difficult and treatment complex. The patient's ability to tolerate allergens, whether ingested, inhaled or absorbed (his threshold) is balanced on one end of the allergy seesaw, with allergenic substances (pollen, house dust, animal dander, mold, one or more foods) plus circumstances that lower the patient's threshold (infection, stress, fatigue) teetering on the other end. If the patient's tolerance threshold is greater than the load of allergens, he will be symptomfree; but if the presence of allergens overwhelms his tolerance threshold, symptoms will appear.

Compounding the Allergy

A good many factors can bounce the allergic patient up and down on that seesaw. His doctor must take his allergic load level into account, if treatment is to be successful. It is often necessary to remove more than one component of the load if the patient is to lose his symptoms. Infection, for instance, may tip the seesaw and overcome the patient's threshold of tolerance. The role infection plays in allergy is somewhat ambiguous, but if it is present, treating the allergy itself without treating the infection is rarely successful. When an individual is ill with an infectious disease, he may react to a food or foods that have never given him problems. Thus, a person suffering from a cold may suddenly find that he cannot tolerate eggs even though he was accustomed to eating them almost every morning for breakfast. Mothers often refrain from giving small children milk when they have a cold on the theory that it "thickens their mucus." What may actually be happening is that the child not only has a cold but the infection has so strained his threshold as to superimpose allergic rhinitis upon his cold symptoms. Underlying sensitivity to milk plus infection tips the child's allergy seesaw out of balance.

The relationship of food allergy to other allergies, such as inhalant or drug allergies, is complex. Allergy to foods may be the sole cause for allergic symptoms, or allergy to foods in conjunction with another allergy may bring on symptoms, or each type of allergy may cause separate symptoms in the same patient. Thus, allergy to foods may be responsible for allergic rhinitis symptoms (cough, stuffy nose, postnasal drip) in itself. Or the food allergy may share responsibility for such symptoms with an allergy to pollen. Or food allergy may cause gastrointestinal symptoms in the patient and the allergy to pollen be solely responsible for the rhinitis symptoms.

One doctor has noticed that there is a close relationship between ragweed pollen and cantaloupes in some of his patients, so much so that he believes that he can predict that a patient who says he cannot tolerate melons will also be allergic to ragweed. But why exactly this is so is not known. It seems to be one of those quirks that turns up in the literature of allergy from time to time.

Allergens such as house dust, molds and animal danders can also tip the allergy seesaw. For example, in the fall when the furnace is turned on in the home, house dust in the air is often drastically increased. Then an individual may suddenly react to eggs because his underlying sensitivity to them plus a minor sensitivity to house dust tips the seesaw below his tolerance level. Another individual may find he cannot tolerate eggs during a long damp spell when mold growth and spore production are high. A third may find eggs uncomfortable when his dog is shedding, wafting animal danders into his environment.

Fatigue and emotional stress may also unbalance the allergy seesaw, lowering a person's tolerance to a food allergen. It is well known that these two factors can lower the body's resistance. The relationship of fatigue and emotional stress to allergy is not clear-cut or simple to demonstrate. But, since flare-ups of allergy symptoms, especially asthma and hives, commonly follow physical and mental exhaustion and/or emotional stress, the possibility is very strong that these two factors play much the same role in susceptibility to allergy that they do in susceptibility to infection.

Changes in temperature, especially chilling, can upset the balance of some allergic persons. An individual may find, for instance, that foods he ate happily all summer no longer can be tolerated once cold weather sets in. Perhaps this is not so surprising. Man has long recognized seasonal influences upon his physical and mental well-being. Spring and fall are times of generally lowered resistance to disease and infection, which may, in turn, affect sensitivity to food. Given that the bodily processes fluctuate to adapt to changing environmental conditions, it does not seem odd that the individual's threshold level might also rise or fall in response to such environmental conditions.

Overindulgence brings its own penalties. Shakespeare said of food in *A Midsummer Night's Dream*, "A surfeit of the sweetest things the deepest loathing to the stomach brings." By overeating a specific food, we can bring allergy down upon our own heads. Thus, a person inordinately fond of chocolate or nuts may sensitize himself to these goodies simply by consuming them too often and in too large quantities. It is quite possible that he will enjoy them for a while, but if he has an inherited tendency to allergy (and sometimes even if he doesn't), the day may well come when he reacts to these delights violently. The more allergenic a food is and the more of it one consumes, the greater the likelihood of developing allergy to it. Researchers established this principle some time ago when they fed laboratory guinea pigs large amounts of skimmed milk. Subsequent feedings of the milk brought on allergic reactions, and one sensitized animal died in a minute and a half after being given the milk. Moderation, then, truly is a virtue!

Even intermittent eating of a food, but in large amounts, may lead to sensitivity. Thus, if an individual, especially a person with a tendency to allergy, consumes great quantities of strawberries or melons in their season but tastes them little if at all during the rest of the year, he may still find that he has become allergic to them. His symptoms will then be seasonal, coinciding with the harvest of these allergenic fresh fruits he too dearly loves.

In much the same manner, although this is controversial, it is thought to be quite possible for a pregnant woman to sensitize the fetus in her womb by overindulging in some foods. Often mothers-to-be think they are doing baby a favor by drinking large quantities of milk, but, alas, if allergy runs in either or both families, baby may arrive into this world with a full-blown allergy to milk. The mother-to-be may overindulge without developing any symptoms of allergy herself, but her overconsumption of such things as eggs and milk and wheat may ensure that her baby will suffer allergic symptoms as soon as he meets these foods. Odd cravings notwithstanding, mothers-to-be, especially when there is a family history of allergy, would do well to eat with great care and not too much or too frequently of any one food, particularly if it happens to be on the list of potent allergens.

Fetal hiccoughs, so often a matter of paternal wonder and laughter, are thought to be a response to foreign protein passed from the mother's blood stream through the placenta into the blood stream of the fetus. This is debatable. One researcher reports that he was able to bring on these tiny, subterranean lurchings a significant number of times by feeding the mother certain foods. This uncertain theory of sensitization before birth may explain why some infants come into the world sensitive to milk and why they suffer an almost immediate onset of croup and colic when there has been too little time for exposure.

The nursing mother also needs to exercise moderation, for she may pass on allergens to the infant through her milk, thus sensitizing him. However (though this too is in question), the breast-fed baby is some seven times less likely to develop allergy than his bottle-fed brother. Nevertheless, the nursing mother must dine with care lest she expose the infant to food allergens. The infant is particularly susceptible to sensitization since his immature gastrointestinal system is often inefficient and apt to allow passage of allergens into his blood stream. And that, as we have noted, may be the beginning of the allergen-antibody battle.

Finally, the condition of the food itself affects its allergenic nature. Thus, cooked foods are less potent allergens than raw, stale foods less potent than fresh. But that is not the whole, strange story. There is an example in the literature of a patient who could eat celery grown in Florida, whereas he reacted allergically to celery grown in Colorado. Another patient could not tolerate Florida oranges but was quite comfortable with those grown in California. Perhaps the epitome of confused cause and effect is the patient who reacted to roasted, salted peanuts but not to roasted, unsalted peanuts or to salted, unroasted peanuts! Trying to sort this one out must have been an allergist's nightmare!

Onset and Duration of Symptoms

Onset of symptoms may occur within minutes of consumption of the allergenic food. This is especially true when the victim is severely allergic to the offender. However, the symptoms may not appear for several hours, normally anywhere from two to ten. And sometimes a person must eat the food two or three days running before any reaction is stirred up.

Duration of symptoms and, to some extent, the degree of distress depend upon how long the allergenic food remains in the body. Complete digestion and elimination usually requires a day or so or longer, if constipation is a problem. Duration of symptoms also depends upon how quickly antibodies in shock organs and the blood unite with the invading allergens and how quickly they are exhausted. The abundance or lack of abundance of IgE antibodies may also be a factor. In general, symptoms from a single ingestion of a food allergen persist at least for several hours and commonly from one to seven days. As the food allergen leaves the body and the antibodies are depleted and exhausted, symptoms disappear.

Sometimes after a reaction, especially if it is severe, no symptoms will be provoked for one or more weeks even if the allergenic food is eaten again. This seems to be because the antibody defenses may be worn out and in need of rebuilding. It's a bit like the lull between battles when armies pull back to regroup and replenish their spent forces. This theory of a brief "refractory" period explains the recurrent nature of perennial food allergy, and it is this chronic reaction to foods eaten daily that presents the most persistent symptoms.

These are the main characteristics of allergy to food. The reader may find some of them rather mysterious. Perhaps he will be comforted to know that allergists are often mystified, too. It is also well to remember that much about the nature and extent of allergy to food is exceedingly controversial.

Checklist

Some foods are more potent allergens than others.

Any food can cause allergy. Under the proper conditions, almost anyone can suffer from allergy.

Allergy to food may appear at any time of life but is more prevalent during infancy and early childhood.

Allergic reaction can take place in almost any body system.

Various factors affect the allergic, either singly or in combination.

Everyone has an allergic threshold.

We can bring food allergy upon ourselves by overindulgence in a food. Moderation in diet is a virtue, especially with the most potent food allergens.

Dietary discretion may be important for pregnant women, for it is thought that the fetus can be sensitized in the mother's womb.

Dietary discretion also may be important for the nursing mother, since it is thought that the infant can be sensitized through the mother's milk.

Three

The Havoc and Hazards of Food Allergy

What actually happens when an individual reacts allergically to a food or foods? What are his symptoms?

Allergy to food can affect any system of the body—gastrointestinal, respiratory, cutaneous (skin), urinary, nervous and even cardio-vascular (heart and blood vessels). Symptoms themselves can range from so mild as to be scarcely noticeable to so severe as to result in collapse and death.

Yes, unfortunately, even that severe!

A grim example was the death, a number of years ago, of a ten-year-old boy in Boston who accepted a dish of ice cream at the home of a friend and died within twenty-five minutes. The ice cream contained peanut butter, an ingredient not listed on the package. The boy was evidently severely hypersensitive to peanuts. According to his father, the boy had been trained early to avoid the foods that made him ill, but neither he nor anyone else could have guessed what the ice cream contained. Deaths from food allergy are rather rare. In this case, the death was totally needless and illustrates the importance of complete labeling of all foods (a subject I return to in Chapter Nine).

Symptoms of food allergy are also symptoms of many other diseases. Before a doctor can determine if allergy to food is the problem, he must first rule out other possible diseases, for some of them may be serious. For instance, the gastrointestinal and respiratory symptoms of cystic fibrosis in young children are very much akin to those of allergy to milk. The process of ruling out other diseases is known as differential diagnosis, but since the problems of food allergy are the concern in this book, I'll not cover this diagnostic procedure.

On to symptoms.

Gastrointestinal Tract

Since the gastrointestinal tract is the body system most commonly affected by sensitivity to food, we begin with it. To be totally logical, we begin, as food allergens do, at the mouth and work our way down. I hope that the length of the list of possible symptoms is not too alarming:

Mouth Area
  itching, burning and swelling of lips, tongue, gums and
    pharynx
  dermatitis of skin around the mouth
  chapped or inflamed lips
  "geographical" tongue (patchy, denuded areas)
  inflammation of mouth, tongue and gums
  canker sores
  bad breath and bad taste in mouth

Throat Area
  mucus in throat (resulting in constant clearing and cough)
  difficulty in swallowing
  a sense of a lump under breast bone often accompanied by
    pain.

Stomach Area
  nausea
  vomiting
  heartburn
  sour sensations
  bloating
  belching
  spasms of the opening between stomach and duodenum (py-
    lorus)

Intestinal Area
  acute abdominal pain (colic in infants)
  subacute abdominal pain
  diarrhea
  constipation
  blood in stools
  mucous colitis

Rectal Area
  anal itching
  rectal bleeding
  inflammation of rectum and anus
  tenesmus (persistent desire to empty bowel and straining
    without result)

There are several disease syndromes associated with possible food allergy. The two most common are celiac disease, characterized by recurrent diarrhea and what seems to be an intolerance to wheat gluten, and ulcerative colitis, characterized by recurrent and often bloody diarrhea. There is also a possibility that sudden crib death in infants may be due to sensitization to milk.

Mouth Area

Contact with allergenic food may cause rash or dermatitis of the skin around the mouth, especially in young children, who quite frequently react to oranges and tomatoes in this fashion. A reaction of angioedema (giant hives) in the mouth area can result in considerable and sometimes dangerous swelling of the lips, tongue, soft palate and pharynx. Foods that cause this odd type of reaction are usually nuts, fish, eggs and fresh fruit, particularly cantaloupes, grapefruit and berries. Sensitivity to food may be the major cause of canker sores in the mouths of older children and adults, although it is thought that viruses also may be responsible. The foods that I believe are a common cause of canker sores can be remembered easily because they begin with the letter "C":

> condiments
> chocolate
> cola (includes all soft drinks)
> catsup (includes all foods with tomatoes)
> corn
> chips (includes all potatoes and fried foods)

Flavorings in toothpastes, mouthwashes, candy and chewing gum may also be responsible.

Swift reactions in the mouth area, clearly connected to a food just eaten, not only often dissuade the allergic individual from consuming any more of the stuff, but are often very noticeable.

An odd feature of allergic reaction in the mouth is the "geographical" tongue, a strange-looking configuration of bald patches surrounded by reddish borders. It probably derives its name from its appearance, for, when in full bloom, the tongue looks vaguely like a map.

Throat Area

One of the most potentially serious manifestations of gastrointestinal allergic reaction involves the larynx, which may swell and choke off the wind pipe. This can be frightening, not to mention suffocating; but fortunately it is rare. More common symptoms are hoarseness and loss of voice. One doctor reports the case of a woman who lost her voice for months at a time. Removal of milk, eggs and wheat from her diet restored her ability to talk normally.

Stomach Area

Symptoms of the stomach are often lumped together and called nervous indigestion. Probably most of these symptoms do represent intolerance to such foods as onions and radishes rather than sensitivity to food allergens. But adults may suffer stomach distress in response to eggs and milk, foods one would never place in the same indigestible category with onions or cucumbers or radishes.

Nausea and vomiting, of course, are symptoms of many ailments. Common especially to children, they usually do not stand alone as symptoms of food allergy but are accompanied by other discomforts such as asthma, hives, headache, abdominal pain or diarrhea. Infants vomit with discouraging frequency, but nausea and vomiting in older children may be of a cyclic type, with sudden attacks lasting a day or two and recurring every few weeks. Such a syndrome may go on for years and may be accompanied by severe headache or migraine. Some doctors believe food allergy makes a large contribution to this syndrome; others consider its role negligible.

Intestinal Area

The number-one symptom of gastrointestinal allergy is abdominal pain; this is true in the infant, the older child and the adult. Much too often such pain is dismissed summarily as being emotional in origin. Not necessarily so, although emotions, tension and stress may aggravate an existing allergy. The pain can be very real, so real and intense that it has been mistaken for appendicitis or obstruction on occasion. The sufferer has sometimes been wheeled into surgery on this basis. Acute abdominal pain is occasionally designated as "abdominal migraine" and is thought to be caused by edema (swelling) of the gastrointestinal mucous membranes, either by direct contact with a food allergen or by the allergen-antibody battle that is going on. When other allergic symptoms are present, such as nasal discomfort or hives, the doctor may suspect that allergy is the correct diagnosis, but he will have to rule out such possibilities as appendicitis, intestinal parasites, inflammation of the colon or intestines and lead poisoning. Allergic abdominal pain can be localized or diffuse. It is usually recurrent, especially in children. Thus, when a child complains that his stomach aches after polishing off a breakfast of eggs and a glass of milk, he may not just be trying to get out of going to school. He may be suffering an allergic reaction to that healthy breakfast he just downed.

Abdominal pain in the infant commonly occurs two or three weeks after birth. One day the baby suddenly turns red in the face, pulls up his little legs and howls. Colic has struck.

There are other good reasons for colic, but allergy to cow's milk is a major one, and it is far more common a cause than many people realize. As the saying goes, cow's milk is for calves, human milk for babies. Usually, colic does not strike immediately. The proud parents may bring a living doll back from the hospital and enjoy him for several weeks, just long enough for him to become sensitized to his formula. The exception is the infant who may already have been sensitized in his mother's womb; it is thought that such a child arrives with his allergy to milk full-blown. In general, it can be said that the later the onset of colic, the milder it will be.

Diarrhea, too, can be allergic in origin, especially in infants and young children. Often as not, milk is the cause. Alas, even soybean milk, commonly used as a substitute when cow's milk gives trouble, can also bring on diarrhea. There are other causes, of course—parasites, growths and infections. Again, diagnosis is made easier by the presence of other allergic symptoms, but they may or may not occur. Gastrointestinal symptoms of vomiting and cramping often do accompany diarrhea, however. Foods commonly at fault seem to be fresh fruits such as apples, oranges and bananas and fresh vegetables such as lettuce, tomatoes and spinach. The basic trio of milk, eggs and wheat are also often indicted.

Persistent constipation may be also due to food allergy. It is commonly associated with other gastrointestinal symptoms such as loss of appetite, as well as headache, allergic tension-fatigue syndrome and asthma. Milk is the chief villain, which bears out the popular notion that milk and its products, especially cheese, are "binding."

Mucous colitis is another symptom. Long believed only a neurotic tendency, since the sufferer's complaints were often generalized—fatigue, weakness, nonspecific aches and pains all over the body coupled with an irritable and nervous disposition—mucous colitis is characterized by the passing of a great deal of mucus in the stools, cramping in the abdomen and diarrhea. It is also often accompanied by other signs of allergy such as hives, hay fever and asthma.

Finally, rectal pain and itching in the anal area seems to be a more frequent manifestation of sensitivity to food than we allergists once thought. Black pepper is a common cause for such symptoms in older children and adults.

It seems reasonable enough that what we eat should affect our stomach and the rest of our gastrointestinal system—although why perfectly good, nutritious food, especially milk, should make us ill doesn't really make much sense. But how can foods cause symptoms in our respiratory systems, our skin and even our brains?

Part of the answer lies in the way our blood circulates. Allergy antibodies lie in wait in the cells of various body tissues and in special white blood cells. When the right food allergen comes along in the blood stream, the IgE antibodies pounce. The battle is on. Wherever the antibodies are clustered in quantity—lungs, skin or brain, the struggle is fierce enough to cause symptoms. And so a bit of egg can be the cause of a stuffy nose or eczema or peculiar behavior, if our blood carries allergens to those parts of the body.

Anaphylactic Shock

One of the most severe allergy manifestations—fortunately rare in food allergy—is anaphylactic shock. It was this reaction that took the life of the Boston boy. Its symptoms commonly are the following:

> widespread hives
> nausea and vomiting
> sneezing, wheezing
> signs of weakness
> complaints of chest constriction
> breathlessness and difficulty in breathing
> anxiety, confusion and collapse

Medical help must be sought immediately. There is no time to lose, for death can come very quickly. Nuts, peanuts (which belong to the legume family) and shellfish are the foods most often indicted in anaphylactic shock.

Respiratory System

The respiratory system seems far removed from our digestive processes, too far to be affected by the foods we eat. Alas, no area of the body is too remote for food allergens! Allergy to food does play a role in asthma, allergic rhinitis and ear problems. Some doctors, probably a minority, consider that role a large one; others believe food allergens are relatively unimportant in respiratory allergy symptoms. Though the controversy still rages—allergy to food does cause respiratory symptoms.

Asthma

This is a severe allergy symptom. For some asthmatic patients, especially children, foods are the culprits. There is no doubt that inhalant allergens play the larger role in asthma, but recurrent, perennial wheezing plus a near constant cold from fall to spring may well be blamed on food allergens as well. When asthma is not relieved by removing house dust or mold or animal danders from the environment, the possibility of food allergy must be considered.

Asthma is a debilitating disease. When the allergen-antibody struggle takes place, histamine or other mediators may be released to cause the smooth muscles wrapped around the bronchi and smaller airways to constrict, narrowing air passages. At the same time, these mediators may cause the mucous membrances lining the air passages to swell, further obstructing the airways, and the mucous glands to produce mucus in great quantity. The asthmatic individual finds himself struggling not only to get air into his lungs, but also to empty the stale air from his lungs. Mucous plugs form because of the oversecretion of the glands, making the effort to expel air increasingly difficult as the intake of fresh air lessens. The characteristic wheezing of asthma is caused by trapped air being forced past the plugs by the contraction of chest muscles. The whole process is exhausting and quite frightening, both to observer and victim.

Asthma attacks may be mild and infrequent or they can be exceedingly severe, frequent and sometimes continuous. Severe attacks may require hospitalization. The attack is often preceded by:

coughing, sneezing, a stuffy or runny nose
yawning
itching

The attack itself is characterized by:

choking and wheezing
straining chest and neck muscles
racing pulse
pale face and blue lips
face and body covered with sweat
a frightening sensation of suffocating

In between attacks, the asthmatic patient may be entirely free of symptoms. In later life and old age, shortness of breath, wheezing and coughing can occur on a daily basis instead of in the usual periodic pattern.

Foods most often indicted as the villains in asthma vary with age. In infants, milk is probably the number-one cause. In older children and adults, eggs, corn, wheat, chocolate, nuts, peas, beans and peanuts can be causes of asthma reactions. Some doctors believe that contaminants in foods, particularly pesticides, are as much to blame as the foods themselves.

Allergic Rhinitis

While pollens and sometimes molds are responsible for seasonal rhinitis (hay fever), allergy to food may well be the culprit in perennial allergic rhinitis, with nasal symptoms occurring at any time of year. A victim of this type of allergy symptom has one cold after another, a constant sniffle especially noticeable in the morning and a constant postnasal drip.

Briefly, in perennial rhinitis, the allergen-antibody conflict affects the mucous membrane of the nose, causing swelling (and thus obstruction) and an excessive production of mucus. The following symptoms are common:

> stuffy nose, but blowing is usually unproductive
> running nose
> itching of nose, eyes and roof of mouth
> excessive watering of eyes
> sneezing and coughing, also usually unproductive
> headaches

Besides being a first-class nuisance, perennial rhinitis can lead to such complications as sinusitis because the swelling of the nasal membranes can block drainage of the sinuses and prepare the ground for infection. When the sinuses are involved, the victim often suffers from headache, postnasal drip, sometimes fever and sometimes asthma. When infection is present, the nasal discharge changes from the clear, watery fluid of allergy to a thicker yellowish or yellowish-green secretion.

Another possible complication of perennial rhinitis is the growth of nasal polyps, watery swellings within the nose that can contribute further to obstruction. These may have to be surgically removed.

Foods most commonly blamed for allergic rhinitis are eggs, milk, wheat, chocolate, beans, peas, tomatoes, onions, salmon, beef, rye, potatoes and citrus fruits—a full market basket of possibilities. Strong odors from such foods as fish, coffee, asparagus, milk and from foods cooking may also precipitate allergic rhinitis.

Impairment of taste, smell and hearing may accompany allergic rhinitis. Hearing loss can be a serious and possibly permanent result of food allergy. Serous otitis is one of the major causes of deafness in childhood: it occurs most frequently in children between the ages of five and ten. It is caused by swelling and blocking in the Eustachian tube, which vents the middle ear into the pharynx. When an allergic reaction causes edema in this tube, fluid accumulates in the middle ear and interferes with hearing. If the allergy is controlled, hearing is usually restored, but permanent damage can occur. Of course, hearing loss can be caused by conditions other than food allergy.

Many a daydreaming, inattentive schoolchild may actually be unable to hear what is going on in the classroom. Since the condition produces little or no pain and few other noticeable symptoms, hearing impairment often goes unnoticed by child and parent alike. For this reason, regular hearing checks of schoolchildren are of great benefit. Special attention needs to be paid to those children who exhibit chest, nose or skin allergies, for they are the ones whose ears are most likely to be affected.

Cardiovascular System

Many people do not realize that the heart itself, as well as blood vessels, can react allergically, particularly to food allergens. Some allergists believe that cardiac allergic reactions are quite common but usually so mild as to be scarcely noticeable. More severe reactions such as tachycardia (abnormal rapid heart action), anginal pain and even occlusion (closure of a heart blood vessel) have been documented. In some cases, angina pectoris seems to have been controlled by eliminating allergenic foods.

Recently I received a case history of just such a heart allergy. I am including it in its entirety here with the kind permission of Dr. K. A. Baird.

Re: Mrs. Isobel G. Baird.

At about age 60 she had considerable trouble with "indigestion." This seemed to be caused by ingestion of cheese, but Swiss cheese caused no trouble. It was then found the indigestion was caused only by eating cheese which was dyed yellow or orange, and thereafter she could eat undyed cheese with no trouble.

At about 63 she developed a number of anginal attacks. These did not respond to nitroglycerine. At that time it was not widely known among cardiologists that this drug deteriorates in a dark bottle and on the shelf. When that was learned and fresh supply of nitroglycerine obtained, the attacks were relieved by it.

She had just started to take vitamin E when she developed an acute coronary occlusion. Recovering from this under standard treatment she continued taking vitamin E (d-alpha-tocopheryl) at the rate of 400 units a day.

At age 65 she had an attack which greatly resembled an acute coronary occlusion but this diagnosis could not be confirmed. Recovery was very slow for about two weeks until it was noted that she was receiving a good deal of egg in her diet. As soon as egg was completely eliminated, recovery was very prompt and complete.

For the next six years she took 1600 units of vitamin E each day. Egg containing foods were avoided and it was found that the unintentional intake of egg would cause an attack about 12 to 24 hours later, consisting of tachycardia, irregular pulse and anginal pain. These attacks would come in short paroxysms which were relieved by nitroglycerine. They were sometimes several hours apart and apparently did no lasting damage because even between them the patient went about her usual activities without special difficulty. Certain other foods were found to cause similar attacks. In particular these were shrimp, haddock, dyes in cheese, pork and venison. By avoiding these known allergens the patient was able to live a reasonably comfortable life with a level of activity or excitement which were kept less than normal on account of the existence of the original coronary damage.

The cardiologist who had not seen her for six years examined her heart as thoroughly as possible at age 71 years and considered it had not deteriorated to any extent in that time. The occasion for this last examination was an oncoming illness which was soon diagnosed to be lymphosarcoma which was rapidly fatal. The cardiologist later expressed his amazement at the fact that during the two weeks in hospital with terminal lymphosarcoma and a good deal of necessary disturbances by examinations, biopsy, etc., this patient did not once have an anginal attack.

Summary: A patient with relatively minor allergy suffered acute coronary occlusion at age 61. Beginning two years later with an acute heart disturbance which seemed to be clinically due to an acute allergy to egg, she suffered anginal attacks which were clinically associated with egg and several other foods but there were no signs or symptoms of further coronary damage, probably due to the large intake of alphatocopheryl.

Diagnosis: Allergic carditis in a post coronary patient.

Cutaneous System

Eruptions of the skin after eating is commonly understood, for since youth we have learned that overindulgence in such delectable things as chocolate and cake and ice cream must be paid for by pimples and a marred complexion. We grow wary in our adolescence of such goodies because so much depends upon a radiant and blooming skin.

Food sensitivities are stamped on our hides mainly by three conditions—eczema, urticaria (hives) and angioedema (giant hives). Of course, food is not the only agent of these sometimes exceedingly distressing skin lesions. Inhalants, bacterial agents and drugs can also be the villains. Physical allergy to heat, cold and light may also bring out such symptoms, hives especially. Nor is a single allergen always at fault. Sometimes food and inhalants or a combination of foods may be causing the havoc. This kind of complexity makes diagnosis no easy matter.

Some foods (tomatoes, carrots, onions, garlic, spinach), when handled by the hypersensitive, can cause contact dermatitis of the hands or, when consumed, around the mouth and chin. A hypersensitive housewife could develop a rash while preparing dinner, and it is not rare to see a baby protesting the spinach that produces a raw, red rash around its mouth.

Allergic Eczema

Allergic eczema due to food can begin at any time of life; but it is more common in infancy and usually can be blamed then on cow's milk. Yet even in old age, when we might think that the time was long past to become sensitive to a food, eczema can appear, with its scratching and digging. Food seems the number-one cause of allergic eczema in infancy. As the child grows older, his problem may become complicated by allergy to inhalants and drugs as well. Or all his symptoms may disappear for awhile only to be replaced by a new allergy, say, to house dust or animal dander or pollen, often with symptoms of allergic rhinitis and asthma. This rather common progression of allergy in children—from colic to eczema to asthma—is called the "allergic march." Milk and eggs may be the agents that start it all in the first place, with cereal next in importance.

Allergic eczema is characterized by diffuse redness with, usually, a pimply appearance. It commonly shows up on the cheeks, on the ears, in the folds of arms and legs, and on the back and upper part of the body. Once established, it tends to persist indefinitely, subsiding to a tiny patch, then flaring up to cover a good part of the body.

Neither the causes nor the mechanism of eczema are thoroughly understood. It is thought that allergens are carried to the skin via the blood system and that an inflammatory reaction is set off when allergens and antibodies clash. Itching is the major symptom. We inflict quite extensive secondary damage to the skin when we scratch and dig to get at the itch. The oozing and sometimes bloody crusts that often follow are actually self-inflicted skin lesions. Unfortunately, they can predispose the skin to infection, which, needless to say, may make matters a great deal worse. Unfortunately, too, the itching seems worse at night, so that loss of sleep adds its toll to the victim's suffering. Thus, it is common for the individual with long-standing eczema to present a picture of nervousness, irritability, fatigue and sometimes even bizarre behavior.

Small wonder that it was once considered that only "nervous" people had eczema, for it isn't easy for the casual observer to know which comes first, the eczema or the nervousness. It is not surprising that an unbroken chain of itching and self-inflicted lesions can make a nervous wreck of the sturdiest of persons.

As with other symptoms of allergy, controversy clouds the role of food in eczema. One school believes that food is the major cause not only in infants but in older children and adults. Another school proclaims that after the first two or three years of life, inhalants are the major source of trouble. As a matter of fact, both factors seem so often to go hand in hand that both usually must be considered and controlled before eczema will exit the scene. Thus for the patient, the argument has a somewhat academic ring.

In any case, it seems safe to say that recurrent allergic eczema that peaks from fall to early spring has a good chance of being caused by sensitivity to food, although house dust may be the offender and must be ruled out. If eczema occurs only during the pollen season, it seems reasonable to assume that inhalants are at work. If the itching and lesions follow the administration of a drug (either orally, by injection or topically as a salve or ointment), then eczema clearly results from a drug allergy. Chemicals and other contactants (allergens we touch) can also produce dermatitis (inflammation of the skin) and so have a clear relationship to eczema.

Yet, even when these connections are clear, an underlying allergy to food may also exist. If it does, management of other allergens will not clear up the problem. Foods most often indicted in childhood eczema are milk, eggs and probably wheat. In adult eczema these foods, plus oranges, potatoes, spinach and codfish, seem to be the most active agents.

Urticaria

Without too much equivocation, we can say that sensitivity to food is the most frequent cause of urticaria (hives) in childhood and, in adolescence and adulthood, may be as important an agent for this skin reaction as are drugs and chemicals. Inhalants may also cause hives, but probably less commonly than the unholy three of milk, eggs and wheat. Infection may also play a role, and some doctors believe that acute and chronic infections can produce urticaria. Parasitic infestation, toxic conditions and other factors may also produce urticaria as well as angioedema (giant hives), but the largest percentage of these skin manifestations are probably allergic in nature and are normally accompanied by other symptoms of allergy, such as hay fever, asthma, gastrointestinal distress and headaches.

Urticaria can be either acute, with hives appearing at once or almost at once after ingestion of food and lasting for only a short time, or chronic, with hives appearing some time after ingestion and persisting for longer than a month. Uncommon foods such as shellfish, seasonal fruits, nuts and peanuts are apt to bring on the acute form. Such items of daily fare as milk and wheat are apt to be responsible for chronic hives.

In general, the following foods are most often involved in the allergic reactions of both urticaria and angioedema:

fresh fruits and vegetables	nuts
chocolate	peas
eggs	pork
milk	wheat
tomatoes	fish
shellfish	

Those that less commonly bring forth hives are:

beans
cheese
corn
mint and licorice
pickles
mayonnaise and mustard
seasonings and spices
cola

Even the odor of some foods, especially onions and garlic, and the cooking fumes of such foods as fish may cause the severely hypersensitive to blossom forth.

More recently indicted by many allergists as agents of urticaria are various additives in food products, particularly dyes of coal tar derivation used to color foods and some preservatives such as benzoic acid and sulfur dioxide. We discuss the problem of additives in Chapter Nine, for it is of growing concern to many physicians and their allergic patients.

Urticaria wheals are often haloed in red and look something like mosquito bites with white centers. They are characterized by itching and burning. They are commonly widespread over the body and are found especially in areas where clothing exerts pressure.

The mechanism of both urticaria and angioedema, like that of eczema, is still somewhat mysterious, but it is thought that, at least in the acute form, histamine is released to cause blood vessels to dilate and fluid to leak into the tissues. Dilation and leakage are responsible for the redness and swelling. Both types of hives occur frequently in association with visceral symptoms such as abdominal pain and serumlike sickness with vomiting, diarrhea, headache and breathing difficulties. Often it takes two allergenic factors working together to produce both these skin reactions. Thus, a person might well enjoy chocolate bars with no problem until ragweed season rolls around. Then every time he munches a chocolate bar, hives blossom. Why suddenly out of the blue? For the answer, we must refer back to the load level of our allergy seesaw. A mild allergy to ragweed plus a mild allergy to chocolate outweigh the individual's threshold of tolerance. Out pop the hives.

One odd fact that we should add here is that women seem to suffer from hives more than men.

Angioedema

Angioedema, or giant hives, is a strange and sometimes grotesque reaction to allergens. Regular, recurrent attacks with intervals of relief indicate that food is probably at the root of the problem.

Edema in this reaction can be quite mild or very severe. When it affects the larynx and mouth, serious obstruction of the airways results. Angioedema can occur in almost any part of the body and in various organs—salivary glands, nerve tissue, membranes of the brain and spinal cord, the gastrointestinal system, to list a few.

An odd reaction to food is a generalized edema affecting the whole body or at least a good part of it. Since it is so widespread, it is often not noticeable to patient or doctor. One physician reports the case of a woman afflicted by this strange reaction, who kept three sizes of clothes handy to fit her constantly varying body size. Another doctor records the case of a man who gained seven pounds when he ate a single peanut. This weird condition is often accompanied by muscle weakness, excessive fatigue and nervous symptoms. There are, of course, other causes for fluid retention and bloating, but food allergy is one cause. Probably to a lesser extent, allergy to drugs and inhalants are also causes.

Urinary System

It may be helpful to parents to know that food allergy is considered one possible cause of bed wetting and enuresis (the involuntary discharge of urine from the bladder). One study reports that 5 percent of allergic children suffer enuresis. Cystitis (inflammation of the bladder), though it can be caused by infection, can also be a reaction to food allergens. And allergy to inhalants can also bring on these problems. But the following foods seem to be the more common agents:

> eggs
> milk
> chocolate
> tomatoes
> food colors and flavorings
> wheat
> citrus fruits
> cola drinks
> some nuts

Sometimes bladder reactions are seasonal, corresponding either with the ingestion of seasonal foods or with pollen or mold spore productions.

Nervous System

Headaches

Allergic headaches are perhaps the most annoying and often the most painful of food allergy manifestations. Just about everyone, children and adults alike, are familiar with the torment a headache can cause, but few realize that allergy is often the instigator of their pain. There are, of course, other possible causes for headaches—acute and chronic infection (of the sinuses in particular), diseases of the nervous system, brain tumors, heart and liver problems, tension and emotional troubles, and others. Normally, headaches with an allergic basis are accompanied by other allergic symptoms such as rhinitis or gastrointestinal disturbances—nausea, vomiting, diarrhea and abdominal distention. But sometimes an aching head is the only symptom.

The pain or ache of an allergic headache is usually situated along the front of the head, even along the bridge of the nose and cheek area, although it may be felt at the top or back of the head. About 80 percent of frontal headaches are due to allergic causes. Dizziness and sometimes visual disorders such as blind areas often accompany an aching head. In fact, some pretty bizarre manifestations can occur. For instance, a patient may know exactly what it is he wishes to say, but when he tries to talk, he is incoherent or says it backwards!

How can an allergy to food (or other allergens) cause such misery?

Two things that happen during other types of allergic reaction can also happen in the cranial area: (1) edema due to the leakage of fluid from blood vessels dilating and thinning in response to the allergen-antibody conflict, and (2) constriction or spasm of the smooth muscles. The nausea and vomiting that can accompany allergic headaches is probably the allergy process.

It is generally believed that emotions and stress play a part in allergic headaches, probably as a trigger rather than as a primary agent. And, of course, an allergic headache itself can produce emotional symptoms of disorientation and confusion.

Opinion is divided as to the relative importance of food and inhalants in allergic headaches. One food or several may be the agents of these headaches, and an additional allergy to an inhalant can complicate matters. The onset of pain may not immediately follow the ingestion of an allergenic food but may arrive hours later. The following foods are most commonly responsible for allergic headaches:

nuts
chocolate
milk
wheat
corn
fish
citrus fruit
eggs
tomatoes

In my experience, wheat seems to be the most common cause of allergic headaches.

"Sinus headache" is a term loosely applied to headaches characterized by frontal pain and pain around the eyes. Sinus headaches can be caused by allergic rhinitis and its concomitant edema and congestion. Unless accompanied by a thick, yellowish nasal discharge and local tenderness, the chances are that such a headache is not the infectious condition of true sinusitis.

Perhaps the most mysterious of all headaches is migraine. Migraine, meaning *half head,* seems to be a disease that plagues only the "civilized." Some doctors believe it walks hand in hand with intellectual ability. If so, women liberationists may be able to make something of the fact that about twice as many women suffer from migraine as do men.

Migraine headaches may begin in childhood; but most often they appear in early adulthood. Somewhere around half the victims report that it runs in their families. Certainly, most of us have known at least one person who retires periodically to a darkened room to wait out the storm of this extremely painful affliction.

What causes migraine is still a subject of controversy. Some doctors believe that sensitivity to food is a major cause; others discount the role of allergy altogether. Still others believe that the percentage of migraine due to allergy is about the same as the percentage of allergic persons in the total population. Thus, they say, if 15 percent of the population is allergic, then some 15 percent of migraine headaches have allergic origins. However, a recent study (1980) of 60 migraine patients demonstrated a significant decrease in migraine attacks, with 85 percent of the patients becoming headache-free, when certain common foods, wheat especially, were eliminated from their diets (see Appendix F).

Migraine typically makes its presence felt about once to three times a month. In between attacks the victim is entirely free of symptoms. Sometimes attacks are preceded by an aura, a disturbance of the senses ranging from vague feelings of tension to visual distortions such as flashing bright lights. The victim may even hear noises. Usually migraine arrives in the morning and rapidly mushrooms into a pounding ache, perhaps generalized at first but then localized in one area of the head. It may or may not be accompanied by nausea, vomiting and other symptoms of gastrointestinal distress. Normally all this misery lasts from about eight to twenty-four hours, but it can linger for several days.

Migraine can be triggered by physical agents such as cold, heat and light, or by tension, stress and fatigue, or by gastrointestinal upsets and infections. The following foods are thought to play a major role:

eggs	milk
wheat	pork

fish	chocolate
legumes	corn
garlic	cinnamon

In addition, individuals suffering this unhappy condition would do well to avoid alcoholic beverages, particularly red wine and champagne. They may also have to forego aged cheeses, especially Cheddar, since these contain tyramine, a substance that seems to precipitate migraine. Tyramine is also present in large amounts in chicken livers and pickled herring, so a migraine sufferer would do well to add these to his proscribed list unless he is sure they have no effect on him.

There is one other type of headache we should mention here—the histaminic headache. The relationship of allergy to this rather strange headache is not yet clear. Some doctors believe food allergy is a basic cause; others doubt that allergy has much if anything to do with it. In any case, the headache itself is a "bummer." It is probably the most severe of all head pains but, fortunately, is of very brief duration, lasting usually only for a few minutes. But those few minutes can be terrifying. The headache often arrives at night, bringing a sound sleeper bolt upright as if he had been stabbed. The pain is so intense that usually he is forced to walk around until it subsides. It is a piercing, burning pain, often on one side of the head at one time, on the other side at another time. It can also occur in the general area of the temple or eye and sometimes in the face. The headache seems to result from the release of histamine with dilation of intracranial and extracranial blood vessels. Fortunately, histaminic headache is uncommon.

Allergic Tension-Fatigue Syndrome

Next to the headaches we have just discussed, this strange syndrome is the most common manifestation of cerebral and nervous system allergy.

It's a little hard to believe that what he eats can change a person's personality, but in a way this is true. For instance, one doctor reports the case of a small boy who was extremely irritable and suffered frequent headaches. The minute the doctor discovered that tomatoes were his problem and eliminated them from his diet, the boy became a tractable, pleasant child. The same doctor also described a little girl who suffered from such severe depression that she refused to go out of the house to play. Once chocolate was totally removed from her diet, she became the embodiment of that phrase, "a living doll."

The mechanism of allergic tension-fatigue syndrome, like that of migraine, is open to speculation. Some allergists believe that it is a definite allergic reaction of localized edema in nerve and other tissue, occurring by itself or accompanied by other allergic symptoms, such as eczema, hay fever and asthma.

Some allergists also believe that they can usually spot the child suffering this condition the minute he walks into their office. This child is pale with dark puffy circles under his eyes (called "allergic shiners"), and he looks exactly what he is, tired. Almost invariably he has a stuffy nose and almost invariably he is nervous, irritable and unpredictable in his behavior.

There are really two sets of symptoms exhibited in this allergic reaction to food (and/or inhalants). On the one hand are the tension symptoms exhibited by the restless, awkward, ceaselessly active child who cannot remain still for one minute. This is the hyperactive child guaranteed to drive teachers and parents alike up the wall. He is physically clumsy—dropping and breaking and falling. His attention span is almost nil. He is argumentive and unable to get along with either peers or siblings. He is the child who seems to wade kneedeep in trouble from the time he gets up in the morning until he is tucked in at night. He can be and often is an unpleasant pest.

The other side of the coin is the drowsy or stuporous child, so tired that he catnaps during the day even though he has had a good night's rest. This is the child so inattentive in the classroom that his teachers accuse him of daydreaming, and his schoolwork may be so poor that they may consider him mentally retarded. He is often singled out by his peers as a "dummy."

The symptoms of the allergic tension-fatigue syndrome are the following:

> drowsiness and inability to concentrate
> fatigue and listlessness
> confusion
> depression
> emotional instability and irritability
> belligerence
> poor coordination
> temper tantrums and schizophrenic manifestations (occasionally)

Foods most often indicted are:

> milk
> wheat
> spices and condiments
> eggs
> chocolate
> cola
> sugar

The sad part of all this is that secondary emotional problems may result, some of them to remain as permanent aspects of the child's personality. It is not hard to imagine, for instance, what being constantly scolded in school and at home can do to the child's self-esteem and confidence.

Children are not alone in suffering from the allergic tension-fatigue syndrome. One pediatrician has noted that parents bringing in their "nervous" and "rundown" children often themselves exhibit the same symptoms. Dr. Walter Alvarez, well-known medical columnist and himself allergic, has spoken of his own "Dumb Mondays," brought about by his once habitual Sunday chicken dinner. This may seem an airy way of dismissing Monday morning goofs, but who can say how much of Monday blunderings may be due to chicken or the equivalent habitual fare on Sundays? It would be interesting to know just how many people have been labeled neurotic and bundled off to the psychiatrist's couch when they really needed an allergist and a change of diet (and/or control measures for inhalants in their environment). That is not to say that all odd behavior and emotional disturbances are caused by the things people eat (or breathe). But perhaps more are than we realize.

In any case, the question of the role of food allergy in behavior and emotional disturbances is presently a matter of heated controversy but of very little scientific basis. Even so, physicians whose practice is chiefly clinical know from experience that certain foods apparently create behavioral problems and emotional upset, although just why or what substances in the specific food remains a mystery. In addition, it may not be the food itself that is the offender as much as it is the additives, intentional and non-intentional. Artificial colors and flavorings in both food and medications have come under fire recently, as we shall discuss later in the book.

Epilepsy

It is now believed by some allergists that a certain percentage of epilepsy cases may be due to allergy, in all probability to food allergy. Some doctors even believe that allergy may be the major cause of this strange disorder; others insist the percentage is very small. In some cases of epilepsy, other symptoms of allergy, such as rhinitis and urticaria, are present, which increases the possibility of allergy as the root cause. Foods reported in the literature as being probable agents of epilepsy are:

milk
eggs
wheat
pork

Emotional Disturbance

While allergy to food may be responsible for a good many of the specific symptoms of the nervous system, other symptoms of sensitivity to food may be so severe as to trail emotional and psychological problems in their wake. It does not take much imagination to comprehend how the itching of a severe case of eczema, for instance, can transform a reasonable and emotionally stable person into an irritable, nervous wreck. Nor is it difficult to understand how a charming, attractive girl can become melancholy and depressed when afflicted by the constant sniffle and postnasal drip of allergic rhinitis. Thus, allergy to food (or whatever) can be either directly an agent of emotional disturbances or indirectly, because of the anguish it causes.

To sum up, allergy to food (and to other things as well) can affect just about any part of the body and, on occasion, more than one system at the same time. To illustrate—I recently had referred to me a six-year-old boy with a history of red blood cells in his urine, a rather worrisome symptom for his parents until the cause was discovered. The child also had a history of allergic rhinitis, so a knowledgeable pediatrician had eliminated some foods and started the boy on antihistamines. The result was the elimination of his symptoms. But the boy was sent on to me for a further investigation of foods and other allergens to which he might also be sensitive. After we had done an allergy workup, we placed him on a diet that eliminated corn, wheat, milk, eggs, peas, chicken, fish, cherries, dates, nuts, broccoli, and his troubles.

Does allergy to food play a role in chronic arthritis? Some physicians believe that it does. Others insist that rather than an allergic reaction to food, the problem is one of a toxic reaction. So far, food as a culprit in this often crippling and always painful disease is only a hypothesis awaiting thorough investigation. Incidentally, a toxic reaction differs from an allergic reaction in that it is an ingredient of the food, caffeine in coffee for example, that is responsible for symptoms, rather than the individual's sensitivity to a particular food.

In the next chapter we discuss how the allergist goes about determining whether allergy to food is at the bottom of these wide-ranging symptoms we've looked at here.

Checklist

Anaphylactic shock is the most severe reaction to allergens and requires immediate medical care.

The symptoms of food allergy duplicate the symptoms of many other diseases. The doctor must first rule out these other possibilities in a process called differential diagnosis.

Glossary

anaphylactic shock:
  State of collapse
angioedema:
  Giant hives, deep swelling
cutaneous:
  Pertaining to the skin
cystitis:
  Inflammation of bladder
dermatitis:
  Inflammation of skin with itching, lesions and redness
eczema:
  Inflammation of skin with intense itching
enuresis:
  Involuntary discharge of urine from bladder
epilepsy:
  Disturbance of consciousness with possible generalized convulsions
larynx:
  Voice organ
migraine:
  Sharp, sudden attacks of headache
pharynx:
  Passage at the back of mouth that functions both as airway from nose to larynx and food route from mouth to esophagus
rhinitis:
  Inflammation of nasal mucous membranes
serous otitis:
  Inflamed condition of ear
tenesmus:
  Persistent desire to empty bowel and straining without result
urticaria:
  Hives
vascular headache:
  General term for migraine, histamine and allergic headaches in which blood vessels dilate and pain nerve endings are stimulated

Four

How To Ferret Out the Villain

The allergic individual who walks into the allergist's office may be a veritable bundle of complaints and symptoms, some very specific, others vague or diffuse. How does the allergist determine (1) whether the patient is suffering from allergy, and (2) what specific allergens are causing his misery?

Well, he has a procedure for going about what amounts to a bit of detective work. First, he probably will listen patiently and sympathetically to the patient's recital of symptoms. This is the beginning of the history-taking process so important in the diagnosis of allergy. Buried somewhere in this history of the patient and his family may be important clues to the "what" and "why" of his problems. The allergist, like a detective, assembles clues, pieces them together and solves the puzzle. Usually.

Symptoms first.

And then suspicion.

Suspicion often is thought to be an all too human failing and not always an honorable one, but sometimes suspicion can be an asset. It is amazing how often suspicion, that small cloud of doubt on the horizon of consciousness, can blossom into full-fledged conviction, and then, often as not, be proved fact. So it is frequently with those allergic to food. Many persons seem to know intuitively what isn't good for them. Perhaps not at the first appearance of symptoms—but after awhile they put two and two together.

"Can't touch it," they say. "Doesn't agree with me."

And they may be quite right. Doctors estimate that patients correctly comprehend the source of their difficulties about 20 percent of the time. Just enough to ensure that attention should be paid to food dislikes and to statements about what doesn't agree with the patient. Babies and very young children will sometimes stubbornly refuse to eat certain foods, especially eggs. Often, to a mother's dismay, her child will spit food out, usually forcefully. Is he just being naughty? Well, maybe, but he could also be protesting the fact that the egg or spinach or tomato is making his mouth and lips burn or itch. Perhaps if she looks closely, a mother might see that her child's face was flushed and even a little swollen. What is happening? An immediate reaction to food allergens. No wonder he won't eat the stuff!

A severely hypersensitive child can react violently to the more potent allergenic foods such as eggs. For instance, he can burst forth abruptly into hives if he just touches an egg shell, much less eats the egg. And there are adults so sensitive that if they merely kiss someone who has recently dined on eggs, they react. Surely that would be enough to take eggs off the breakfast menus in highly allergic families.

There is an interesting contradiction to the clues suggested by food dislikes, and that is the theory that some people actually become addicted to the foods that cause their allergy disease, even as alcoholics become addicted to their liquor. According to this theory, not only does the victim crave the allergenic food, he even derives temporary relief from his symptoms when he eats it. Proponents of this theory suggest that a variety of symptoms of allergy disease are akin to the withdrawal symptoms of the alcoholic. When the victim consumes more of the allergenic food, he finds relief, just as the alcoholic obtains relief by downing a "touch of the hair of the dog" that bit him the night before. If this theory is valid, the habit of "craving" a food would naturally be difficult to break. And, of course, if the allergic individual kept on "craving" and eating, his symptoms would remain chronic.

In general, however, food likes and dislikes are the tip of the iceberg. It seems reasonable to suppose that most adults—like stubborn children—simply do not eat what they dislike and so avoid what makes them ill. Children, of course, are harried or bribed into stuffing down things considered especially good for them no matter what their own inclination may be. Dislikes in their case may be a particularly valid clue in tracking down food sensitivities.

Usually, though, allergy symptoms are caused by the basic foods of our daily fare, such staples as milk, eggs, wheat and corn. Most patients sensitive to these foods rarely have the slightest suspicion that this is so. The more exotic a food, the more chance the average allergy sufferer can suspect the guilty item. This shouldn't be surprising. What is eaten less often can be pinpointed much more easily than foods consumed more or less daily and responsible for chronic symptoms.

If hives follow the first strawberry shortcake of the season, there isn't much doubt about the connection, but if hives come and go the year round, it is hardly likely that an individual will recognize that the cause is wheat contained in a large variety of the foods he eats every day.

Thus, some people who arrive at the allergist's office convinced that they know what is causing their problems may be quite correct. But most sufferers arrive bemused and perplexed.

With symptoms and suspicions noted, the allergist may turn next to the patient's family history, both on the paternal and maternal sides. His quetsions may have to be specific, for often in the past such things as asthma were called "weak lungs" or the "tizzy," and allergic rhinitis had an unfortunate way of being dismissed as "just one cold after another" or the "catarrh," while a somewhat constant tendency to gastrointestinal upset was considered a "weak stomach."

Questions about the illnesses of grandparents and parents may seem to the patient to have little bearing on his own problems. But when the allergist presses him about aunts, uncles, cousins and his own children, he may really begin to wonder what all this has to do with him. Such questions are important, for they not only help to rule out other disease possibilities such as cystic fibrosis, diabetes, congenital heart disease and the like, but they may establish the presence of an inherited tendency to allergy. As we have already noted, a confirmed history of allergy on both sides of the family predisposes strongly. If allergy appears on one side of the family only, the patient's chances may be reduced yet still run much higher than for those with no family history of allergies.

Thus, the questions about Aunt Hettie's hay fever or Grandmother's fearful headaches or Father's face that swelled up like a balloon whenever he came close to a cat, all have bearing on the patient's problem. So, down through the aches and pains of the preceding generations until we get back to the patient.

In the patient's own history, specific symptoms are easier to come by. If the patient is a child, it is relatively easy to establish, via his parents, the early signs of allergy—infantile eczema, colic, even fetal hiccoughs. Feeding habits of the child during infancy may also have bearing on his present problem. The poor feeder, as well as the baby with colic, may have been exhibiting symptoms of allergy early on. Frequent changes of formula, bouts of diarrhea, problems with homogenized milk when it was begun—All are possible indications of early sensitivity.

Adult patients, of course, may have some difficulty providing this kind of early information, but other symptoms that have followed—eczema, allergic rhinitis, asthma—can be catalogued with more authority. The doctor may wish to know the patient's general health history and when symptoms first appeared and, if possible, under what circumstances. He would probably ask about any previous or current medications or drugs the patient might be taking including laxatives, aspirin and even the mouthwash he uses. Then, he may concentrate on the symptoms themselves.

Do they come on gradually? Or suddenly? How frequently? How long do they last? Under what circumstances do they begin? When the patient is in bed? Exercising? At work? Do the symptoms seem related to various activities such as house cleaning, mowing grass, driving on the freeway? Do they follow exposure to such things as dust, hay, mold? Do they follow a specific meal? Do they seem related to emotional upsets? Physical ailments? What time of the day do they occur? (If in the morning, pollen could be to blame or eggs for breakfast or occupational or schoolroom inhalants.) What time of the week? (Weekends suggest the fish on Fridays or chicken on Sundays or picnic foods.) What time of the year? (Seasonal pollens or seasonal foods?)

The allergist may surprise the patient by asking when and where he is free of symptoms, for this may be as important as the preceding questions. If he is free of symptoms at work, then the cause may be found at home. And vice versa. If he is better at the homes of friends or on vacation, then home is where his harassment probably is. If he is better indoors than out, then pollen or pollution may be the answer. And so on.

Clues are what the allergist is after, and he seeks them with question after question. When he is done with symptoms, he may turn to the patient's environment.

Where does he live? In what sort of surroundings? In a low spot or ravine? On a hillside? In the woods? Urban or suburban? In what kind of house? Brick? Stone? Wood? Is there a basement? How is it heated? Is it a relatively new house? What kind of energy is used to cook with?

Again, the patient may wonder, what has this to do with allergy?

Quite a bit. A house built on low ground may invite mold; a house on a hillside may invite pollen. Urban areas are more heavily polluted, and pollution is becoming an important factor these days in allergy. If the house is old or built of stone or has a basement, mold may well be at least part of the patient's problem. Home heating and cooking equipment often have a good deal to do with allergy. Forced air stirs up large amounts of potently allergenic house dust; fuel oil creates potentially allergenic fumes; electric heat is just about incapable of causing problems; natural gas has caused a number of problems for persons bending over hot stoves, including exhibitions of peculiar behavior.

By now the questions have become rapid fire.

Are there any pets in the house? Even a bearskin rug? Horsehair couch or mattress? Has the patient noticed any connection between his symptoms and cold? Heat? Sunlight? What is his occupation? In what sort of place does he work? Are chemicals or fumes involved?

Occupational allergy runs high among certain workers—those in metal and chemical industries, bakeries and dry cleaning establishments. If the patient is a child, it may even be important to know the father's or mother's occupation—for either parent may bring home allergens on his clothing. One doctor cites a case in which the father of an asthmatic child worked as a grain elevator operator. Whenever he worked with soybeans, he had to change his clothes in the basement and wash his hair each evening when he came home to avoid precipitating an asthma attack in his child.

By this time, the patient may be getting restless. What has all this to do with his suspected allergy to food? The allergist is trying to get the "big picture." A person allergic to one thing is very often allergic to something else. Not only must the allergist search for clues to the suspected food sensitivity, but he must be sure no other allergy lurks in the background. He knows that he may not be able to alleviate all symptoms by removing one cause alone.

When food is already suspected, the most important questions of all, naturally, will relate to the patient's diet. Likes, dislikes and suspicions have already been explored. Now the allergist gets down to the nuts and peanuts of the patient's dietary history to find out exactly what he eats, how much and how frequently. The doctor will probably pay particular attention to the foods most commonly indicted in allergy—those we noted at the beginning of Chapter Two:

milk	fish and shellfish
eggs	berries
wheat	peas
chocolate	citrus fruits
nuts	corn

And perhaps the following:

pork	beer and wine
chicken	spinach
mustard	tomatoes
legumes	cherries
cola drinks	tomatoes

The doctor may also ask about nebulous symptoms the patient may not have noticed—gas or nausea, a feeling of fatigue or unwellness, or a mild headache following ingestion of a food. These may be the earliest symptoms of a sensitivity to a specific food, and they are the easiest to ignore.

All in all, the process of history-taking is a long and detailed business, often taking up an hour of both the patient's and the doctor's time. However, it is a vital procedure in diagnosis.

And when the allergist has the "big picture," what then?

Then comes a thorough physical examination with special attention to the body system or systems affected. Here, again, the doctor is seeking clues. For instance, the mucous membrane of the nose in allergic rhinitis looks different than when the patient is suffering from an infection. In allergy, the membrane usually appears pale and boggy; in infection it will probably be red and inflamed. In general, the allergist is as busy ruling *out* other possibilities as he is ruling *in* allergy.

The patient may also present an allergic portrait or facial aspect, especially if he is a child. This is the allergic facies, a recognizable physical appearance that may consist of the following features:

> long face
> high cheek bones
> somewhat pointed chin
> noticeable overbite
> pallor
> dark, puffy circles under the eyes called allergic shiners
> watery eyes

Allergic children very often have long, silky eyelashes, and sometimes, a horizontal crease near the end of the nose, created by a constant rubbing of the nose in a distinctive upward gesture called the allergic salute. This allergic salute is so characteristic that the allergist usually can recognize it a block away. Often, however, parents never notice this ceaseless gesture in their own child.

Other possible signs of allergy are:

> mouth breathing
> snoring
> a tendency to frequent coughing or clearing of the throat
> instability in weight due to retention of fluids during severe
>   bouts with allergy

The allergist, more than likely, will include some laboratory tests with the physical examination. Their extensiveness will depend upon his suspicions and the patient's symptoms. Among other things, he will probably take smears of blood, nasal secretions or stool, depending perhaps upon which body systems are exhibiting symptoms. In addition to ruling out other disease possibilities, what he is looking for in these smears is the increased presence (above normal counts) of eosinophilic cells, which would indicate sensitized tissue. Eosin means *red,* philos means *to love;* these somewhat large eosinophilic cells have a unique property of soaking up red stain, thus making themselves highly identifiable. They often are found in allergic persons. However, since their increased presence may also be indicative of internal infestation by parasites, they are not conclusive evidence but just one more clue in a growing pattern.

The allergist may also include an urinalysis in his allergy work-up, since infection of the urinary tract may cause symptoms of vomiting, diarrhea and abdominal pain similar to those of allergy.

Then there are skin tests. As a diagnostic tool, skin tests have come a long way in allergy, but the one exception is allergy to food. In this case, they are not really reliable. In fact, some doctors do not even bother with them when they strongly suspect sensitivity to food. Others, however, believe that they are of help in providing suspects, even though the procedure is just as likely to overlook genuine culprits and even indict foods that are not guilty. But skin tests are reliable for inhalant allergies and so are useful to ensure that such allergens are not working in conjunction with food allergens.

Exactly why skin tests are not reliable in food sensitivity is unknown. One suggested reason is that in the preparation of the test extracts, the allergenic properties of the food are nullified. Another theory suggests that their unreliability is due to a less direct connection between the skin and gastrointestinal tract than exists between the skin and the respiratory system. Whatever the cause, results of skin testing in food allergy must be taken with a grain of salt, if you will excuse the figure of speech.

Then why do them for foods?

Those doctors who use them believe that, while they are not reliable diagnostic tools, they may confirm (or not confirm) the presence of a sensitivity to food or foods, in conjunction with dietary trials and the patient's history. For instance, some doctors deliberately feed the patient large amounts of a food that has caused a marked positive reaction in a skin test to determine whether or not the patient is truly sensitive to that food. The skin test pointed the way but could not be completely trusted. In addition, doctors who use skin testing for food believe it an objective test and that results may indicate some evidence of allergy. I believe that marked skin reactions to certain foods, such as eggs, are significant.

The procedure of skin testing is quite simple, although the patient might not think so when he first sees the tray loads of paraphernalia in the treatment room. Equally horrifying may be his first look at the list of substances the allergist proposes to test for. However, the process is so quick that a list of some two hundred extracts can be disposed of in one or two office visits. Nor should the patient flinch at the sight of the scarifier for scratch testing or the hypodermic for intradermal testing, for normally no blood is drawn.

The scratch (or prick) test consists of making a tiny scratch on the skin, usually on the patient's back or his inner arm below the elbow. A drop of extract of the substance to be tested is then applied and rubbed gently into the scratch. The patient waits for about twenty minutes in the office until it is time to read the results. If nothing has happened at the scratch site, the test is considered negative. If, on the other hand, something resembling a mosquito bite has appeared, the result is positive, and the patient is considered potentially allergic to that substance.

If there is a negative reaction to a scratch test, the allergist may move on to intradermal testing of that substance, for the intradermal procedure is more effective in detecting a weaker sensitivity to an allergen. However, since with this method a potent food allergen can give rise to a severe reaction, it is employed with caution.

The intradermal test consists of injecting a small amount of the extract into the upper layer of the skin, usually on the upper arm. The results are normally in in about ten minutes. Again, the appearance of a mosquito bite or hive indicates a positive reaction.

When skin testing to some foods has positive results, the allergist will usually cross these foods off the diet he prescribes. Or he may challenge the patient then and there by giving him a significant quantity of the food to consume to see if it does indeed cause symptoms. The drawback of simply accepting the positive results of intradermal or scratch tests is that, because they are unreliable, the patient may not be allergic to the food at all and will be deprived for no good reason.

Even if the skin test results are negative, the patient may be sensitive to the food in question.

Recently, a new diagnostic method worthy of the computer age has been developed. Essentially a laboratory test, it is an in vitro procedure (in a glass, i.e., a test tube), which measures the IgE antibodies that are the hallmark of allergy. This test, the Radioallergosorbent test, mercifully dubbed the RAST, couples a bit of the patient's blood with various allergen extracts on separate paper discs, incubates them for a few hours and washes away the extraneous material to leave only the patient's antibodies to a specific extract. After several additional steps in the process, the radioactivity of the discs is measured. The higher the count, the more IgE antibodies are bound to a given extract. A scale has been developed so that the relative degree of IgE present on the disc can be assessed. Above normal amounts are indicative of hypersensitivity to a food.

As the reader is certain to suspect by now, this is a complex and somewhat time- and money-consuming procedure, perhaps best employed for the unfortunate patient who suffers from multiple food allergies. Probably a good many allergists still place their faith in the basic diagnostic tool for food allergy—diet followed by a careful reintroduction of foods.

Elimination diet sounds a bit grim, and in truth some of the diets prescribed can be spartan indeed, so much so that they could cheer only a veteran weight watcher. In fact, for severe cases, some doctors prescribe spring water or sweetened tea only until the body has a chance of clear itself of allergens. Other doctors restrict their patients to a menu containing four or five foods, especially when symptoms occur more or less daily, and if symptoms continue, they drop the lot and substitute four or five others.

Most allergists simply prescribe a diet that eliminates (1) those foods suspected on the basis of the patient's history, his likes, dislikes and suspicions; (2) those foods that are considered potent allergens; and (3) probably those foods indicated in positive skin tests and challenge tests. Often, the allergist gives the patient not only a list of foods he should not eat but also a list of all the things he may eat. The diet needs to be tailored to the individual patient, for his general health and nutritional needs must be taken into account. A growing child, for example, or a man in an occupation that requires a high caloric intake, may need a quite different diet than does a sedentary office worker or an elderly patient.

We should add here that diet prescription is no do-it-yourself procedure—not only must specific health and nutritional needs be considered but also particular vitamins or other nutritional supplements to ensure a balanced diet may be prescribed by the doctor.

Usually, the patient is asked to remain on the elimination diet for a period of fourteen to eighteen days, the time necessary to clear his system entirely of allergenic foods. If symptoms persist after this interval, the doctor probably will wish to remove still other foods. When all symptoms have vanished, then it is time to reintroduce foods one by one into the diet, usually starting with fruits and vegetables. Normally, the allergist recommends that three- to five-day intervals separate the reintroduction of each new food. This is to allow time for a reaction to occur, if it's going to.

When a reaction occurs immediately after a food is reintroduced, the patient is apt to be jubilant. Aha, here is the villain! Now all I have to do is not eat it!

Were it that simple.

Often as not, the reaction occurs hours later or even two or three days later, and the cause-and-effect relationship is not that clear. Suspicion may be enough, however, to remove it from the diet, then add it later when the patient is once again symptomfree. If, after two or more such trials, the patient's symptoms reappear upon eating this particular food, then it can be considered a cause of his allergic reaction. If, on the other hand, symptoms appear after the first trial but not the second, it may be that he either can tolerate moderate amounts of the food or that there were other factors at work to bring on his symptoms the first go around—such as an inhalant allergy or infection. As with positive results in skin testing, so in elimination trials: It is not wise to jump to immediate conclusions and to deprive the patient unnecessarily of what may well be a valuable or pleasurable part of his diet.

All in all, reintroduction of foods is a trial and error procedure, working back to what may be considered a normal diet with as few proscribed items as possible. On the return trip, those foods that cause illness are discovered. The elimination diet is both test and remedy, an instrument of discovery and of relief.

To illustrate, let's go back to our long suffering, egg-sensitive gentleman whom we met in Chapter One. He, you will remember, would develop asthma when he ate eggs for breakfast. As he passes through all the above diagnostic procedure, we discover that his father swelled up like a balloon in the presence of a cat; his mother had allergic rhinitis from fall to spring; and he, himself, skin tested positively to egg—so positively in scratch test results that his allergist chose not to attempt an intradermal test. Eggs, of course, are now immediately excluded from the elimination diet he is given. So are the other potent allergenic foods of milk, wheat and chocolate. Home goes our gentleman to remain on this diet for two weeks, but when he reports back, his symptoms are still intact. Obviously, something else beside eggs is at fault. Out come the rest of the commonly allergenic foods. Again, home for two weeks on this somewhat depleted menu. Ah, but this time there is a minor miracle. For the first time in years, our gentleman is symptomfree.

That's wonderful, but what was it beside eggs that caused his symptoms? What else is it that he must avoid?

To find out, the allergist puts, say, orange juice (and other citrus fruits) back into his diet. For a week our friend enjoys his glass of juice at breakfast and all goes well. No sniffle, no wheeze.

Now corn is tried for a week, and again all goes well. One by one the eliminated foods are brought back into our gentleman's life to remain there as long as his symptoms do not reappear. He makes it without incident down the list to fish; suddenly his symptoms flare and he is coughing, sniffling, wheezing, short of breath. Fish, too, is a villain.

This is a simplified and very brief illustration, but perhaps it will suffice to give the reader an idea of how elimination diets are both test and remedy.

During this whole procedure, the allergist may ask the patient to keep a diet diary, a record of foods eaten and when and what sort of symptoms, if any, followed their consumption. In this way, the relationship between foods and symptoms are not only clearer but are a matter of record for the doctor. It is important that everything that goes into the mouth, goes into the diet diary, and that includes such things as chewing gum, toothpaste and mouthwash, laxatives and vitamin pills, unless specially prescribed.

On page 50 is a copy of the kind of diet diary I ask my patients to keep. Note my own preference for reintroduction of foods.

Do elimination diets ever fail?

Well, yes. Sometimes symptoms don't vanish; they simply change in degree with changes in the diet. Often this is because the patient still suffers from an undiscovered allergy to drugs or inhalants. His symptoms stay with him through the thick and thin of an elimination diet.

There are also times when an elimination diet is helpful but not completely successful. For example, if a patient is known to be allergic to ragweed and the elimination diet is doing no good, it may be necessary to wait until the ragweed season is over for the best results. Yet, an underlying allergy to food may be aggravating his hay fever, so that the diet may be helping even if he is not symptomfree. When the patient has an additional allergy to an inhalant, especially to pollen and house dust, to contend with,

ELIMINATION DIET
and
GENERAL RULES FOR FEEDING AN ALLERGIC PATIENT

DR. CLAUDE A. FRAZIER   **ASHEVILLE, N. C.**   **DOCTOR'S PART**

1. When a food is added to the patient's diet, the food must be eaten daily for 5 days. Eat a small portion the first day and a large portion at least twice a day for the next 4 days.
2. Introduce one food at a time into the diet of the patient, and do not add any other food for 7 days. The purpose is to see how each particular food affects the allergy, and of course if it makes it worse, it should be omitted. No new food may be considered as a part of the patient's regular diet until the trial period of 5 days has been observed. If the food causes no symptoms within 5 days of trial, it may be added to the permitted diet after eliminating 2 more days.
3. Add one of the foods listed to the patient's present diet every 7 days.
4. Any food which causes any symptoms should be stopped promptly. Wait until the symptoms caused by the food on trial have subsided completely before trying the next food (2 days).
5. It is not necessary to try any food you do not like, or do not want to add to the normal diet.
6. All foods should be thoroughly cooked before being fed to the patient.
7. Unless you are certain of the ingredients in a certain dish, do not give it to the patient.
8. During the first year of life, only a few foods should be given.
9. When a new food is offered, it should be a single food, and not mixtures. Some prepared vegetables have more than one vegetable present, and if the allergy became worse with the mixed foods, we would not know the single offending food.
10. Excessively large amounts of any food should be avoided. This also applies to milk.
11. No patient should be starved because of his allergy, and allowed to get into a state of malnutrition.
12. Keep a record of the effect of each food added in the chart below.

DATE	FOOD ADDED	EFFECT

it is difficult to track down a food allergy. Sensitivity to food may be playing a much smaller role in producing allergic symptoms than is the inhalant.

Sensitivity to food is also difficult to track down when a patient is suffering from an infection or just recovering from a severe illness, for there is often a lull in a person's allergic symptoms following some viral infections, which is thought to be the body's response to stress.

Finally, antihistamines prescribed to treat the patient's allergic symptoms may have to be discontinued during the period of the elimination diet lest they mask reactions.

In general, however, it can be said that if the will is strong and the flesh not too weak, the elimination diet with careful reintroduction of foods is the best of all possible ways to ferret out guilty allergens. The whole idea is to eliminate any possible cause of allergic reaction, clear the body of lingering allergens, and then start fresh to find out just which foods in the patient's everyday diet are causing his symptoms. And because common, daily foods cause the most trouble generally, eggs, milk, wheat and chocolate are usually the last to be reintroduced. All in all, the elimination diet is a relatively simple process, but it does require patience and will power. Not only is it a long drawn-out process, but it may also require a certain rigid abstinence on the part of the allergic. Still, to be free of symptoms in the end is usually well worth time and trouble. Once the villains are discovered, the patient advances to simple avoidance, the cardinal principle in all allergy.

Did I say *simple* avoidance?

Avoidance is not very simple in this modern era of burgeoning new food products, many of them combinations of mysterious derivation. The allergic person must become an expert dietician, if not a trained chemist. Normally, we don't pay too much attention as to what exactly is in our daily bread, but when we are allergic, we must. For example, here is a brief list of things the corn allergic must avoid:

    corn as a vegetable
    corn cereals
    cornstarch (in puddings, canned applesauce, stews, soups)
    cornmeal and bread
    popcorn
    corn chips
    corn oil (in margarine, for example)
    corn syrup

Thus, to avoid corn, the corn sensitive will have to read food labels with care, and with the fervent hope that they are complete and all ingredients are listed. In Chapters Five, Six, Seven, and Eight I try to be helpful on this score by describing food products in detail, discussing ingredient possibilities and how to avoid some of the more common foods such as milk, eggs and wheat. The first commandment of food avoidance is—read labels. If the product does not list ingredients, those with more than a very mild allergy will do well not to buy it. Or try it. "Try it, you'll like it" may not hold true in this case.

The allergic must not hesitate when dining out to inquire about ingredients in restaurant meals. Nor should the severely allergic person be shy about asking his hostess at a social gathering what her offerings may contain whenever there seems to be doubt.

Once the allergic individual and his doctor, through their joint efforts, have established what food or foods play a part in the patients' allergy, then it is time to settle down to avoidance and good health.

The younger the patient, the more favorable the long-range outlook can be, for children often develop a tolerance to foods that initially brought on an allergic reaction. One exception is the egg-sensitive baby. If he exhibits a marked skin reaction to eggs, he will probably be allergic to them for years to come.

Adults, on the other hand, commonly have to look forward either to a lifetime of abstinence or to a judicious balancing of gastronomical satisfaction with allergic distress. It is possible, though, for an adult to achieve a certain degree of tolerance after he has abstained from a food, usually for several months. Then, after a little experimentation, an allergic person may find that he can tolerate small amounts of proscribed foods at set intervals or that he can develop a certain amount of tolerance by rotating foods and diversifying the diet. In this way, it may be possible to eat allergenic foods in moderate amounts now and again.

Keeping in mind that every doctor has his own way of doing things, we can say that the rotation diet runs something like this: The allergist has determined that fish is the patient's problem. If he has had a severe reaction to fish, such as shock or acute uticaria (hives), then the chances are that he will be told never to try fish again. But if he suffers chronic asthma or rhinitis or the like and has no severe reaction, the allergist may recommend that fish be eliminated from his diet for a lengthy period of time, even after symptoms have vanished. This could be weeks, months, even a year. Then the patient may be advised to try fish again at three-day intervals. I, myself, would tell him to eat fish no more than twice a week. If no reaction occurs, he now has a reasonable assurance of remaining symptom-free. He must be wary, though, of consuming too large an amount at one sitting. He must curb his taste for fish and be moderate.

Such a rotation of foods can help keep the allergy-prone person from becoming sensitized in the first place. And it can help the already food allergic person from developing sensitivity to new foods, if he spaces all potently allergenic foods three to seven days apart. Thus, a patient who is sensitive to fish should also not eat eggs or chocolate, for example, any oftener than every three days or even less often, depending upon the severity of his allergy.

This may sound hopeful, and certainly those allergic to such staple foods as milk, eggs and wheat can re-check for possible tolerance every three or four months. But often, even if the original culprit can be tolerated, a new food villain or, even more likely, a new allergy is apt to surface. Young children tend especially to lose their allergies to food only to gain other sensitivities—to an inhalant, for instance. In any case, however the patient experiments, he should do so only under the direction of his doctor and only if has not suffered acute, severe reactions in the past.

There are several other diagnostic methods, but the winds of controversy howl about them and their reliability is also in question. One, the sublingual provocative food test, consists chiefly of placing a drop of the suspected food under the patient's tongue, then assessing the result. Simple? Yes, but unhappily some have found that a drop of a placebo, in this case of distilled water, was just as apt to produce symptoms of reaction as were drops of the suspected food.

Another test, the cytotoxic test, like RAST is an in vitro procedure. After a twelve-hour fast, blood is drawn from the patient and coupled with various food extracts on slides, then examined under a microscope. If there are certain changes in white blood cells or white blood corpuscles (leukocytes and lymphocytes) to a specific food extract, this indicates a possible allergic reaction. It fits nicely into our technological age; however, it is likely again that most physicians rely mainly on the elimination diet.

Finally, I shall assume a doctor's firm and authoritative stance to assure all allergic patients of the importance of not fudging (perhaps an unfortunate choice of words) on the elimination diet the doctor prescribes or on later avoidance measures that he may suggest. If you would be well, you will simply have to exercise will power. And you will have to be scrupulously honest about your diet diary if you wish to discover the cause of your problem. To be weak in all this is to admit defeat. You will have wasted your money and your doctor's time. A few weeks or months of abstinence from life's goodies is a small price to pay for freedom from the havoc allergy can cause. And, as we discuss in Chapters Five, Six, Seven, and Eight there are ways to substitute to keep the pleasurable in one's diet.

Checklist

Food likes and dislikes may sometimes indicate sensitivity.

The allergist's diagnostic procedure includes (1) history-taking of the patient's symptoms and diet; his family's allergies, his own health, occupation and environment; (2) physical examination;

(3) laboratory tests; (4) skin tests; and (5) elimination diets and reintroduction of foods.

Skin tests usually are not as reliable in food allergy as in allergy to inhalants.

Allergy symptoms are most frequently caused by common foods such as milk, eggs, wheat and corn.

There is often an allergic appearance or facial aspect, especially in children.

It is important to follow to the letter the elimination diet the allergist prescribes.

The diet diary is often vital to establish a clearcut cause-and-effect relationship between foods consumed and symptoms suffered.

Five

Allergenic Foods

When young Tichborne lamented that his "feast of joy is but a dish of pain," he had something to grieve about, since he was on his way to his own beheading for attempting to assassinate Queen Elizabeth I. Still, many a person allergic to one or more foods, especially the common ones that make up our basic fare, echoes that sad lament on his way to the dinner table—at least until he learns how to manage his allergy. But avoidance of a food is no simple matter in this era of prepackaged and prepared foods. Not only that, but a person's reaction to an allergenic food is likely to seem as changeable as a chameleon's reaction to an enemy.

As an example, let's examine the apple. Avoidance seems simple enough. You simply omit apples from your diet. All well and good, but does that mean avoiding such delights as apple pie, apple jelly, baked apples, and cider?

Not necessarily. You may be allergic to apples in the raw and in cider, but perfectly able to tolerate them in applesauce and pie, for cooking often changes the allergenic nature of a food.

But we haven't exhausted the possibilities. Some allergic persons need only peel the apple to be able to enjoy it. The peel brings on reaction, which makes us question whether the individual is truly allergic to the fruit itself or simply to the residue of chemical pesticides still adhering to the peel. These compounds do not always wash off as easily as we might like to think they do.

But saddest of all is the allergic individual who cannot even attempt to peel his apple without symptoms—eyes that water, a nose that runs, a skin that blossoms with hives. The odors of foods can bring on allergic symptoms. In fact, food odors probably play a far greater role in allergy than most people realize or can believe. It may strain credibility to be told that, even if you do not realize that you are smelling an egg frying two rooms away, you are suffering an attack of asthma because of it. Minute particles of that egg are in the air, and you are inhaling the allergens that cause your asthma. If you are severely allergic, it does not take much to set you off.

One doctor reports that one patient of his need only enter a vegetable store to react to spinach piled in its bin. Even if he didn't handle the stuff or only stayed in the store a few minutes, he suffered an attack of asthma. An even odder case is that of a young child so hypersensitive to eggs that her parents could not eat them anywhere in the house without bringing on such severe itching that the child would be aroused from a deep sleep. The poor parents tried to satisfy their fondness for eggs by waiting until the child went to bed, but even though they shut doors between kitchen and bedroom, the first egg to hit the pan brought the child awake crying and scratching.

Thus, food inhaled can be just about as allergenic as food ingested. The following are most often indicated in this rather strange phenomenon:

eggs	fish
beef	pork
cauliflower	spinach
beets	tomato
onion	peas
peanut butter	nuts
some spices	

Fruit is one of life's great pleasures. While undoubtedly good for most of us, it can be the cause of much misery for some. Following that fairly stable rule of allergy, it is the fruit most commonly eaten that usually causes the most trouble—apples, bananas, oranges. But seasonal fruits such as strawberries and melons do elbow their way into the troublemaker category, perhaps because not only are they delicious but their season is short, leading to a fierce temptation to gorge on them in every conceivable shape and form. Fruits that contain seeds are more allergenically potent than those that do not. Thus, apples are probably more allergenic than bananas. Allergic reactions to orange juice may be caused by a seed crushed in the juice-making process rather than by the juice itself. It is thought that the seeds harbor the active allergens.

Fruit pulp may be used as a filler in baked goods and bread. Fruit juice is used in many beverages, ranging from ginger ale to table wine.

Bananas have always seemed to me to be an innocuous fruit, good enough to be served mashed to small babies. But there are numerous reports of banana damage ranging from gastrointestinal distress to anaphylactic shock, the latter, admittedly, a rarity. One physician has reported the case of a teenage girl with a past history of uneventful banana consumption, who suddenly developed life-threatening symptoms after munching on a banana at school. The unfortunate youngster ended up in a hospital.

Among vegetables, legumes, tomatoes, celery, cabbage, cauliflower, white potatoes, mushrooms, carrots, squash and lettuce are generally considered the chief villains in food sensitivity. Doesn't seem to be much left in the garden to eat, does there? These are the vegetables most frequently included in such food products as soups, stews, casseroles and flavorings.

Just handling these vegetables may bring on a reaction in the highly sensitive, some allergists think. Not only may the hypersensitive react when inhaling the vegetable odor, but even touching the food may bring on contact dermatitis or hives. To illustrate, one doctor reports the case of a patient who not only suffered from hives when he ate a tomato but also whenever he touched one. Another doctor tells of a woman who developed asthma the minute she entered a dining room where raw celery had been placed upon the table.

Legumes are potent allergens. One legume that can cause all kinds of trouble for those few who are sensitive is the soybean, that wonder bean so versatile that it is incorporated in all kinds of unlikely products from steering wheels to salad dressing. In a world running short on protein, soybeans are a kind of latterday miracle, except to the Chinese, who have been eating soybeans for thousands of years. For this reason, kwashiokor (a dreadful protein deficiency disease) does not occur in China as it does in much of Africa and some parts of South America.

How is it that the Chinese have so successfully utilized this protein-packed legume, where nobody anywhere else, until recently, caught on to it? Probably because the Chinese are a patient and creative people, and it takes both of these traits to make the soybean edible. Combining various forms of the bean with various strains of fungi and bacteria, the Chinese produce gourmet cheeses, pastes, sauces and curd dishes. And they eat well!

Health food buffs have introduced the soybean as a protein substitute for meat. They have developed some tasty ham, steaks, and the like from the soybean that seem like the real thing. While such substitutes have replaced only about one percent of the meat proteins consumed annually in the United States, we may be seeing the beginning of a dietary revolution.

Here are some of the foods in which you may find the soybean today:

salad dressing	bacon chips and flavorings
salad oil	coffee substitutes
margarine	ice cream
doughnuts	Chinese food (naturally)
whipped toppings	mayonnaise
macaroni	cooking oils
baked goods of various kinds	shortening
cakes	pancakes
chili	hot dogs

soup   lunch meats
breakfast foods   pork sausage
candy   sauces
meat loaf   cheese preparations

Quite a list for the soybean allergic to avoid. But that's not all for the ubiquitous soybean. One strange case has been reported of a lady who could tolerate cola drink if it came in a returnable bottle but was unable to enjoy coke in the "no deposit, no return" bottle. The reason? The throwaways were made of plastic in which soybeans were an ingredient, and she was unfortunate enough to be one of the few highly sensitive to soybeans. It may seem strange that soybean contamination could pass from container to beverage, but it doesn't take much of the allergen to set off the severely allergic.

Factories turning out the great variety of products incorporating soybeans can also generate enough soybean pollution of the air in their immediate neighborhoods to affect those highly sensitive to the bean.

Pulverized soybean in liquid form looks like cow's milk and is used as a milk substitute for those allergic to milk. Soya flour is employed widely for the allergic and nonallergic person alike.

The other legumes are also potent allergens, especially the peanut. So potent are peanuts (a legume, remember—not a nut) to the unfortunate few severely allergic to them, that a person can carefully pick out everything but peanuts from a bowl of nuts and yet suffer a reaction because the nuts he ate were in contact with the potent peanut. It is conceivable that the very sensitive cannot enjoy the company of those who have recently consumed a peanut butter sandwich. What a blow this would be to a large family. Let one child be hypersensitive and out goes the mainstay of all the rest.

Adults allergic to peanuts may have to forego their coffee-break doughnuts unless they can be certain the doughnuts have not been fried in peanut oil. However, just how much of the allergenic quality of vegetables is retained in the refining process to obtain their oils is open to question.

One practice, made prevalent with the success of food processors, and inherently dangerous for the individual allergic to peanuts, is that of slicing peanuts so thinly that they resemble almonds. Sprinkled on cakes and cookies and the like they are potential booby traps for the unwary.

With the exception of the peanut, most vegetables do not cause severe reactions. But allergy to nuts is a different story. It is fortunate that such sensitivity is not too common since reactions to nuts can often be sudden and harsh. I once treated a man so hypersensitive that if someone so much as cracked a walnut in the same room with him, he would suffer a serious reaction. Women allergic to almonds must be doubly wary, for not only are almonds used widely in foods and flavorings but some cosmetics contain almond oil. And since nuts are commonly employed in candy and bakery products to enhance flavor and provide crispness, the nut-sensitive must approach goodies with caution. Not only that, but ground nuts are often used as filler in such things as bread and coffee substitutes.

In general, nuts most frequently cause symptoms of asthma, rhinitis or hives.

Seeds, which we rarely think of as nuts or vice versa, can also be powerful allergens. Sunflower seeds, touted as exceptionally healthy fare, can be especially dangerous for those hypersensitive to them. So can those ubiquitous sesame seeds, as a good many young people with a yen for hamburgers have discovered. Cottonseed and flaxseed are likewise potent allergens, as we shall see.

Wheat takes its place beside milk and eggs as one of the common allergens, perhaps because most of us in this country consume wheat in one form or another with every meal. The great American sandwich, be it hot dog and roll or hamburger and sesame bun or ham and cheese and whole wheat, may well be responsible for a good deal of allergy. Some people who react allergically to grass pollen may also be unable to tolerate wheat. Why? Because wheat is a member of the grass family, and if a person is allergic to one member of a botanical family, he may also be allergic to several or all of the rest of the family members. In any case, since wheat sensitivity is so common, I discuss it in detail in a separate chapter, as I do milk and eggs (see Chapters Six, Seven, and Eight). These three foods—milk, eggs and wheat—present the greatest avoidance problem nutritionally and the greatest challenge to cooks.

Those allergic to wheat are often also sensitive to the other cereals, especially to corn. That corn should be a problem for a good many people in the United States is not too surprising, considering its wide employment in many dishes and products, especially in the South. Let's take a look at the problem of avoidance of corn.

Corn as a vegetable? That's easy enough to avoid.

Corn as cereal? That's not too difficult. Corn flakes are clearly forbidden, but the corn allergic have to remember that the brand name may not contain a clue and that corn is an ingredient in many cereals. Read the labels and ingredient listings!

Cornstarch? That's more difficult. There is no way of knowing, for instance, if it is in ice cream or sherbet. It is almost sure to be found as a thickener in soups, gravies, creamed foods, puddings, jellies and jams and even in catsup.

Corn as syrup, meal or oil? It can be in the following products:

margarine	coffee substitutes
baking powder	salad oil
almost all canned fruits	commercial breads and
some sausage, ham and bacon	pastries
some hot dogs and lunch	some frozen fruits
meats	Karo

candy
peanut butter
chewing gum
mayonnaise
Chinese food
corn chips
tamales
enchiladas
beer
some gins

pancake syrup
sweetened cereals
powdered sugar
marshmallows
tacos
tortillas
Cracker Jacks
bourbon
some other whiskeys

If an individual is allergic to both wheat and corn, he will probably be sensitive to the other grains as well. While allergy to rye, for instance. is more prevalent in Europe where rye flour is used more extensively in bread, a number of people seeking a fashionable figure via Ry Krisp may have ended up both slender and sensitized. Rye can be found not only in rye bread but also in the following:

some breakfast foods
vodka
whiskey
gin

Oats, of course, are found in oatmeal and are mixed with wheat and other grains in some prepared foods. Oats and barley—often given infants when they start off on solids—may sensitize but, like rice, they are not very potent allergens.

Barley can be found in some of the following foods:

coffee substitutes
soups, puddings, cakes and breakfast foods as pearl barley
Scotch whiskey
beer
malt and malt beverages

Rice may occur in breakfast foods mixed with wheat or other grains.

Buckwheat, though not a cereal, is commonly lumped in with the other grains. Allergy to buckwheat can be so severe that most allergists are cautious about skin testing for sensitivity to it. Fortunately, such sensitivity is rare. Very small amounts can bring on violent reaction. There is a report in the literature of a patient so sensitive to buckwheat that he reacted to cornmeal ground by the same stones that had ground buckwheat earlier, nor could this same man tolerate wheat or corn batter pancakes cooked on the same griddle used earlier for buckwheat cakes. Neither corn nor wheat uncontaminated by buckwheat bothered him in the least.

Buckwheat is found in a number of unlikely places and has some odd uses. Buckwheat hulls used as packing material may also turn up mixed in black pepper. Buckwheat is also used as filler in some foods. And bakers sometimes dust the bottom of their bread loaves with buckwheat flour to keep them from burning. Buckwheat honey is full-bodied, dark and delicious, but is not for those allergic to its source. One individual is reported to have suffered a violent reaction after eating only one mouthful of bread spread with this superior honey.

Cottonseed and flaxseed are two other potent allergens. Cottonseed, especially, turns up in a variety of food products. Cottonseed flour or meal is found in:

> some commercial cookies and cakes
> most doughnuts
> a good many sweet rolls and diet breads
> some candies as a thickening agent
> the casings of sausage (often)
> packaged foods on which the label merely reads "flour" without specifying the type

While cottonseed oil is not very allergenic and affects few people, it may affect the highly sensitive. It, too, is employed in a variety of foods: margarine, salad dressing and as a cooking oil for all kinds of things from nuts and potato chips to breaded deep-fat fried seafoods.

Flaxseed can also be a potent allergen but fortunately is not widely used in foods. It is in Roman meal and some other cereals. It can turn up in laxatives and cough medicines. On occasion, the milk of cows fed flaxseed feed may affect the severely allergic.

Not too many people react uncomfortably to spices and condiments, but enough do to cause most allergists to automatically rule them out of elimination diets. Hives can be the lot of those sensitive to pepper (or perhaps to the buckwheat often incorporated in pepper products). The old-fashioned mustard plaster applied to the chest of the ailing probably has started up sensitivities to mustard as a food.

Flavorings such as vanilla and peppermint may cause such allergic manifestations as swelling of the lips and mouth or spasms of sneezing. Flavored toothpastes and mouthwashes are also often culprits. One reason may be that they contain chemicals that can be primary irritants as well as being allergenic. They cause burning sensations of the mouth and throat as well as edema.

Honey, the favorite sweetener of the natural food cultists, has an odd way of producing allergy in some people. We have noted that bees that feed upon buckwheat blossoms produce a fine honey guaranteed to create havoc among the buckwheat sensitive. Beekeepers who supply their charges with solutions of cane or beet sugar over the winter may market honey that causes reaction among those sensitive to either sugar. Thus, food chains may have relevancy in allergy. What the bee or the cow consumes may be important to the allergic, who in turn consumes their products.

Honey isn't the only bee product to pose a problem. The rising tide of health foods has produced bee pollen to restore health and happiness for all; all, that is, except for the allergic, who, as always, must be wary. Bees have a habit of collecting pollen from a variety of sources, one of them being dandelions. Dandelions are cousin to ragweed, and pollen acquired from this source may do the opposite of curing one's hay fever. In the southwestern region of the country, bee pollen is often laced with mesquite pollen, picked up by the busy bee in its search for food. Mesquite pollen is an allergen powerful enough to cause anaphylactic shock in several unfortunate health seekers.

Individuals allergic to fungi can react not only when they inhale the spores but also when they ingest foods containing yeast or fungi (mushrooms). Yeast in bread and other bakery products and in beer, and fungi in cheese that make them delicious (Roquefort and Camembert) can cause symptoms in the allergic. So, unfortunately, can antibiotics used either as medications or ingested as residues in foods.

Now for the main course: Fish and shellfish cause allergic reaction in quite a few people, far more so than do meats. Sensitivity to both, particularly to shellfish, can be violent. While some people are allergic to seafood in general, others are selective about the matter and react only to a specific kind of fish, or to two or three kinds. Some may be able to eat flounder, for instance, but not cod. Or shrimp but not lobster. However, this selectivity is probably uncommon, though interesting.

Sensitivity to fish may be so acute that even the smell of fish, raw or cooking, can trigger reaction. The allergic may react to food inhaled as well as to food ingested. Either way the allergen enters, the battle with antibodies can take place. And fish can be smelly. One doctor records the case of a patient who had to make a detour around the local fish market to avoid reacting. Another doctor speaks of a teenage girl who suffered facial swelling and severe asthma from the odor of fish frying or even from the odor of raw or canned fish.

Cod liver oil, time-honored source of vitamin D, is contraindicated for those allergic to cod.

A person highly sensitive to fish may need to be wary of certain fish glues. Licking a postage stamp with such glue possibly could bring on acute symptoms in the hypersensitive. Not only smell and taste play a part in allergy to seafood, but touch has a role. A skin dermatitis called crabhand has been noted among some commercial fishermen.

Among meats, pork leads the way allergenically and beef comes next. Some persons allergic to meat must also forego gelatin, since it is composed of animal products—hooves, horns, hides and the like. Also, since sausage and bologna and other pickled meat products are amalgamations of meat products, individuals allergic to either pork or beef will have to approach them with caution, if they approach at all.

In this era of inflating prices and meat shortages, some people have been turning to horse meat. They should be warned that, among those who eat a great deal of horse meat, higher incidences of reaction to horse sera, as in tetanus toxin, occur than among beef eaters. The French probably have a far greater problem with serum sickness than do, say, the English, because of the comparatively larger consumption of horse meat in France.

Vegetable gums turn up in the strangest places and make life complicated for the allergists. Widely used in food products, they are also contained in a number of cosmetics. For instance, a woman patient may suffer, say, rhinitis whenever she eats a frozen cream pie or whenever she sets her hair. The relationship? A vegetable gum, perhaps karaya, used to thicken and give bulk to the pie, may also be an ingredient in the hair set lotion. In the first instance, she ingests the gum; in the second, she inhales it. But in both cases the result may be the same—rhinitis.

I will list all the gums in the botanical list of food families on pp. 64–72. Actually, only three really give much trouble—karaya, arabic (acacia) and tragacanth. A person sensitive to karaya might have difficulties with such things as gum drops and dental plate adhesives. His difficulties most commonly arrive in the form of hives or gastrointestinal distress. He will also have to remember that karaya is an ingredient in some toothpastes. Nor does he want to undergo the experience of the middle-aged lady who spent three months making hurried trips to a hospital emergency room with severe allergic reactions before it was discovered that her denture paste was the culprit.

Gum arabic, used a great deal in medicines, candy and the printing industry, might conceivably cause the highly sensitive to react—with other than the usual dismay at political and social absurdities—while reading a freshly printed newspaper.

The gums may be found in laxatives (mineral oil) and in foods as fillers and binders (cheese, some ice creams, some salad dressings, cream pastries and icings). They often appear on the label, if they appear at all, under the loose heading "vegetable gum." Although an individual may be sensitive to only one type of gum, he will have to avoid all foods with this cryptic label.

In general, the vegetable gums cause the following symptoms:

gastrointestinal distress
migraine-type headaches
hives
rhinitis and asthma

Normally the symptoms of rhinitis and asthma occur only when the gum fumes are inhaled as when hair set lotion dries or while unfolding a freshly printed newspaper.

Foods, like people, come in families, and these family relationships have important connotations for the allergic. How come? Because biologically, plants and, to a lesser extent, animals are so akin that an individual allergic to one food stands a good chance of being allergic (in varying degrees) to other or all members of that food family. This phenomenom is called cross reactivity.

Thus, a patient told that his daily orange juice at breakfast is the cause of his allergic misery has not heard the whole story yet. He may, at least to some degree, also be sensitive to lemons and grapefruit and other members of the citrus fruit family. If eggs bring forth eczema, so may a chicken. But it's not that simple, unfortunately. The individual who reacts to eggs with eczema, may also react to eating hen meat but not to rooster or capon. And a person allergic to milk can usually tolerate beef, but he who reacts to beef will more often than not also react to milk. All in all then, cut and dried rules are hard to come by. We can only say that, in general, if we know the biological relationship of foods—their family tree, so to speak—we can much more easily predict which foods go together to produce allergic reactions.

With much gratitude to Kathleen Miller, I reproduce here the following botanical list of foods that she prepared for the Allergy Information Association of Ontario, Canada, an association eminently generous in providing information and help to those suffering allergy.

Botanical List of Food Families

Family	Food	Related Plants or Extracts
Apple	Apple (Cider, Pectin), Crab-apple	
Berry	Blackberry, Boysenberry, Dewberry, Loganberry, Raspberry, Saskatoon Berry, Youngberry	Bramble
Pear	Pear	
Plum	Almond, Apricot, Cherry, Nectarine, Peach, Plum, Prune	
Quince	Quince (Pectin)	Japanese Quince
Rose	Blackthorn, Sloe (Gin), Strawberry	Rose, Woodruff, Sweet Brier, Cinquefoil

All Sub-Members of Rose Family

Amaryllis		Amaryllis, Belladonna Lily, Daffodil

Family	Food	Related Plants or Extracts
Ammoniacum		Gum Ammoniacum, Spirits of Ammonia
Arrowroot	Arrowroot	
Arum	Poi, Taro	Arum, Jack-in-the-Pulpit
Balsam		Frankincense, Olibanum
Banana	Banana	Abaca, Manila Hemp
Beech	Chestnut	Beech, Oak, Horse Chestnut Trees
Water Chestnut	Ling Nut, Singhara Nut	
Chinese Water Chestnuts	Chinese Water Chestnuts used in Chinese foods	
Birch	Filbert, Hazelnut, Oil of Birch	Birch Tree
Borage	Borage, Comfrey Tea	Forget-me-not, Alkanet, Bugloss, Lungwort
Brazil nut	Brazil Nut	Tree yields Red Dye
Buckthorn	Buckthorn Tea	Buckthorn Syrup, Cascara Sagrada
Buttercup	Aconite, Lenten Rose, Celandine	Aconite, Lenten Rose, Celandine, Buttercup, Clematis, Columbine, Delphinium, Larkspur, Monkshood, Peony, Hepatica
Buckwheat	Buckwheat, Coccolaba, Rhubarb	Knotweed
Caper	Caper	
Carnation		Carnation, Pink, Sweet William
Cashew	Cashew, Mango, Pistachio	Poison Ivy, Poison Sumach

Botanical List of Food Families *(continued)*

Family	Food	Related Plants or Extracts
Chicle	Chicle Gum from Sapodilla Tree, also called Marmalade Plum Tree	
Citrus	Citric Acid, Citron, Citrange, Citrangequat, Grapefruit, Kumquat, Lemon, Lime, Limequat, Orange, Pummelo, Shaddock, Tangerine, Tangelo	
Coca		Cocaine
Cola nut	Chocolate, Cocoa, Cola Nut, Kutira Gum	Rope Fibre
Coffee	Coffee, Royoc, Indian Mulberry	
Composite	Globe Artichoke, Jerusalem Artichoke, Burdock, Camomile, Chicory, Dandelion, Endive, Escarole, Lettuce, Oyster Plant (vegetable oyster), Safflower Oil, Salsify, Sunflower Seed or Oil, Tarragon, Yarrow, Boneset Tea, Lad's Love, Fever-few, Lavender Cotton, Wormwood	Aster, Bachelor's Button, Mum, Chrysanthemum, Cornflower, Dahlia, Daisy, Gaillardia (blanket flower), Gazonia (treasure flower), Heliopsis, Helipterum. Layia (tidy tip), Marigold, Pyrethrum, Ragweed, Sunflower, Zinnia, Cosmos, Blessed Thistle, Elecampane, Tansy, Lad's Love, Fever-few, Lavender Cotton, Wormwood
Curry powder	Not one spice, but a blend of many different spices	
Ebony	Date Plum, Persimmon	Ebony Tree
Elm	Slippery Elm Tea	Chinese and Siberian Elms are resistant to Dutch Elm Disease

Family	Food	Related Plants or Extracts
Foxglove		Digitalis, Figwort, Snapdragon, Verbascum (purple mullein)
Fungi	Moldy (natural, hard) Cheeses, Mushroom, Yeast	Toadstools, Decaying Plants
Gentian	Gentian Tea	Centaury
Geranium		Geranium, Nasturtium, Pelargonium
Ginger	Cardamom, Ginger Turmeric	
Gooseberry	Currant (black, red and white), Gooseberry	
Goosefoot	Beet, Beet Sugar, Spinach, Swiss Chard	Lamb's Quarters
Gourd (melon)	Cantaloupe (muskmelon), Cocozelle, Cucumber, Casaba, Cassabanana, Curuba, Honey Dew Melon, Spanish Melon, Persian Melon, Pumpkin, Squash (all varieties), Vegetable Marrow, Watermelon, Zucchini	
Grains	Barley (Malt, Whiskeys, Ale, Lager, some Liqueurs), Cane Sugar (Brown Sugar, White Sugar, Molasses, Rum), Corn (Cerulose, Corn Oil, Cornstarch, Corn Syrup), Bourbon, Dextrose, Glucose, Millet, Oat, Rice (wild rice), Rye, Sorghum, Wheat (Bran, Gluten Flour, Graham Flour, Wheat Germ, Cake Flour, All-Purpose Flour) Bamboo Shoots, Pumpernickel	Grass (all varieties) Citronella, Lemon Grass

Botanical List of Food Families *(continued)*

Family	Food	Related Plants or Extracts
Grape	Cream of Tartar, Grape, Raisin, Brandy, Port, Sherry, Wine, Champagne	
Heath	Blueberry, Cranberry, Dangleberry, Huckleberry, Uva-ursi, Wintergreen, Bearberry	Azalea, Heather, Rhododendron
Heliotrope	Garden Heliotrope (valeriana) used in medicine as Allheal or St. George's Herb	Valerianella (Lamb's Lettuce or Corn Salad)
Honey	Honey, Bee Nectar, Beeswax	Royal Jelly
Honeysuckle	Elderberry	Honeysuckle
Hypericum	St. John's Wort Tea	
Iris	Saffron	Crocus, Gladiolus, Iris, Orris (used as scent in cosmetics)
Laurel	Avocado, Bay Leaf, Camphor, Cinnamon, Laurel, Sassafras	
Legume	Acacia, Arabic, Kidney Bean, Green Bean, Lima Bean, Navy Bean, Soy Bean (soya flour and oil), Wax Bean, Locust Bean Gum, Carob, Cassia, Fenugreek, Licorice, Black-eyed Pea, Chick Pea, Green Pea, Split Pea, Peanut (and oil), Karaya, Suakin, Talca Gum, Tamarind, Alfalfa, Indian Breadroot, Lucerne, St. John's Bread, Urd Flour, Mung Bean, Tragacanth	Cassia (used in laxatives and cathartics), Mimosa, Milk Vetch, Clover, Senna (sometimes used for artificial cinnamon flavor)
Lily	Aloes, Asparagus, Chives, Garlic, Indian Cucumber Root, Leek, Onion, Sarsaparilla, Shallot	Lily (all varieties), Hyacinth, Trillium, Tulip, Yucca, Solomon's Seal, Adder's Tongue

Family	Food	Related Plants or Extracts
Linden	Linden Tea	Basswood and Linden Trees
Linseed	Flax, Flaxseed, Linseed	Linen
Macadamia nut	Macadamia Nut, Queensland Nut	Protea Plant produces a Sugar
Mallow	Althea Root Tea, Cotton-seed, Cottonseed Flour Gumbo, Okra	Cotton, Hibiscus, Hollyhock
Maple	Maple Sugar and Syrup	Elder and Maple Trees
Mint	Balm, Bergamot, Basil, Catnip, Chinese Artichoke, Horehound, Marjoram, Menthol, Mint, Peppermint, Rosemary, Sage, Savory, Spearmint, Thyme, Pennyroyal Tea, Betony (Chinese Artichoke)	Lavender, Flowering Mint
Morning Glory	Sweet Potato, Yam	Morning Glory
Mulberry	Breadfruit, Fig, Mulberry	Rubber Plant
Mustard	Cabbage, Cauliflower, Celery Cabbage, Chinese Cabbage, Collard, Broccoli, Brussel Sprout, Horseradish, Radish, Kale, Sea Kale, Kohlrabi, Mustard, Mustard Greens, Rutabaga, Turnip, Garden Cress, Pepper Cress, Pepper Grass, Watercress	Heliophila, Mustard Seed
Myrtle	Allspice, Bayberry, Clove, Eucalyptus, Guava	Blue Gum, Kino
Nettle	Hop, Oregano	Nettle, Verbena, Hashish, Marijuana
New Zealand Spinach	New Zealand Spinach	

Botanical List of Food Families *(continued)*

Family	Food	Related Plants or Extracts
Nightshade	Brinjal, Eggplant, Cayenne, Capsicum, Chili Pepper, Red Pepper, Banana Pepper, Bell Pepper, Green Pepper, Sweet Pepper, Paprika, Pimiento, Tabasco, Tomato, Potato	Tobacco, Belladonna, Nicotiana, Thorn Apple
Pepper	Black and White Pepper only	
Nutmeg	Mace, Nutmeg	
Olive	Black Olive, Green Olive, Ripe Olive, Olive Oil	Lilac, Privet
Orchid	True Vanilla, Rum Guaiacum	Orchids (all varieties)
Palm	Coconut, Date, Sago	
Papaw	Papaya	No Relatives
Parsley	Angelica, Anise, Carrot, Celery, Celeriac, Celery Seed, Caraway Seed, Chervil, Sweet Cicily, Coriander, Comino, Cumin, Dill, Fennel, Ferula Gum, Gum Galbanum, Kummel, Lovage, Parsley, Parsnips, Samphire	Asefetida, Musk-root, Sumbul
Pine or Cypress	Juniper, Gin	Fir Trees, Pine Trees (all varieties), Resin, Turpentine
Pineapple	Pineapple	
Plantain	Plantain Tea, Psyllium	
Pomegranate	Pomegranate	No Relatives
Poppy	Poppy Seed	Argemone, Opium, All Poppies, Morphine
Ruta	Rutin Tea	

Family	Food	Related Plants or Extracts
Seaweed	Dulse, Kelp	Irish Moss, Carrageen, Carragheenan
Sesame	Sesame Seed and Oil	Beni, Benne, Gingelly, Gingily, Teel or Til Oils
Styrax		Gum Benzoin or Benjamin
Tapioca	Castor Bean, Tapioca	Cascarilla, Cassava, Castor Oil, Chinese Tallow or Vegetable Tallow (candle wax)
Tea	Green Tea, Pekoe Tea	
Violet		Pansy, Violet
Walnut	Butternut, Hickory Nut, Pecan, Black Walnut, English Walnut	
Willow		Aspen, Cottonwood, Poplar, all Willow
Witch Hazel		Sweet Gum, Witch Hazel

Vegetable Gums

Gum	Family	Uses
Acacia (minosa)	Legume	Perfume, Tanning, Timber
Arabic	Legume	Dyeing, Fruit Drinks, Mucilage, Printing
Suakin	Legume	
Talca	Legume	

Vegetables Gums *(continued)*

Gum	Family	Uses
Karaya (milk vetch)	Legume	Mucilage, Pharmacy, Straw Hats, Textile Stiffener
Tragacanth	Legume	Same as Karaya
Carob (locust bean)	Legume	Chocolate substitute
Ammoniacum	Ammoniacum	Cement, Medicinal Stimulant (Spirits of Ammonia)
Gum Benjamin or Gum Benzoin	Styrax	Incense, Medicinal use in Expectorants, Inhalants, and External Antiseptics, Scent of Vanilla in Lotions, Toilet Water, Tooth Powders
Chicle	Chicle	Chewing Gum
Eucalyptus	Myrtle	Aromatic Spirits, Resin called Kine, Tannin, Timber
Ferula (fennel)	Parsley	Anti-spasmodic, Stimulant, Asefetida, Musk-root or Sumbul.
Galbanum	Parsley	Same as Ferula
Guaiacum	Orchid	
Irish Moss	Seaweed, dried and bleached	Cosmetics, Laxative, Tooth Paste
Carrageen or Carragheenan		Extracted from Irish Moss
Kutira	Cola Nut	One variety for Rope; Chinese variety for Drinks, Jellies and Sweetmeats
Olibanum	Balsam	Frankincense
Quince	Rose (sub-member)	Pectin
Sweet Gum	Witch Hazel	Astringent, Medicinally for Chest Complaints, Sedative, Tonic, Skin Diseases, Perfume, Timber

Cross reactivity or cross sensitivity can be a mysterious business. It isn't hard to understand that if a person is allergic to oranges, he might not be able to tolerate the other citrus fruits. They clearly go together. It becomes a little more difficult to comprehend that if an individual is sensitive to lettuce, a member of the composite family, he might not be able to enjoy camomile tea (if anyone ever drinks it anymore) or dandelion wine or tarragon sprinkled in his chicken with wine. And it might be almost unbelievable that the person unable to tolerate onion without allergic reaction not only may have trouble with garlic but also not be able to eat asparagus. Nor drink sarsaparilla.

Since the cola and coca bean are close kin, those allergic to chocolate most likely will be unable to tolerate cola drinks. A double blow!

Cross sensitivity in meat is not as strong as among the plants. Thus, a person allergic to beef may be able to enjoy veal, or vice versa.

In the gourd family are a number of common and popular foods, but only those we eat uncooked—watermelons and cucumbers— really give trouble. Cooked squash and pumpkin pie rarely disturb. Oddly enough, pickling in vinegar seems to render cucumbers harmless, so that he who reacts to cucumber salad may be able to enjoy pickles.

An interesting cross reactivity exists between cashew or pistachio nuts and poison ivy. Both the ivy and the nuts, when handled, can cause contact dermatitis.

The following are examples of possible cross reactivity:

Allergic to	Be wary of
chicken	eggs
eggs	hens
milk	beef
poison ivy	cashew, pistachio nuts
peanuts	peas, beans and, sometimes, soybeans
almonds	peaches and prunes
buckwheat	rhubarb
apples	pears
grapes	raisins
coconut	dates
tomatoes	white potatoes
carrots	celery
mustard	cabbage, cauliflower

It won't always be the case that an individual allergic to one member of a food family, will be allergic to all members. The chances are that he won't, but he may. Thus, a knowledge of food families and cross reactivity is an assist to avoidance. To be forewarned is to be forearmed.

Checklist

Cooking usually makes food less allergenic.

Just peeling or handling foods, as well as inhaling their odors, can bring on allergic reaction.

Sensitivity to peanuts, buckwheat, nuts and shellfish can be especially severe.

Foods are botanically related. Sensitivity to one member of a food family may mean sensitivity, at least to so some degree, to all members of that family. Such an allergenic relationship is called cross reactivity or cross sensitivity.

Six

Milk—The Almost Perfect Food?

In its booklet, "Family Fare, A Guide to Good Nutrition," the U.S. Department of Agriculture recommends the following daily milk consumption:

> Children under nine should consume the equivalent of two to three 8 ounce cups of whole milk daily.
> Children nine to twelve should consume the equivalent of three or more 8 ounce cups daily.
> Teenagers should consume four or more.
> Adults two or more.
> Pregnant women three or more.
> Nursing mothers four or more.

Such phrases as "the milk of human kindness," "the sweet milk of concord," and "the land of milk and honey" display something very like reverence for the cow and her product. Yet this almost perfect food can be pure poison for a surprisingly large number of people, especially the newborn. I have found milk to be the most common cause of gastrointestinal allergy and colic in infants.

Because it is such an integral and revered part of the American way of life, it is not so easy to avoid cow's milk. Most of us, young and old alike, start our days with a bit of milk—in our coffee, over our cereal or as a beverage cold from the refrigerator. A great many children and, I suspect, a good many adults too, drink milk at lunch, if not at supper. Snacks of ice cream or cheese or a glass of milk are common in homes and offices across the land. And, of course, milk is incorporated in a great variety of foods, especially baked goods. It is difficult to escape. But there are a great many people who must, at some time or other in their lives.

Most of the world's peoples cannot drink milk comfortably—not because they are allergic to it, but simply because they have never adapted genetically to its lactose content. They lack the proper enzymes to digest cow's milk. This problem is called lactose intolerance. Only those tribes that became herdsmen of cattle seem to have adapted gradually, throughout centuries and probably through genetic or natural selection, to cow's milk.

A study of lactose intolerance in Africa showed that the inability to digest cow's milk coincided with the area of tsetse fly infestation, a pest that effectively banned the keeping of cattle. Thus, no adaption to the drinking of milk was needed. But many of the milk-intolerant tribes could and did enjoy fermented milk products, such as yogurt, because the lactose content is greatly reduced by the fermentation process.

Thanks to our European, cattle-raising heritage, most Americans are properly equipped to enjoy milk. But there are many who are not adapted. They may be in for trouble when they try to accommodate themselves to what amounts to the national beverage.

Because the ability to digest cow's milk in its raw or pasteurized form is not universal, American gifts of powdered milk ended up as whitewash for houses in Guatemala and emptied the classrooms in Colombia. Thousands of sickened schoolchildren are no diplomatic asset. But we have only recently become aware of the unacceptability of our gifts of powered milk to many peoples across the earth.

Symptoms of lactose intolerance mimic those of allergy to cow's milk. When a doctor is confronted by such symptoms, he must rule out this congenital condition before he can settle on a diagnosis of milk sensitivity. What are those symptoms? The more specific and easily recognizable are:

> eczema
> colic
> croup
> diarrhea, often with blood or mucus in the stool
> constipation
> frontal headache
> serous otitis
> asthma

More diffuse symptoms of milk sensitivity may be:

> loss of appetite and refusal of feedings
> pallor
> failure to thrive
> irritability
> allergic tension-fatigue syndrome
> bad breath
> excessive sweating

Severe allergy to milk can cause almost instantaneous swelling of the lips and mouth upon drinking a very small amount. There are accounts in the literature of allergy of children who have suffered collapse and death after being fed milk. In fact, it is now believed by some physicians that severe sensitivity to milk may be one possible cause for the as yet unexplained "crib deaths," the sudden and mysterious deaths of infants in their sleep for no discernible reason. Though the role of allergy in these tragic deaths is still an hypothesis, studies have shown that antibodies to cow's milk turn up in above normal amounts in the sera of the small victims of this malady. It is supposed that the infant may have suffered anaphylactic shock in reaction to the milk.

Recent studies have also shown that serum antibodies are unusually high in Mongoloid children, a finding that may open some intriguing doors to this equally strange and sad affliction. Nor does the grim indictment end here. Some researchers have suggested that marasmus, a very severe malnutrition condition of young children (most common between the age of 6 to 18 months), may be due in part to sensitivity to milk. A child with marasmus wastes away until he becomes a living skeleton.

If the reader finds his beatific vision of sleek cows knee-deep in grass, embodying good health, damaged, let me reassure him that not only are these problems controversial but such grim reactions are exceedingly rare.

Other, less severe forms of allergy to cow's milk, however, are quite common. It is variously estimated that anywhere from two to six percent of American infants, for instance, exhibit sensitivity to cow's milk. Considering that a 15 lb. baby consumes the 150 lb. adult's equivalent of two gallons of milk a day, it is not surprising that so many babies do becomes sensitized. Oddly, many children allergic to cow's milk often love it and, if they can, drink it in quantity. Unfortunately too, infants allergic to milk often develop allergy to other things.

The allergic usually react to two main fractions in cow's milk, whey and casein. Or they may react to only one of the two and not at all to the other.

The whey fraction, which contains lactalbumin along with a small amount of lactoglobulin and other proteins not significant as allergenic factors, causes the most trouble. Nonetheless, the whey sensitive are more fortunate than the casein sensitive on two counts: (1) they may be able to tolerate goat's milk because its whey fraction differs from cow's milk; and, (2) since whey proteins can be altered by heat, they may be able to tolerate evaporated or boiled milk. They have a "whey out."

When milk is heated, the skim or film that forms across the top is the whey. It is out of this whey that cottage cheese is made. Those sensitive to whey may have to forego the delights of soft, unripened cheeses but may be able to tolerate such hard cheeses as Edam. Processed cheeses, however, besides containing a great deal of water, may also contain whey returned during the manufacturing process as well as other green and aged cheeses. Processed cheeses will probably be taboo for those allergic to either fraction, though for genuine cheese lovers, this may be no great loss.

Casein is usually stable under heating. Thus, evaporated and boiled milk are no answer. And since the casein sensitive react to the "curd," the hard cheeses must go by the board. Nor is goat's milk any help.

Whey sensitive might react to:

cottage cheese
cream cheese
ricotta
Gervais
Neufchatel

Casein sensitive probably react to:

Edam
Parmesan
Cheddar
American
Gruyère
Swiss
Romano

Whey sensitive could probably tolerate the cheeses in the second list.

In addition to whey and casein, there are other constituents of milk that can cause allergic reaction in the sensitive. Some doctors estimate that cow's milk allergy has increased five to six times over in the last decade or so and they point out that this increase coincides with the burgeoning use of pesticides, fertilizers and drugs, some of which find their way into cattle feed and fodder, and, thus, into milk. Cottonseed allergens can turn up in milk when cows are fed cottonseed meal. Likewise, cows fed on bran may conceivably produce milk that would be allergenic to the wheat sensitive. Perhaps the oddest documented case of all is that of a patient who developed hay fever when he drank milk produced from cows who had browsed on ragweed tops.

That such things should find their way through a cow's complex digestive system does seem strange—until we remember the garlic flavor of early spring milk. One researcher has estimated that a cow fed onions will give onion-flavored milk five or six minutes later.

Some drugs, particularly antibiotics, employed for ailing cows, have found their way into milk to affect adversely the unsuspecting drug sensitive. Until recently, penicillin used to treat mastitis among dairy herds showed up in significant amounts in the milk produced by those herds. Because those severely sensitive to the drug were endangered by this practice, usage of this antibiotic has been somewhat curtailed.

In general, however, the milk proteins and some polysaccharides (carbohydrates) not broken down and disposed of with reasonable promptness by the gastrointestinal mucosa are the most apt to stir up antibodies. Cow's milk has almost three times the protein content of human breast milk. Obviously, then, it has the potential for stirring up far more allergic reactions. When the gastrointestinal system is immature or inefficient, as in infants and young children, or when it is inflamed by infection, cow's milk protein is most likely to be inefficiently disposed of and thus bring on the conflict in body tissues, including gastrointestinal mucosa.

Small wonder that infants and young children are the most frequent victims of allergy to cow's milk. They not only drink most of the stuff, but their digestive apparatus is far more susceptible and far less efficient than their elders'. But nobody is ever too old to react to cow's milk, especially if it is not heat-treated. If an older child or adult suffered reaction to milk during the first fourteen months of his life, allergy to milk could still be active and should be considered with other possibilities if he turns up with symptoms of allergy.

A puzzling aspect of this persistence of milk sensitivity is that when it does accompany the allergic individual into later life, it often does so with symptoms other than those it caused in infancy and early childhood. The body systems affected may be totally different. Thus, the individual who suffered diarrhea from sensitivity to milk as an infant may drop that symptom and pick up rhinitis instead. Headaches in the older child or adult may replace the loss of appetite that was so worrisome in the baby. Or asthma may take over from eczema. Often the child is thought to have "outgrown" his sensitivity to milk, but what really may have happened is that he has simply exchanged his early symptoms for a new and different set. To complicate the picture even further, he may also develop allergy to inhalants as well, such as dust or pollen or animal danders.

There does seem to be a tendency for milk allergy to run in families. One doctor reports the case of four generations of allergy to milk in one family. And I can offer the following case as a good illustration of a family beset by sensitivity to milk: Because his mother had asthma as a child and two of his siblings were allergic to cow's milk during their infancy, one young patient of mine was given Prosobee (a soybean milk substitute) from birth. (Oddly enough, his twin brother showed no signs of allergy.) When the child was six months old, he developed itchy eyes and nose, sneezing, wheezing and rattling in his chest accompanied by a smothering sensation. It was noticed that all this followed his eating foods that contained milk, for example, baby food custard and ice cream. Later, when he ate bread or biscuits, he would develop immediate wheezing that lasted for several hours. It also was noticed that he could tolerate cornbread if it was made without milk. Unfortunately, he also developed attacks of wheezing immediately following the ingestion of chocolate and pears. And his eyes and nose would itch and he would begin to wheeze when he got near dogs and when he was out in the grass, especially during damp weather. Not too long ago, when this boy was given cow's milk by mistake, he developed wheezing almost at once and had to be hospitalized for four days. Not only did he follow the milk allergy of his siblings, but he developed the asthmatic symptoms of his mother in reacting to milk (and later, inhalants).

Cow's milk can arrive in the individual's life with no effort on his part. If the pregnant woman drinks milk in quantity, she may be sensitizing the fetus then and there. Because of this possibility, some doctors recommend that a woman drink no more than a pint of milk a day during her pregnancy and that she boil it at least ten minutes to lessen its potency. However, a recent theory suggests that fetal tolerance can be produced only if the fetus is exposed to potent allergens early in the pregnancy, say, the first trimester (see Chapter Eleven).

It is pretty sure that the nursing mother who drinks cow's milk in quantity may sensitize the infant, for the protein can pass through her milk to the baby. Particularly if allergy runs in the family, the nursing mother must exercise caution about the amount she drinks. She probably should follow the same regimen as a pregnant woman with regard to milk.

Allergically speaking, the breast-fed baby has a great advantage over his bottle-fed brother. Eczema is likely to run some seven times higher among infants on the bottle than it does among those on the breast. This statistic seems to support the adage—Cow's milk is for calves, human milk is for human babies. However, a recent study seems to refute the belief that cow's milk is the villain; the study found no significant difference in the incidence of allergy diseases among children fed breast, soybean and cow's milk (see Chapter Eleven).

Cow's milk is not the best thing going for other animal young. We've mentioned the case of the bottle-fed baby walrus that developed facial dermatitis from cow's milk. Captured on an ice floe in the Bering Sea, this young walrus was transported to San Diego where she not only developed skin trouble but also a kind of walrus rhinitis. A walrus with a runny nose must have puzzled the zoologists. They tried all sorts of things to cure her sniffles. They changed her environment and daily care, but only when they removed her bottle did the itching stop, the sniffing cease. Without cow's milk, she became a healthy, happy walrus, whatever that might be.

What is even stranger is that cows themselves sometimes can be allergic to their own milk. Farmers and veterinarians are familiar with this problem. Among certain cows, overproduction in the udder leads to absorption of their own milk with a resulting allergic reaction to milk protein particles. What kind of reaction do these cows exhibit? Hives—if you can imagine cows with itching welts and bumps. And they also suffer a kind of bovine rhinitis, somewhat on the pattern of the sniffling baby walrus.

An itching, snuffling baby walrus, a herd of sneezing, hive-ridden cows may seem a far cry from the distress of a human infant whose cow's milk formula is literally curdling his pleasure at being in this world. Yet, the knowledge that man is not alone in suffering from allergy to cow's milk can be helpful, at least scientifically. A good many dogs, cats and guinea pigs have been made allergic to cow's milk, all in the interests of finding out why it happens and how it can be prevented, and all with the intention of removing this bane from the lives of so many new young humans.

Once the individual is sensitized to cow's milk, how is this allergy treated?

To begin at the beginning, which is where allergy to milk usually makes its start—the doctor finds himself confronted by a bottle-fed infant with eczema and/or colic. The doctor, after ruling out other possibilities, diagnoses milk as the villain.

So, what can be done for this thoroughly miserable baby and his almost equally miserable parents?

First, his parents must realize that there probably will be a trial and error period, hopefully brief, during which the baby's formula will be changed and the baby's symptoms observed. With luck, the whole thing may be resolved overnight. If the whey fraction of the cow's milk is the villain, then all that may be necessary is to switch from homogenized cow's milk to evaporated milk or simply to boil the homogenized milk for at least twenty minutes to make the protein elements more easily digestible. If this simple maneuver is unsuccessful, it may be possible to substitute goat's milk for cow's in the formula. Finally, there is a predigested synthetic milk substitute on the market called Nutramigen. It contains hydrolyzed casein, arrowroot starch, corn oil, sucrose, vitamins and iron. One or the other of the above switches should ensure a happy baby and, in turn, a good night's sleep for harassed parents.

But it may not be the milk in the formula that is causing the trouble. The doctor may also wish to tinker with the carbohydrate content of the formula, be it corn syrup or whatever. Cane sugar, for instance, is less allergenic than corn. The doctor may also investigate the baby's feeding habits, since too rapid feeding, intake of air, and just plain too much food or too much sugar in the formula can also cause colic. Thus, formula tinkering involves more than changing the milk.

If the casein fraction of cow's milk is causing the trouble (and this is far less common), then we have a different story. Goat's milk is similar to cow's milk in its casein fraction, and so is out as a substitute. Nor does heating help, since casein is relatively stable. In all probability, the doctor will turn to soybean milk sub-stitutes first. Soybean milk is chemically very close to mother's milk, and when carbohydrates and the proper vitamins and minerals are added, it can also be the "almost perfect food."

Since products are apt to change names overnight or merge with each other, and since their ingredients are switched or something new and different is added, I list just a few of the soybean milk substitutes presently available. This should not be considered an endorsement of any particular brand. I intend this brief list only to suggest to the harried mother of an allergic infant that there is help. Incidentally, all of the following have vitamins and iron added:

> ProSobee, Mead Johnson Company
> Sobee, Mead Johnson Company
> Isomil, Ross Company
> Mull-Soy, Borden Company
> Soyalac, Loma Linda Company

Unlike Oriental babies, who, if they must be bottle-fed, are nurtured on the soybean, Western infants have come late to this versatile legume. Better late, I suppose, than never.

Soybean milk comes in several forms. The easiest to use is the canned liquid kind, either ready to use or concentrated so that it needs to be diluted in the proper amount for the baby's age and weight. It can also be used undiluted in coffee or over fruit or cereal. Other types come in flour or powder form and, while messier to use, they have the advantage of being considerably cheaper. Water is added in the prescribed amount to the powder and the whole is heated just enough to ensure proper mixing.

Alas, often enough the perfect rose is accompanied by a thorn. One fifth, approximately, of the children allergic to cow's milk turn out also to be allergic to soybean milk substitute. Soybeans are quite capable of their own brand of mischief—scalded buttocks and diar-rhea, as well as other symptoms of allergy. It is for this reason that many doctors recommend that soybean milk be strongly diluted at first, especially if the infant has already been suffering from diarrhea.

Now what if the child is allergic not only to cow's milk but to soybean milk substitute as well?

Then we turn to a meat-base formula, a sort of meat soup actually. An example is MBF, put out by the Gerber Company. It contains strained beef hearts, sucrose, sesame oil, tapioca, calcium ascorbate and vitamins A and D. There is a slight tendency for those allergic to milk to be also allergic to beef. For these rare few infants, Gerber puts out a formula called Lambase, which, as its name implies, uses strained lamb as its foundation.

Thus, the parents of a milk sensitive infant will find, now and in the future, plenty of help. Most of the companies manufacturing milk substitutes publish helpful recipe booklets, a boon for the feeding of infants and older allergic children and adults as well. In Appendix B, I give the names and addresses of as many of these companies as I can corral.

When it comes to avoiding cow's milk, infants on a bottled formula are relatively simple to manage. But once the baby puts that bottle down, life can become complicated, for milk is everywhere. It lurks in some form in a thousand food products, and the sensitive can come upon it unaware and in all innocence.

First, there is milk in its overt form:

> homogenized, nonhomogenized and raw
> skim milk and buttermilk
> powdered milk
> malted milk, cocoa and chocolate milk

Then there is cream:

> regular
> half and half
> whipping

And butter and most margarines (some diet margarines are milk-free).

And cheese, as we have seen:

> cottage cheese, cream cheese
> natural cheese
> processed cheese

Then there is milk somewhat or totally concealed:

au gratin foods
biscuits and their mixes
some boiled salad dressings
bread, rolls and other bakery products
cakes and cake mixes
canned fish balls
chocolate bars and many opaque candies
cookies
cream pies
cream sauces and some gravies
cream soups, chowders and bisques
doughnuts and doughnut mixes
fritters
ice cream and sherbets
macaroni, noodles and spaghetti

meats: meat loaf (often) processed meats, such as hot dogs, luncheon meats and sausage (dried milk is often used as a filler and binder) milk-fed veal (as in Wiener Schnitzel)
mashed potatoes
muffins and their mixes
pancakes and their mixes
puddings such as rice, tapioca, custard, Blanc Mange
pudding mixes
rarebits
scalloped dishes
souffles, omelets and often scrambled eggs
waffles and their mixes

The reader allergic to cow's milk may browse through this long list and yearn for the good old days before allergy was "invented." However, unless he is severely sensitive to milk, there is no great need to despair. Some doctors like things spartan and may recommend that bread, for instance, be avoided. But most probably say that bread is okay for all but the hypersensitive. The majority operate on the principle that bread usually contains traces of milk and causes little if any trouble, but that without bread (and a few other bakery products) in moderate amounts, the diet is so grim that children and adults both find it too difficult to maintain. Margarine and some butter is usually permitted for the same reason. Thus, there is a certain balance to be struck between the severity of the diet and the severity of allergic symptoms. Usually, the allergic person learns this for himself—what he can and cannot tolerate and how far he can step beyond the bounds of his avoidance diet without adverse effects. It is very much an individual matter. Each will walk his own tightrope.

Of course, some manufacturers produce products on the list above that do not contain milk in any form. Be a label reader! If milk is not listed among the ingredients eat hearty. But if the ingredients are not listed and you have any doubts at all, you would be wiser to forego the pleasure, especially if you react to milk strongly.

Label readers should know that the following terms mean milk in some form is an ingredient:

> lactose
> caseinate or sodium caseinate or casein
> lactalbumen
> lactoglobulin
> curds
> whey

Nor are the "nondairy" products always milkfree. Some, such as the following, contain caseinate (milk protein):

> Cool Whip
> Coffeemate

On the other hand, the following are okay because they do not contain either milk or caseinate:

> Coffee Rich
> D'Zerta Whip

When the child or adult must adhere rigidly to a milkfree diet, the doctor will probably prescribe calcium tablets, to make up for the diet's deficiency, plus vitamins, especially vitamin D. It is important to take only those the doctor prescribes, for some vitamins contain milk powder filler.

Perhaps by now the reader allergic to milk is exasperated, even frustrated: "Well, what *can* I eat?"

There is the world of fruits, vegetables and meats (except processed meat and beef for that rare individual who is cross reactive). And there are substitute milks. It is often simply a matter of replacing one thing for another.

For instance, the older child or adult should have little difficulty coming up with a new beverage to take the place of the accustomed glass of milk. Fruit juice, coffee (black and for adults only, naturally) and tea can fill the gap. The younger child who still drinks milk in quantity may be enticed over to soybean milk or even meat base substitute, if that proves necessary. Soybean milk can even be whipped in the blender to resemble a milkshake. Soybean milk in whatever form is greatly helped by chilling, and while the taste may take a little getting used to, it is no insurmountable problem. Try the various brands to find one that suits best.

Milkless cereal at breakfast may rock the imagination a little at first. We are all thoroughly accustomed to muting the cheerful snap, crackle and pop of these dry products with a generous flow of milk. Try fruit juices such as apricot nectar instead. Or stewed fruits, which are especially good mixed in with hot cereal such as oatmeal.

Unless strictly policed, childhood is the time of uninhibited consumption of goodies, of complete unconcern for the limits a desire for a fashionable figure sets, of no thought for an overloaded heart. Children are apt to gorge on allergenic fare, particularly milk and chocolate. And so these are usually the first to be eliminated when a doctor prescribes a diet for a child with a suspected allergy to food. No more chocolate bars and candy, chocolate milk, flavorings and syrups or cola drinks. For many a child, the very staff of his "good life"! Children are likely to take such deprivation to heart, especially when it is flaunted in their faces by their free-eating peers. So, when the child on a milkfree diet stands empty-handed and forlorn among his friends who are making their ice cream cones sound even better than they are, quickly give him a fruit ice or a popsickle. And when all about him are enjoying their chocolate bars, pour him a generous fistful of hard candy or gumdrops, jellybeans or peanut brittle or hand him a lollypop. Show him that he has not lost the world. Do not let him feel totally left out.

For the older child and adult, there is a chocolate substitute made of carob, a powder ground from the pod of a tree belonging to the locust family. When it is toasted, it tastes much like chocolate. There is also a soybean chocolate. Both of these goodies may be found in health or natural food stores.

It is also well to note that kosher products such as kosher margarine, bread, and processed meats labeled "parve" or "pareve" do not contain milk traces. Nor do many diet margarines.

Then there is gelatin, a wonderful, somewhat magical food with which you can make "cream" pies and sherbets and forget the milk.

When it comes to substituting for milk in cooking, soybean milk can generally be used just as canned or regular milk would be. Water left over from cooking vegetables is a very good substitute for milk in many recipes. It can be used not only in sauces and gravies but in such baked goods as biscuits. It not only adds to the flavor, but you will have succeeded in utilizing some valuable vitamins and minerals that would otherwise have gone down the drain.

For baked goods, too, there are synthetic butter flavorings on the market to give that taste vegetable oils sometimes fail to provide. Even ice cream using soybean milk can be made in the old-fashioned home freezer or in a refrigerator ice cube tray (see recipe in Chapter Thirteen).

It may come hard at first, but it is quite possible to live without cow's milk. A milkless menu might run something like this:

Breakfast:
Fruit or fruit juice
Hot cereal made with water or cold cereal with fruit juice or soybean milk
Bacon and eggs
Milkfree bread, biscuits or muffins
Coffee (black) or tea

Lunch:
Soup, milkfree
Any unprocessed meat, without gravy or with milkfree gravy
Any vegetable (not buttered or creamed or with margarine containing milk)
Any fruit
Cookies, milkfree
Coffee (black), tea or fruit juice

Dinner:
Any unprocessed meat
Potatoes, baked or fried
Any vegetable as at lunch
Muffins, milkfree
Fruit or gelatin or milkfree dessert
Coffee (black), tea or fruit juice

Not bad. And anyway, it may not be forever, this milkless menu. You may be able to fit yourself into the following scenario—With admirable will power you have successfully avoided both milk and your allergic symptoms for a good while, perhaps for as long as a year or more. You are healthy and delighted to be so, but . . . there are many things you miss, even yearn for. You are growing weary of being so cautious, of stopping dead in your tracks in the middle of busy supermarkets to read labels (all in very fine print guaranteed to strain your vision), of asking waiters in restaurants if there is any milk in the day's special you've chosen or declining graciously the milk-rich cuisine of your favorite hostess. But don't do anything rash. Consult your doctor. He may surprise you by relenting a little. He may even suggest that you experiment, depending, of course, on how severe your symptoms have been in the past. "Try out a few baked goods," he may say. "Those least likely to contain much milk." Or he even may okay a little dried skim milk or buttermilk with meals. Naturally, if your symptoms return in a rush, all bets are off.

When you do return to foods that you have been sensitive to in the past, there are several things to keep in mind. First, your tolerance to that food will be low. It will be easy to exceed it. Thus, you can only consume very small amounts infrequently. Second, there may be an initial period of a few months' tolerance, which could embolden the unwary and encourage them to plunge joyously off their avoidance regime with never a thought for tomorrow. Alas, this brief, symptomfree period may be no more than a false tolerance. You may find yourself back where you started.

Finally, after a period of avoidance and freedom from symptoms, allergy may change its form when the allergenic food is once more consumed. Thus, if you originally suffered from hives whenever you drank milk, you may exchange hives for rhinitis when you experiment after a symptomfree period. It is well to recognize that allergy may still be with you, although the symptoms may be new and different. It has been my experience, however, that this is more likely to happen to children than to adults.

You must be cautious and exceedingly moderate when you do reintroduce milk back into your life. You must accept the sad fact that you may be among the unfortunate whose symptoms will return in full force or in a new guise. On the other hand, you may be one of the lucky who can tolerate a little milk now and again—an expanding of your food horizon, but no panoramic view.

If you turn out to be allergic to milk and perhaps also to one or two other less basic foods, you can always count yourself fortunate in comparison to those who are not only allergic to milk but also to eggs and wheat as well, the three basic foods. Theirs is a substantial avoidance problem.

Checklist

There are two main allergenic fractions in milk—whey and casein. An individual may be sensitive to one fraction and not the other.

The whey fraction causes allergy symptoms among the majority of the milk sensitive, but it is the easiest to manage since heat treatment may mute its allergenic properties. In addition, those allergic to this fraction in cow's milk may be able to tolerate goat's milk.

Allergy to milk is most common in infants and children under three years of age.

Allergy to milk that persists after childhood often exchanges the original set of symptoms for a new set.

Although the matter is in question, it is probable that pregnant and nursing women should be wary of drinking milk in quantity, especially when there is an hereditary tendency to allergy.

Soybean milk and meat-base formula are usually satisfactory substitutes for cow's milk in the infant's formula.

Although the statement that breast-fed babies are less likely to suffer allergy than bottle-fed infants is currently in dispute, it can be said that breast feeding is preferable for the allergy-prone and the nonallergic infant alike.

The milk sensitive individual, after a period of abstinence, may be able to reintroduce milk into his diet in very small amounts consumed infrequently and still remain symptomfree. He must remember, however, that his tolerance may remain low.

Seven

Which Comes First, the Chicken or the Egg?

This may be the riddle of the universe, but in allergy there isn't much doubt—The egg comes first and it often comes on strong. Allergy to egg is common and very often violent. Like allergy to milk, it strikes early in life, often when egg and infant are introduced to each other. On the plus side, allergy to egg that begins in one's tender years may disappear. Or it may persist for a lifetime. One doctor reports the case of a man in his sixties severely allergic to eggs since the age of five. Over fifty years of egg avoidance!

Samuel Butler once wrote that "A hen is only an egg's way of making another egg," which may be one way to answer the riddle this chapter's title poses. If a person is egg sensitive, he may have to pass up the hen, although he can enjoy capon or rooster meat. There is a cross reactivity, although not very strong, between egg and hen. Why this is so is not thoroughly understood. Why should sensitivity carry over to the hen and not to either capon or rooster? One school of thought believes the flesh of the hen is contaminated, so to speak, by the allergen of unlaid eggs. Another believes that eggs and hen meat simply share a common allergen. Whatever the reason, for some people it means no eggs for breakfast and no chicken in the pot, at least not a plump hen.

Eggs, like milk, have two main allergenic fractions whose properties differ dramatically. Unlike milk, the difference can be seen. With a little manual dexterity, the fractions can be easily separated, yolk from white. Egg white does the most damage most of the time. Raw or cooked, egg white can be extremely allergenic. Cooking does help somewhat, but when a person reacts to cooked eggs, say, baked in a cake, then he is considered highly and severely sensitive, so much so that his doctor will probably be very cautious about skin-testing for egg. As we have noted earlier in the book, skin-testing for egg allergy usually has more validity than for other foods. A positive skin test to eggs in infancy may be bad news. It is often a bad prognostic sign of severe, prolonged allergy that may last for years. In particular, it may signal allergic eczema and other allergies to come. Unfortunately, those with severe allergy to eggs often do not lose that sensitivity.

Egg yolk claims fewer victims than the white, and when it does, its effects are less drastic. In fact, some allergists believe the yolk rarely causes allergy diseases. Others believe that, while it is not nearly as potent as the white, it does, nevertheless, create enough trouble to be considered significant. The first group holds that the yolk cannot be separated without contaminating it with some of the egg white and that only a tiny amount of that white can go a long way with the hypersensitive. Thus, like a good deal else in allergy, the relative potency of white and yolk is still open to question.

Eggs are a close second to milk in most commonly causing allergy in infants and very young children. I, myself, have found them to be the most common cause of eczema in children. This is a misfortune, for, like milk, eggs are highly nutritious and an exceedingly valuable source of protein. Both yolk and white are richly endowed with this building block of life. Eggs are an even better source than milk of vitamin D and of iron, both important for the growing child. At one time, infants of three months were fed raw egg yolk as a preventive measure against anemia and rickets, but it was soon discovered that a goodly number of babies developed rashes and other symptoms of allergy. Doctors backtracked a bit, and many began to recommend no eggs until the child reached six to nine months of age. Then, usually, they recommended cooked yolk, not raw. Rashes began to fade from the scene, at least in part.

Why can babies tolerate eggs at six to nine months when they may react to them allergically at three months of age?

One school of thought believes that infants develop a kind of protection against food allergens as they grow older, even in so short a period as three months. This theory states that their gastrointestinal tract matures and grows more efficient with the passing days in the disposal of food particles, especially proteins. Again, this is no absolutely certain thing.

Even though the incidence of rashes and other signs of egg allergy has diminished since the halcyon days of early and frequent feeding of raw egg yolk, a good many allergists and pediatricians are recommending today that babies be fed no eggs until they reach one year of age and then only hard-boiled yolk to begin with. They advocate this especially for youngsters with a family history of allergy in any form. They also recommend that nursing mothers refrain from indulging in too many eggs, since, like cow's milk, the protein allergens can be passed into the breast milk to sensitize the baby. And again, as with milk, they believe that the pregnant woman should eat egg moderately lest she sensitize the fetus. And, once again, this is a matter of controversy. We discuss measures that conceivably might head allergy off in more depth in Chapter Eleven.

Like milk (and wheat), eggs are a basic food in the American diet, thus making them a common cause of allergy and often a severe one. To illustrate, here is an early description found in allergy literature. Because he suffered diarrhea, an infant of ten days was given a little egg. He received no more egg until he was fourteen months old, but evidently that first taste was enough to sensitize him. The second time around, after he'd taken a bite, he immediately refused to eat more and within minutes was clawing at his mouth. His tongue and mouth tissues swelled quickly to many times their normal size, and hives literally covered the poor tyke's face, centering around the mouth. Months later, when again he ate egg, he vomited swiftly, but his mouth and tongue again became swollen and hives blossomed. On his fourth encounter (and let us hope his last experience with egg), he became very ill, suffered all the above symptoms, and became mentally dull to boot.

That a tiny bit of egg, a mere taste, could do all this seems incredible. Yet, there are cases on record of individuals going into shock and collapsing after consuming minute amounts of this potent allergen. There are actually cases on record of egg sensitivity so exquisite that reaction is caused when the allergic person is kissed by someone who has recently eaten eggs. This comes very close to being the fabled "kiss of death." Some people are so hypersensitive that the smell of an egg cracked open can set them off. Or the touch of an eggshell or a bit of egg white can cause contact dermatitis. The egg sensitive might even have to forego the luxury of egg shampoo, for it, too, might bring on allergic symptoms.

I would recommend that anyone severely allergic to eggs, and especially children, wear a warning bracelet or tag to this effect. There is always the possibility of loss of consciousness if shock occurs, and there is always the possibility that a vaccine grown on egg might be administered with adverse results to a child severely allergic to egg. A Medic Alert warning tag is a good idea for anyone who is severely hypersensitive to any allergen, be it food, an inhalant, a drug or insect venom. The Medic Alert Foundation (P.O. Box 1009, Turlock, California 95380) puts out such a tag and also maintains a file at its offices of the allergic person's detailed medical history. In case of an accident or illness, and in the event the patient is rendered unconscious or incoherent or is heavily sedated, the attending physician can call Medic Alert headquarters collect for detailed information concerning the patient's allergic history. The headquarters is operated twenty-four hours a day.

What sort of symptoms does allergy to egg usually bring on?

Most frequently those involving the skin, the gastrointestinal system and the respiratory system:

> eczema
> hives
> colic
> vomiting and diarrhea
> perennial rhinitis
> asthma

And these symptoms can appear very quickly, often within minutes after ingestion, especially of raw egg.

So, when a person turns out to be allergic to eggs, what's to be done?

Avoid! Avoid!

At least, avoid until the symptoms vanish, and the allergy has been controlled.

Yes, fine. But what does one avoid?

Alas, quite a bit, for eggs, like cow's milk, are everywhere. In one form or other quite a few of them can turn up in the market basket. Be a label reader. If the ingredients of the product are not listed on that label, it would be wiser not to be a hero and dare the unknown. Better to pass up the mysterious for the frank and open, the product that has nothing to hide.

If the following appear among listed ingredients, egg protein lurks in the product somewhere:

> albumin
> vitellin or ovovitellin
> livetin
> yolk
> powdered or dried egg
> globulin
> ovomucoid
> ovomucin

Egg white or eggshells are often used to clarify coffee, both in restaurants and by hostesses anxious to please. Some soups, such as bouillon and consomme, are also clarified with egg albumin. Be sophisticated enough to make the proper inquiries when dining out. It is often more embarrassing to burst forth in hives or swell up like a balloon than to ask a discreet question or two.

Egg white is also used abundantly to glaze all sorts of things or to help brown pies and cookies or to add luster to candies. Thus, the egg sensitive must be wary of bright, brown and shiny baked goods.

The following products frequently, but not inevitably, contain eggs:

baking powder, but not all kinds (Cellu is eggfree)

bread and breadings

cake mixes (not all) and cake flour

candy, especially divinity, glazed, fondant and paste

coddled foods

cookies, especially macaroons

creamed foods (often)

cream sauces (often)

croquettes

deviled foods

doughnuts

dumplings

French frying batter

French toast

frostings (a good many)

glazed coffee rings, rolls and bread

hollandaise sauce

macaroni, noodles (often) and spaghetti

malted beverages (such as Ovaltine and Ovomalt)

marshmallows

meat loaf, meat jellies and molds; Wiener Schnitzel

meringue

muffins

pancakes and some pancake mixes

pies—cream, custard and pumpkin

popovers

pretzels

puddings—custard, Bavarian cream and Blanc Mange

root beer when egg is used to produce foam

salads (such as tuna fish and chicken)

salad dressings (some)

scalloped dishes

soups (such as mock turtle and noodle)

souffles, omelets

tartar sauce

timbales

waffles and some waffle mixes

whips

And last but not least, egg is also a constituent of the laxative Agoral.

The egg-sensitive individual has a lot to avoid. And not always just in the food department either, for egg turns up in some odd places to cause contact dermatitis in the sensitive. Even such things as sensitized photographic film, printed cotton and silk, some dressed furs and possibly egg shampoo can all bring out the rash and itch and lesions of allergy because they contain eggs.

In the chapter on milk allergy, we noted that soybean milk, water and fruit juices could be substituted for milk. Unfortunately, it's not so simple to substitute for eggs. But don't despair. Ingenuity has come up with an egg replacer, a product known cheerfully as Ener-G Egg Replacer, manufactured by Ener-G Foods of Seattle, Washington. Its listed ingredients are arrowroot flour, potato flour, tapioca flour, modified vegetable gums, leavening and vegetable color. It contains no egg or egg derivative, and the company makes no claim that it is nutritionally the same as eggs. It simply makes life easier and a bit tastier, especially in cooking baked foods such as cookies and cakes.

One ingenious lady wrote the Allergy Information Association of Canada that she substituted one teaspoon of vinegar for each egg called for in some cake mixes. She reported that her cakes came out delicious if inelegantly crumbly. Others who cook for an eggless diet simply omit the eggs when cake mix instructions call for them, but handle the finished product with care. Egg is a binder, and cakes without eggs are a little like bricks without mortar. They tend to come apart crumb by crumb. Still, even if you must eat them with a spoon, they'll taste fine. Another recommendation, if you don't mind the taste in the end product, is to use mashed banana instead of egg. It will keep the cake in one piece quite well.

Eggs not only bind in baked goods but they add volume. An eggless cake is apt to look emaciated. To meet this problem, simply substitute an extra half teaspoon of baking powder (eggless) for each egg called for in the recipe. That should plump out the cake suitably. Eggs are also often used as thickening agents in such things as creamed dishes and sauces. Extra flour added, or even better, cornstarch, can do the egg's job.

Here is a home recipe for an egg replacer: To two tablespoons of flour add one half teaspoon of shortening plus one half teaspoon of eggfree baking powder plus two tablespoons of liquid. Mix well, dump in.

Since egg yolks are an excellent source of iron, the doctor may prescribe iron drops for the infant and young child on an eggless diet. And since eggs are so rich a source of protein, adults who must pursue an eggless diet may be concerned about missing out on this essential part of food. However, the following items can remedy any deficiency in an eggless menu:

milk and milk products, especially cottage cheese and other natural cheeses	bean sprouts
	meat
fish	chicken (other than hen, perhaps)
liver	soybean products
peanuts	Brewer's yeast
peas and beans	brown rice
sesame seeds	wheat germ
whole rye flour	oats and barley
sunflower seeds	

Bean sprouts can be made at home, year round, with nothing more than a jar and a piece of nylon netting in place of a lid. In spite of its Oriental connotations, growing sprouts is a simple process. Whole dried peas, beans and lentils can be purchased at any supermarket; and other, more exotic fare such as alfalfa, fenugreek or mung beans can be found in health or natural food stores. Put a tablespoon of beans or seeds in a pint jar, fill half full with lukewarm water and let the beans or seeds soak overnight.

In the morning, drain the water off through the nylon netting, fill the jar again with lukewarm water, rinse, then drain well and let stand. Rinse and drain the jar twice a day for about four days. The beans or seeds will sprout and be growing by then. Store the sprouts in the refrigerator in a plastic bag or dry container, as any other vegetable. Sprouts are best raw and are delicious in salad. The Chinese, who have been around for a long time, know a good protein source when they stumble on it.

Another source of protein is sesame seeds. They are not as yet a potential rival of the soybean, either as a protein or in variety of employment, but sesame seeds are rich in protein and a good source of calcium. Sesame oil is exceedingly digestible. The Turks are supposed to use sesame butter as is or in cooking, much as we use cow's milk butter. Like the Chinese, they are on to a good thing, especially for the allergic. Unless, of course, the allergic is allergic to sesame seeds, as we noted earlier.

If bean sprouts are not your dish and sesame seeds don't thrill you (and youngsters especially may feel both are on the "blah" side), you can ease your concern about missing out on the protein eggs ordinarily afford by tackling one or the other of the various protein concentrates that are on the market. Some of these include vitamins, some do not. Your doctor would be the best judge of which to use, if any. These concentrates are usually vegetable materials and come either in cookies, bars, powder or tablet form. They are not nearly as exotic (or probably as cheap) as a jar full of homemade bean sprouts or a handful of sesame seeds, but they are no doubt less trouble and will fill the protein bill. Here are, without either endorsement or recommendation of any kind, several of these products and their parent companies:

> Protein Snacks (tablets), Sears, Roebuck & Company
> Protein Bars and Cookies 30, Sears, Roebuck & Company
> Protein 60 Powder, Sears, Roebuck & Company
> Protein Wafers, Hudson Vitamin Products
> Sustein (powder), Hudson Vitamin Products
> Protana (powder), Universal Nutrition

There are, no doubt, a good many other such products that your doctor may suggest if he believes that you need them. I do not normally recommend such products myself because I believe that most of my egg-sensitive patients make up for protein deficiency with the other foods listed earlier. These protein powders should probably be considered "incidental information," useful for the few on severely limited diets.

Well, what does an eggless menu look like?

Breakfast:
    Fruit or fruit juice

Cereal, hot or cold
Bacon
Toast (but never French) using eggless bread
Coffee, milk or tea

Lunch:
Soup, eggfree
Any meat (except chicken from a hen)
Any vegetable
Any fruit or gelatin dessert and eggless cookies
Milk, coffee, tea

Dinner:
Any meat as for lunch
Any vegetable
Eggless muffins or biscuits
Fruit or fruit pie
Coffee, milk or tea

With a little ingenuity, eggless recipes such as those in Chapter Thirteen and a lot of careful label reading, no one on an eggless diet need starve.

And the future, will it have to be eggless?

Not necessarily.

Although those severely allergic to eggs may not be able to risk the pleasure of reintroduction of eggs in any form into their diet, a good many persons with milder reactions who cannot eat eggs today may be able to eat them tomorrow. In this matter, everyone is an individual and goes his own stubborn and separate way. Thus, it may be that after a period of abstinence and of being symptomfree, the mildly sensitive might be able to take on bread and other bakery products again without problems, especially if they will pass up such egg-rich delights as angel food and sponge cake, eclairs and custard pies. Infrequently and in moderation, hard-boiled eggs may be tolerated, especially the yolks. Some people may have no problems when they return to eggs if—and it's a big if—they eat them only once in every five or seven days. And if they remember that this may not be wise during pollen season, periods of heavy pollution or following a severe infection. An underlying inhalant allergy or an infection can overwhelm the individual's tolerance. This may also be true if he suffers allergy to some other food and tries to eat both eggs and this other allergen at the same meal or even during the same day. Thus, an understanding of one's other allergies and one's own tolerance level and how it can be affected is essential for successful maneuvering around potential difficulties.

As a test to see if a patient is able to tolerate eggs again, some doctors suggest that he eat a little egg white. If symptoms return, tolerance is still too low to reintroduce eggs into the diet.

When the time for experimentation arrives, the egg sensitive must remember the following:

1. Tolerance to eggs usually will be lower than normal. Eat sparingly of eggs in any form and, preferably, never raw. Moderation and infrequency of consumption are the keys. Once sensitized, one rarely if ever can consume eggs as of yore.

2. It is quite possible to enjoy a period of false tolerance for a few weeks or even months before symptoms return. Time alone will tell.

3. It is also quite possible that old symptoms are exchanged for a new set when the tolerance threshold is broached again. For example, initially the egg sensitive may have suffered hives every time eggs passed his lips. But after a period of abstinence, diarrhea may appear when eggs are reintroduced. These new symptoms are really manifestations of the old allergy.

Before we conclude this discussion of eggs and allergy, we must examine one final problem such sensitivity can present its victims —immunization. Parents of egg-sensitive children should be aware that these children may suffer allergic reactions, sometimes severe, from vaccines grown on egg or chick embryo. However, this possibility seems to be rare, so rare that many doctors feel there is little if any difference in reaction between allergic and nonallergic children. Some doctors, on the other hand, believe that there is a certain hazard for the egg sensitive in immunization with measles and influenza vaccines. In this era of mass school immunizations, it is probably just as well that school authorities be aware of a child's allergic problems. I, myself, believe and recommend to parents and school administrators that if an allergic child can eat eggs without trouble, even though he may skin test positive to egg allergens, he is not more likely to have a reaction to measles and influenza vaccines than any nonallergic child. It is well to remember also that any child can react adversely to one or another of the vaccines routinely given throughout childhood.

If there is any doubt about the matter, I skin test to play it safe. If a child does give a positive skin test to eggs, the doctor may decide to administer the vaccine in divided doses, beginning with a dose one tenth or less than the full immunization. If a child definitely has an allergic reaction to eating eggs, then I think that it is best to avoid any vaccine grown on eggs. And if the child has suffered a severe reaction to eating eggs, then I do not believe there is a need to skin test. In fact, it might be dangerous. Thus, if the child is severely allergic to eggs, even divided doses may be dangerous for him, since it takes very little of the allergen to cause him to react. I would recommend avoidance of any vaccine grown on egg for him.

Vaccines usually grown on egg or chick embryo cultures are:

influenza
Rocky Mountain Spotted Fever
typhus
yellow fever

Vaccines often grown on such cultures are:

measles
mumps

Fortunately, most vaccines can be grown on cultures other than egg or chick embryo—on such things as rabbit, dog and monkey tissues—so it is often possible to simply use another vaccine for the severely egg sensitive. One thing is certain, the egg-sensitive child should be protected by a full immunization program, including measles, and this is as vital for him as it is for any other child.

One peculiar and, fortunately, rare problem might arise for the child or adult allergic to chicken and other fowl and, perhaps, eggs. The safest and most widely used anti-rabies treatment is a vaccine grown on duck embryo. Compared to the severity of the disease itself, allergic reactions are relatively minor. One doctor does recommend that during and for several weeks following the rabies vaccine series, antihistamines be administered in large doses to help ward off potential allergic difficulties. But the whole problem may vanish when a new vaccine prepared in human cells arrives.

Finally, allergy to eggs, like allergy to fish, nuts and buckwheat, may last a lifetime. Usually, if an infant shows a marked positive skin test, his sensitivity may not only dog him the rest of his days, but may well be severe. He is usually likely to develop other allergies also. If an individual's reaction to egg is severe, he would be wise (1) to wear a Medic Alert warning tag or bracelet, (2) approach immunizations with certain vaccines with caution and (3) not attempt to reintroduce egg into his diet. This is especially true if the ingestion of egg causes swelling of the tongue or throat and hoarseness or symptoms of shock.

Suppose you or your child are one of those people for whom eggs can be extremely dangerous, and suppose that accidentally you have eaten egg. What should you do? Or if it is your child, what can you do for him? The first procedure is to get rid of as much of the egg (or any other potent allergen that threatens) as possible. Induce vomiting. The chances are that vomiting is already occurring, but if not, put your finger down your throat (or the child's throat) to begin the process. With a very small child, it is best to turn him upside down so that he cannot choke on vomited matter. As a next step, administer an antihistamine and, if you should have it on hand, ephedrine or the like. Seek medical aid immediately.

It must be remembered that for the severely allergic, ingestion of even a small amount of the allergen can be a hazard to life.

Checklist

Egg allergy is common, especially in children, and is often severe.

Symptoms of egg allergy tend to appear swiftly upon ingestion.

Symptoms usually occur in the skin and gastrointestinal and respiratory systems.

Egg white is a more potent allergen than egg yolk.

If ingredients are not listed on the labels of food products, do not buy, especially if you are severely allergic.

Other foods and special products can ensure that there will be no protein deficiency in an eggless diet.

It may be possible, though usually not for the severely allergic, to reintroduce eggs into the diet after a period of abstinence. But in all probability, they will have to be eaten infrequently and in moderation.

Those severely allergic to eggs would do well to wear a warning tag or bracelet, such as Medic Alert.

Caution should be employed in immunization procedures for those egg sensitive who cannot eat eggs and especially for the severely sensitive. When possible, vaccines grown on something other than egg or chick embryos should be employed or divided doses of egg-cultured vaccines used.

An infant with a marked positive reaction to skin-testing to egg is very likely to be sensitive for a prolonged period, even for his lifetime. That sensitivity is apt to be severe.

Severe sensitivity to egg can be a life-threatening situation. If egg is inadvertently ingested, induce vomiting, take antihistamines and seek medical help at once!

Eight

Our Daily Bread

No other food family plays as large a role in keeping the human race from starvation as does the grass family. Its cereal grain members—wheat, corn, rice, oats, rye and barley—are the staples of the human diet the world around. When harvests are lean, famine stalks. Unfortunately, like Janus, the grass family sports two faces —the benign that feeds us, the angry that makes us ill. No other food family is quite so diligent in causing the human race discomfort, perhaps simply because the cereal grains are staples, consumed everywhere in great quantity. In Sweden, allergy to rye is likely; in Mexico, to corn; in Asia, to rice. In the United States, wheat and corn are the chief villains. Since more wheat finds its way into our diets than does corn, it claims the greatest number of victims, numerically if not in severity. Some allergists believe that wheat is responsible for anywhere from 30 to 50 percent of the allergy diseases they treat.

Corn may run a fairly close second as a cause of allergy, while the other cereal grains—oats, rye, barley and rice—appear to be far less allergenic, but then we simply do not consume them in the kind of quantity that we do wheat and corn. One of the cardinal rules of food allergy is that sensitivity is most likely to occur to foods consumed in quantity over a long period of time.

Cross reactivity among the members of the grass family is not very strong. But it appears that a person allergic to both wheat and corn is very likely to end up allergic, at least in some degree, to other members of the family—which makes life difficult when it comes to substituting another member of the family for wheat and corn.

Sugar cane belongs in the grass family. Sugar can cause allergy, although white or granulated, sugar is so thoroughly refined that most, if not all, of its allergenic properties have vanished in the process. Occasionally, crude brown sugar or molasses can cause allergic reaction. Only a few persons are allergic to carbohydrates rather than the usual protein content of food, and they will have trouble with sugar.

Most Americans eat wheat in some form at every meal and, unfortunately for the national waistline, a good bit between meals. About a quarter of our daily caloric intake is supplied by this ubiquitous grain. Man may not live by bread alone, but a good many of us make a stab at just that. Those unable to handle their protein efficiently may wish they had followed that other adage— Variety is the spice of life.

Wheat, like milk and eggs, contains several allergenic fractions, the main two being gluten and starch. Gluten is probably the more potent allergen and causes the most damage. It is a vegetable protein found in all the grains, but its characteristics, oddly enough, differ from one grain to the next. The gluten found in wheat, as well as in oats, barley and rye, not only causes allergy but also is responsible for an intolerance similar to the lactose intolerance some persons exhibit to milk. There are people who simply cannot handle gluten because of a malabsorption problem of the gastrointestinal system. Strictly speaking, celiac syndrome, as this condition is called, is not allergy. But some doctors believe that there is a limited relationship between this intolerance, and gastrointestinal allergy.

Celiac syndrome symptoms usually appear in children between the ages of six months and six years. The disease is characterized by chronic indigestion, a failure to thrive, fatty stools, muscle weakness, a distended abdomen and general emaciation. It is called a syndrome because these symptoms result from varied causes, gastrointestinal allergy probably being one of them. Other possible causes for celiac syndrome might be:

  metabolic defect
  cystic fibrosis
  parasitic infestation
  mechanical obstruction in gastrointestinal tract

Whatever the cause, the condition can be very distressing. And wheat, the gluten in wheat, and milk may play an important part in its unhappy sequence of symptoms. Those allergic to wheat and those intolerant of gluten follow similar paths of avoidance and diet to alleviate their symptoms. What helps the former, of necessity helps the latter.

As with sensitivity to milk and eggs, allergy to wheat may begin when the infant first meets wheat in his diet. That first bite of cereal, that first teething cracker may start the allergy ball rolling, and, as with the other two basic foods, symptoms may disappear as the child grows older. Or often as not, they may continue into adulthood. Fortunately for both child and adult, allergy to wheat is not apt to be severe.

Symptoms most commonly caused by wheat when it is ingested are:

> eczema
> gastrointestinal allergy
> asthma

Wheat can also cause contact dermatitis, perennial rhinitis and asthma among those who handle it a great deal. Bakers, for instance, sometimes suffer skin lesions running from fingertip to elbow. Farmers, threshers, bakers, millers and housewives may develop rhinitis and asthma, not because they eat wheat but because they inhale it. "Miller's asthma," as it has been called, has been around a long time. It may not always be due to the grain itself, however. Mold spores on the grain or silica or mineral dusts on the grain husks are possible causes for this condition. In the case of wheat flour, even the chemicals that are used in bleaching or the mildew that infests the grain may bring on symptoms. It is not always easy to pin down the villain. It may be possible to desensitize those who must work around wheat or flour, but for the ordinary wheat allergic there is really one good solution—avoid it.

Because wheat is so versatile and because wheat gluten makes bread and other bakery products rise with a flourish, avoidance is difficult. Wheat gluten is especially invaluable in baking because it holds dough together and imprisons leavening gases, thus producing a light yet cohesive product. Thus, wheat lurks in many a product, including soybean baked goods so eagerly sought by those allergic to wheat and/or the other cereal grains. One has to suspect its presence even in rye or potato bread. It is estimated that some 40 percent of so-called "other grain" baked goods contain wheat. Wheat-sensitive persons must develop a suspicious nature toward all that rises! If it is baked and it has risen—avoid it.

One interesting problem connected with allergy to wheat and/or gluten intolerance is the possibility that glutenlike proteins may be created within the body in conjunction with other proteins in the diet. For instance, the protein of malted barley, even though there is no gluten present, may bring about a reaction in the gluten sensitive and/or the gluten intolerant.

Another potential problem is the possibility of "wearing out" the other cereal grains when they are substituted for wheat. Thus, some people sensitive to wheat may substitute corn cereals for breakfast and cornbread for wheat bread and corn muffins for biscuits. But they may soon find themselves sensitive to corn, especially since corn is highly allergenic. But it can happen with the other cereal grains as well, with rice the least potent of all. The mildly wheat sensitive usually make out all right using other grains as substitutes. But those with more severe reactions may soon find themselves in the "wearing out" process. In the end they may have to resort to soybean and potato flours for their starch substitutes and meat and other proteins for their protein and vitamin B needs.

Why this "wearing out" of one grain after the other?

Because members of the grass family share similar proteins, and the person strongly sensitive to one may cross react to the others when he consumes them in anywhere near the quantity he would consume wheat.

So, how and what to avoid?

When he contemplates all the food products on the supermarket shelves that contain wheat, the wheat sensitive may well be appalled. How is it possible to avoid wheat in some form? What on earth would be left to eat?

If any of the following are among the ingredients listed on a food product's label, the wheat sensitive must avoid it:

> wheat flour (or just plain "flour")
> graham flour
> gluten flour
> enriched flour
> hydrolized vegetable protein or hvp (gluten and/or wheat is often present)
> monosodium glutamate or MSG

Those sensitive to or intolerant of gluten will not only have to avoid the above but malt syrup, oats in any form, rye and barley.

To reissue an old warning, if the ingredients are not listed, be stubborn, refuse to buy. You possess an inalienable right to know exactly what it is you intend to eat.

The following foods are likely, but not inevitably, to contain wheat and/or gluten:

baked beans
beverages such as Postum, malted milk, ale, beer, some wines, coffee substitutes, gin
biscuits and biscuit mixes
bread, bread crumbs, breadings
butter sauce often
cakes, cake mixes, cake flour (less allergenic than bread flour)
candy (sometimes)
cheese spreads and sauces

chili con carne
cookies
crackers and cracker meal
cream sauces (often)
creamed vegetables
croquettes
custards (sometimes)
doughnuts and doughnut mixes
dumplings
egg dishes, often thickened with flour
fritters

fruit, stewed and thickened with flour
fruit in pies and jams (commercial)
gravy
ice cream (sometimes) and ice cream cones
macaroni, noodles, ravioli, spaghetti and vermicelli
meats:
  canned poultry, fish and meat
  floured meats, such as Swiss steak
  processed meats, such as luncheon meat and hot dogs
  premolded hamburgers
  sausage
  meat loaf (often)
  any stuffed poultry, fish or meat
melba toast

pancakes and pancake mixes
pies and pastry
popovers
pretzels
puddings (often thickened with flour)
rusks
salad dressings (sometimes)
scalloped dishes (often)
sherbets (sometimes)
soups:
  with noodles
  some bouillon cubes and extracts
  some soup mixes
  bisques
  chowders
  creamed soups
waffles and waffle mixes
whiskey
yeasts (sometimes; Fleishman's is wheatfree)
zwiebach

By the time you have reached the end of this list, you may be shaking your head in despair and wondering how you are going to keep from wasting away. I admit it's a long and comprehensive list. Still, there are millions of human beings who never eat wheat in this world, so there are other things that can be substituted. Nor is it too difficult, once you get the hang of it, to bake and cook with these substitutes. It does, I am also willing to admit, take a little extra effort and a bit of daring experimentation. Perhaps even more, it takes a measure of bulldog stubbornness and a dedication to that old motto —If at first you don't succeed, try, try again.

Happily, some wheat sensitive persons can tolerate melba toast because the dry heat seems to alter protein molecules, making them more digestible. Those mildly sensitive to wheat can probably substitute the other cereal grains, perhaps indefinitely. All-rye bread (often canned) can take the place of wheat bread and rolls. Such cereals as oatmeal, cream of rice, rice flakes and cornflakes can easily take the place of wheat cereals at breakfast. Corn can, at least for a time, replace wheat in a good part of the diet.

And then there is an exotic fare, a recent and interesting addition to the list of suitable substitutes for wheat as a cereal—poi. Here may lie an answer to the problem of "wearing out" other cereal grain substitutes for wheat. Poi, a Hawaiian food, is made from the taro plant. It is the underground bulb or corm of the plant and looks something like a potato. It turns out to be an excellent source of carbohydrates. On a visit to Hawaii some time ago, Dr. Jerome Glaser, noted pediatrician and allergist, discovered that many Hawaiian infants are practically raised on poi. Hawaiian doctors praise it highly as an infant cereal substitute, not only for allergic babies and those suffering gastrointestinal problems, but for normal babies as well. Dr. Glaser also noticed that ethnic Hawaiians were, in general, tall, handsome, intelligent, healthy and had especially good teeth. He noted, too, that poi had long been a staple food of the Islands. Putting all this together, he came to the conclusion that they had a good thing going in poi. After somewhat inconclusive studies, which seemed to show that at the very least youngsters fed poi rather than true cereal grains did as well as their counterparts on rice or other grains, he concluded that poi was a good substitute for wheat and/or the other cereal grains for the allergic. He did think that taste might be a barrier for the allergic older child and adult.

Plain or exotic, there are adequate substitutes for wheat. The greatest difficulty comes, at least for the cook, in making do without wheat flour.

Bread made without wheat flour may be more difficult to concoct and a far, far cry from the soft, fluffy, rather gooey white product we Americans prize so and which, often as not, engenders the scorn of people of other lands whose bread is apt to have a good deal more body and less whipped air. Without the use of wheat flour the American loaf is hard to come by. Still, an otherwise tasty and nutritious loaf is quite possible. Rice flour makes a good raised bread, and quick breads such as biscuits and muffins can be created with other flours and leavened with extra eggs and baking powder. The following flours can all be pressed into service with varying degrees of success:

rice flour
barley flour
potato flour
oat flour
soya flour

Cornstarch and tapioca and arrowroot flours are apt to produce heavy baked goods somewhat on the order of the bride's fabled lead-weight biscuits. Nor can a respectable cake be made from flours other than wheat or rice, but cookies can, and they should satisfy the frustrated sweet tooth of the wheat sensitive. The best bet is to make a mixture of flours, using two or more grains, for baking. Mix, store in a container and use in almost any recipe that calls for wheat flour. For instance, the following mixture yields a good all-purpose flour (except for making light bread):

    1 cup cornstarch
    2 cups rice flour
    2 cups soya flour
    3 cups potato flour

Allergy cooking experts recommend that such a flour be baked at lower temperatures than wheat flour and for a longer period of time. They also warn that the end product will be a bit crustier than with wheat flour and perhaps more inclined to crumble. Also, they say, since substitute flours have a higher fat content, it pays to experiment a little in cutting down on the shortening called for in the recipe.

Various flours can be substituted directly for wheat flour, but the proportions are a bit different. Here is a table of exchange for one cup of wheat flour:

    1⅓ cups rolled oats
    1 cup rye meal
    1¼ cups rye flour
    ¾ cup soya flour
    ⅝ cup potato flour
    ⅞ cup rice flour
    ½ cup barley flour
    ¾ cup cornmeal
    1 cup cornstarch

An alternative may be the various ready-mixed flours. See Appendix A.

Perhaps you are wondering why I haven't suggested buckwheat flour as a good substitute for wheat. The answer is simple enough. Buckwheat is not a grain but a member of the rhubarb family. It can be a potent allergen. Potent allergens the allergic can do without, and the chances are good that buckwheat would only add to their troubles. So, while buckwheat makes a fine flour, I do not recommend it to those sensitive to wheat.

Cornstarch, for those not allergic to corn, and potato flour make good thickening agents in puddings and gravies. Not as much of them is needed to thicken the pot. Here is a substitution table for one tablespoon of wheat flour:

    ½ tablespoon cornstarch
    ½ tablespoon potato flour
    ½ tablespoon rice flour
    ½ tablespoon arrowroot flour
    2 teaspoons quick tapioca

For breading foods, substitute crushed corn flakes or rice flakes or another flour or a bit of the flour mixture above. If a person is very allergic to wheat, meat fried in fat used earlier to fry meat rolled in wheat flour can be enough to set him off. When dining out it is wiser to choose the broiled entree. Social life is complicated enough without superimposing a headache or gastrointestinal allergy upon it or a case of the hives or the grotesque swelling of giant hives!

Most of the substitute flours can be obtained at grocery stores, supermarkets and even drug stores, but the best bet may be the health food and natural food shops that have spread across the land like dandelions on an indifferently kept lawn. Even in these shops of exotic fare, be sure to read the labels.

Here's a general menu for a wheatfree diet:

Breakfast:
> Any fruit or fruit juice
> Any wheatless cereal without malt
> Bacon and eggs
> Wheatfree biscuits or muffins
> Coffee, tea or milk

Lunch:
> Any processed meat
> Any unthickened or creamed vegetable unless wheat flour is
>   used
> Wheatfree light bread
> Fruit and wheatfree cookies
> Coffee, tea or milk

Dinner:
> Any soup, without noodles and wheatfree
> Any unprocessed meat prepared without wheat flour
> Any vegetable as at lunch
> Canned rye bread or wheatfree light bread or quick breads
> Pudding, custard or ice cream (wheatfree)
> Coffee, tea or milk

Not exactly famine fare!

As in milk or egg allergy, your doctor may recommend that, after a period of abstinence ranging anywhere from a few months to a year or more, you try wheat again in very small amounts and infrequently, perhaps beginning with a less allergenic form such as Melba toast. Your tolerance is apt to be low or it may even be false. Your symptoms may return after a few months, either as they once were or in a new form. The name of this game, is caution and moderation.

Admittedly a wheatfree diet is not easy to maintain. It can be a bother and a burden, but it is not impossible. And those allergic to wheat who can still enjoy eggs and milk should comfort themselves with the knowledge that their lives could be a great deal more difficult, not to say Spartan, if they had to add these two other basic foods to their list of "no no's." To be allergic to all three—eggs, milk and wheat—is really a "bummer."

With her kind permission, here is the advice of Mrs. James R. Wall, who recently wrote me that she has been coping with a quite limited allergy diet for her asthmatic husband since 1934.

> Think positively. Make a list of all foods by classification of allowable foods. As far as possible eliminate forbidden foods from your supplies. When this is impossible, as when all the family do not go on the diet, isolate the permitted food. . . . Read labels and recipes carefully. Many innocent-sounding products will have a joker of one forbidden ingredient. Sometimes a small modification in a recipe or substitution of an allowable ingredient will make it usable.

These are the wise suggestions of a woman who has "been there." Maintaining a nutritionally sound diet is of vital importance in all these substitutions and menu manipulations. There is little sense in getting rid of allergy symptoms to replace them with symptoms of malnutrition. The allergic must exercise care not to toss out the proverbial baby with the bath water. Thus, in all probability, if a person must remain on a restricted diet for any length of time, his doctor will provide vitamin and mineral supplements and perhaps protein concentrates, such as we discussed in Chapter Seven, as well. He will probably wish to be assured that ample amounts of the following are supplied in the avoidance diet:

ascorbic acid (vitamin C)
vitamin B complex
vitamins A and D
fluorides
iodides
calcium salts
iron salts

There has been some controversy about the possible role of vitamins as an antiallergy therapy. Some doctors have thought that the allergic condition could be influenced by large doses of vitamins, especially of vitamin D. Others have found no evidence of vitamin deficiency in their allergic patients and so discount the benefits of massive doses as treatment. What all seem agreed upon, however, is the importance of a vitamin-mineral balance in an avoidance diet to prevent deficiency diseases of one sort or another. Generally speaking, when we eat a well-balanced diet, we get all the vitamins and minerals we need. but when the diet is restricted, deficiencies can crop up. So, though this chapter began as a discussion of allergy to wheat, I will digress a little and discuss vitamin and mineral needs. It is germane in any discussion of avoidance diets.

Vitamin A, as most of us know, is essential to good night vision. As children, we are often told that if we eat our carrots, we'll be able to see in the dark almost as well as the cat—a theory guaranteed to intrigue most youngsters. The basic idea is correct, though a little far-fetched. Vitamin A does a great deal more than provide efficient night vision. It also aids in resisting infection by maintaining the health of the skin and mucous membranes. It also stimulates production of cortisone and ACTH, hormones that incidentally, help prevent allergic reaction. If the allergic individual can tolerate fish, he will probably be able to ingest enough vitamin A with fish and vegetables in his diet. If he must avoid fish, there are synthetic vitamins. As a matter of fact, synthetic, water-soluble vitamins are less likely to cause allergy.

The following foods are especially rich in vitamin A:

beef liver	mango (a good excuse for
broccoli	some exotic fare?)
sweet potatoes (baked)	carrots (especially raw)
squash (winter)	spinach
cantaloupes	apricots
persimmons	peaches (fresh)
tomato juice	papaya

Vitamin D, as most of us also know, is vital to the building of body and bone. It is essential to the absorption of calcium in the gastrointestinal tract. The calcium, among other things, helps restrain leakage of fluid from the blood vessels into the tissues, which helps the allergic since leakage is often part of the allergic reaction. Most persons who include fish in their diet regularly will probably obtain enough vitamin D. Then there is always cod liver oil and calcium tablets. The former, however, hasn't the best taste in the world. Moreover, cod liver oil has been known to cause allergy in infants on its own. So, if there is a need for it, synthetic vitamin D may provide the best solution.

Vitamin B complex performs a good many yeoman chores in maintaining our health. Its various members are especially important in the maintenance of a healthy nervous system and as barriers against infection, in the assimilation of carbohydrates and the utilization of the end products in protein breakdown and in preserving the health of skin and mucous membranes. Foods especially rich in vitamin B are:

pork
fresh peas
spinach
avocado
tomato juice
orange juice
artichokes
sweet potatoes (baked)
Irish potatoes
coconut (fresh)

Vitamin C is one vitamin that has generated enough controversy in the last few years to make most people thoroughly aware of vitamins. Whether or not it can prevent the common cold or reduce cholesterol levels in the blood or relieve arthritis pain is still unresolved. But it is essential for good health. (I personally think it helps to prevent colds, but I realize that this belief is not shared by all doctors.) Vitamin C does seem to stimulate the production of cortisone and ACTH and evidently helps to keep blood vessels happy. Fortunately, its intake is not restricted for those on eggfree, milkfree and wheatfree diets. Fruits, especially the citrus family, contain vitamin C aplenty, and vegetables such as green peppers and broccoli are rich in C.

Mineral traces are equally essential to good health. The human body needs the following:

zinc	sulfur
sodium	copper
iodine	fluorine
magnesium	manganese
potassium	phosphorus
calcium	iron

Sounds a bit like a metal working shop, doesn't it? Well, it just about is. Mineral traces are the essential ingredient of all cells and of the enzyme system, among other things, and form a good deal of our bones, teeth and fingernails. Because we excrete mineral salts daily, we must continually consume them in our food. This is especially true for growing children. Those on a restricted diet can replace the mineral traces lost by deleting eggs, milk and wheat from the diet by adding extra meat. Or, when meat becomes scarce or prices itself right out of the family budget, the doctor can suggest mineral supplements.

Let us admit what seems to be quite obvious—It is not easy to eat, drink and be merry on an eggless, milkless, wheatless diet. When all three basic foods must be avoided, things can become hectic and some of life's pleasure be lost. Your doctor may then consider a procedure called either desensitization, hyposensitization or extract therapy. This process works very well for allergies to inhalants, such as pollens or house dust, and is employed with excellent success to relieve the miseries of hay fever. It is not, however, very successful in food allergy. But we should take a look at it if we intend to cover the field. Besides, it's a rather interesting procedure in itself, for it operates somewhat on the principle that a hair of the dog that bit you may indeed be the cure.

For food allergy, there are two methods of desensitization (rather, attempts at desensitization)—oral and by injection. The oral method is simply to eat gradually larger amounts of the food or foods that are causing the allergy. You don't just pull your chair up to the table and, say, consume great quantities of foods containing wheat. Nothing quite so enjoyable. The allergen is prepared in extracts and placed under the tongue in measured amounts by a dropper. The amount at the beginning is very small and is increased every few days, perhaps every four days, depending upon your doctor's preference.

The second method is to inject measured amounts of the food extract and gradually increase the strength of the injections until a tolerance level is reached.

It must be said that no one is quite sure how these desensitization procedures work to bring about tolerance, if and when they do. One theory is that, because of the deliberate injection or ingestion of allergens in small, increasing amounts on a daily basis, the allergic person develops blocking antibodies that unite with the allergens to prevent the release of chemicals or mediators that cause the allergic reaction. Another theory is that continued reception of small amounts of allergenic food by the body produces a refractory period during which the allergic person is immune to further action in the allergen-antibody struggle. A good analogy from the sport of boxing: Two exhausted boxers hang on to each other and shuffle around the ring to catch their breath and regain their strength to renew the fight. And so may the battle between allergen and antibody be stalled.

Neither of these theories is firmly established. Nor does either method, oral or injection, really produce much in the way of a cure. Some doctors believe desensitization for food allergy can be accomplished in some cases, but it is not an accepted procedure by most allergists. Still, when a person is allergic to the three basic foods plus, perhaps, corn, he may be willing to try almost anything! For the severely allergic, desensitization is risky, especially for those severely sensitive to eggs.

Where do I stand on desensitization?

I personally do not believe in the procedure. I do not use either of the methods. If you've been complaining to your doctor that your best friend has been desensitized to ragweed pollen, and why can't you be desensitized to your allergy to milk, eggs and wheat, now you know the answer—it simply does not work well enough or often enough in food allergy to be worth the time and trouble (and possible risk).

Cromolyn sodium, a new drug for us, but extensively employed abroad, has proven very effective in protecting many asthma sufferers and is fairly effective in preventing symptoms of food allergy for some patients. In the first instance, it is inhaled from a special spin-inhaler, but for food allergy it is taken orally. Several recent studies indicate that the drug has been successful in suppressing symptoms for persons allergic to eggs and cow's milk, but its overall effectiveness is still an open question simply because, as of this writing, it is still comparatively a new drug. Time and an increase in clinical application will eventually take the measure of its general efficacy for the food allergic.

Avoidance is the best, the safest, the surest way to leave food allergy symptoms behind. Again, I recommend Mrs. Wall's cheerful attitude: "Think positively." Time will arrange all things, including an eggless, milkless, wheatless diet, Spartan and unattractive as that might seem at first. Yes, it may be difficult, inconvenient and even grim initially, but after a while such an avoidance diet becomes so much second nature that nothing very vital is missed—except of course one's miserable symptoms.

Checklist

Wheat in one form or another probably makes up approximately one quarter of our daily caloric intake.

Wheat gluten is essential to light breads. It is the ingredient that makes bread rise.

Gluten intolerance, though not an allergy, calls for the same sort of avoidance measures and restricted diet that does allergy to wheat.

Allergy to wheat may begin early in life and continue into adulthood, but it is seldom severe.

Those with a fairly strong sensitivity to wheat may develop sensitivity to the other cereal grains substituted for wheat in their diet.

Wheat can cause allergic symptoms in sensitive individuals, not only by eating, but also by inhaling and touching it.

Most restricted of all is the diet of those unfortunate few allergic to eggs, milk and wheat plus corn.

It is vital to maintain vitamin and mineral intake when on a restricted diet for any length of time.

Desensitization, while a useful tool in inhalant allergy, especially to pollen, is not very successful in food allergy.

Nine

This Is Food? The Case of Food Additives

Emerson once said, "To different minds, the same world is a hell, and a heaven." For most people, food can be one of life's great pleasures. But, as we have seen in the last few chapters, for a good many persons, it can be a dismal torment. Members of the latter group seem to be on the increase.

Why is this?

To a large extent in this case, man is his own worst enemy. Modern man incorporates into his food many substances he might not be so eager to consume if they were presented to him all by themselves on a platter. He does this intentionally with additives. He does this accidentally with chemicals that find their way onto his table through carelessness or heedlessness or both. Man is both habit-ridden and a perfectionist. If a cow gives white butter, man adds a dye, for butter must come to the table bright yellow to fit a habitual perception that butter is yellow. Man prefers his apple coated with pesticide to an apple free of chemical poisons but marred by a gall or a worm hole. It may well be that we are paying an increasing price in illness (and allergy is only one of several serious diseases involved) in exchange for preconceived notions of how food should look and an inability to tolerate what may often be very minor imperfections.

Not that Nature is always an ally to be trusted. She has a bad habit of sandbagging some of our best efforts. We grow a perfect food and she adds a fungi to make us ill. She tempts us with delicious fruits that contain chemicals, such as the salicylates, to trigger our allergy.

However, it is not always the food itself to which the allergic react but to components in the food, many of which need not be there. It is often not enough to simply know what food you are

113

eating or what foods are in a product. It is often also necessary to know what may have been deliberately added to color, flavor, fill, bind, preserve and accentuate that food, what touch Nature may have added to make you ill or what chemicals used in growing the food may arrive on your table as residues.

Here is Dr. John J. Miller's eloquent estimate of our present problem:

> This was not such a problem some fifty years ago when most people lived on farms or had their own gardens. Insecticides were seldom used and herbicides were unknown. Administering antibiotics to livestock and feeding of hormones would have been considered a sacrilege. Well water was made safe by chlorination without addition of other chemicals or removal of valuable minerals. Practically nobody drank softened water. Moreover, pollution of the atmosphere was not a health hazard, and the functions of the Food and Drug Administration were: (a) preventing the marketing of unclean foods; (b) prohibiting dishonest advertising; and (c) curtailing the sale of substitute or imitation foods. Schools taught the improved production of natural foods and the art of preparing them to the best advantage in the kitchen. Only the basic foods were obtainable in the grocery stores; and farmers butchered their own livestock, had grain ground at the local mill; traded high quality eggs and butter for sugar and well cured cheese. Wagon salesmen provided coffee, tea, and spices, but no carbonated beverages. Dental caries were rare, and the degenerative diseases that now plague the nation were practically unknown. Only occasionally was a man rejected for military service, whereas now rejections involve almost half of all draftees.

But Dr. Miller is not just indulging in nostalgia; he goes on to pinpoint the controversy that swirls around a good many modern food products:

> School training, which should promote health, largely ignores these dangerous conditions. Do schools explain to pupils that wheat seeds are dosed with mercury compounds to prevent rot; that insecticides are sprayed on the growing wheat crop; that stored wheat is fumigated with methylbromide, carbon disulfide, carbon tetrachloride or methoxychloride; that flour is bleached with chemicals; that the vitamins and minerals lost in the milling process are only partially replaced in so-called "enriched flour or baked products"? Where are the lessons telling the farmer that he is undermining the health of his family in not raising his own fruits and vegetables; in taking his good milk and cream to market, then bringing home the commercial substitutes? How come nowadays even

the farmers buy bread, cakes and cookies from town bakeries or bread wagons that profitably serve farm areas, instead of baking their own at much less cost? Why has the soft drink business of the U.S. grown from 1.3 billion dollars in 1957 to 3.5 billion dollars in 1967 [to over ten billion by 1978], which means the high intake of sugar or sugar substitutes? What can be done now to get rid of the toxic nitrates and fluorides in the water used for drinking and cooking? Who will stop the use of insecticides and herbicides on over 80 percent of the farming area? Under conditions today, the family physician is the only person who knows enough about the needs of the human body—together with the inadequacies and hazards of available foods—to help solve the problems of nutrition.

Why is Dr. Miller concerned?

Well, first and foremost, there are a surprising number of malnourished Americans walking about the land. They are suffering from inadequate diets not simply because of poverty but also because of impoverished food products. Second, many doctors believe that there is a correlation between our modern American diet and the greatly increasing incidence of degenerative diseases. Finally, probably one out of seven Americans suffers allergy of some sort—it ranked seventh as a medical reason for rejection in the draft. Allergy is on the rise. Dr. Stephen Lockey, a long-time advocate of more caution in the use of additives in food and of the synthetic substances in particular, has estimated that around 12 percent of the population is susceptible to allergic reactions in some degree to food additives. In *Jane Brody's Nutrition Book* (W. W. Norton & Co., Inc., 1981), the author notes that the average American adult consumes 150 pounds of additives annually, over 90 percent of which are sugar or salt. That's quite a mound of colors, flavors, fillers, enhancers, antioxidants, blenders, and preservatives—a regular platterful!

However, before we wander off into the wasteland of additives, we should first make note of some of Nature's nasty ways with food, some of which are allergenic in nature but most of which are toxic.

In Chapter Ten we noted the importance of vitamins and trace minerals to human health. Many of us do not realize that the chemical composition of fruits and vegetables varies, depending upon the conditions of the soil in which they are grown and even the air where they are grown. It has been repeatedly shown that soils depleted by constant use often grow foodstuffs of inadequate nutritional value. While man extracts some billion metric tons of metals from the earth each year plants may well extract five times that amount. Quality of soil, then, is not only vital to the plants themselves but to those that eat the plants, be they animal or man. For instance, a study suggested that, when on a winter diet of grain (an acidotic diet that may result in a disturbed acid-base balance), animals were more suspectible to sensitization than when on a summer diet of grass and green fodder (an alkalotic diet that increases the body's alkalies above normal).

There are natural substances in our foods other than mineral traces and vitamins that affect us for better or for worse. A good many people react to fungi—prolific and leafless plants with countless spores—especially when they inhale them. Ingesting fungi can also cause allergic reaction. Molds not only thrive in dark closets and damp basements, but are also inclined to make their home on stale bread, cheese, grains, fruits and vegetables. They are not always unwanted invaders, for they are responsible for tastiness and zip in cheese and wine and beer, not to mention our daily bread.

Penicillium, a fungus that appears as a bluish fuzz on old bread and cheese and is a source of the antibiotic, penicillin, is a common allergen. Such gourmet delights as Camembert, Roquefort and Gorgonzola cheeses are the better for harboring this mold but not for those who are sensitive to it. Fortunately, it does not itself seem to affect those allergic to the penicillin derived from it (a potentially severe allergy). But those sensitive to the fungus (not the antibiotic) may have to give up the pleasure of some of the better cheeses.

We Americans have an ambivalent attitude toward fungi. We cuss the kind that gives us athletes' foot even as we bless the kind that raises our bread and bubbles our beer. But those unfortunate enough to be allergic to them seldom have cause for gratitude, from the time the snow melts in the spring until it flies again in autumn. Oddly, some mold sensitive persons can enjoy beer in winter but guzzle it at their peril once warm weather arrives. Why? Because their exposure is vastly increased (and therefore their threshold lowered) during the mold spore season of warm weather when the air is filled with fungi spores; it is at its lowest in the winter. This state of affairs seems to turn the pleasure of beer drinking around backward but so it must be for those whose tolerance to the fungi is low. They often, alas, cannot drink their mold and breathe it at one and the same time without reaction.

The mushroom lover may suffer the same upside-down enjoyment if he develops a sensitivity to his favorite fare. He will be able to enjoy his treat (canned or imported) during cold weather but be unable to enjoy the search, seizure and satisfaction of mushroom collecting and consumption during warm weather. Thus, it may not be possible for him to inhale and ingest his treat at one and the same time without illness.

Those sensitive to the fungi may have to avoid the following foods:

mushrooms	wine
melons, particularly cantaloupes	beer
cottage cheese	cider and any beverage containing yeast
cheese	pickled meats such as pastrami, corned beef, pickled tongue
sour cream	
buttermilk	

vinegar and all products containing it, such as mayonnaise, catsup, pickles, relishes, salad dressings and sauerkraut

smoked meats and fish
bread and bakery goods with yeast

Foods stored in the refrigerator or elsewhere, especially where it is damp, may start up a colony of the ubiquitous fungi. Thus, highly mold-sensitive folk have the perfect excuse to feed leftovers more than a day old to the family dog!

Another of Nature's mixed blessings is salicylate, which is a constituent of food and also an ingredient of aspirin. Aspirin sensitivity can be exceedingly severe, so severe that virtually a crumb can result in shock and even death. Thus, many allergists recommend that those allergic to aspirin avoid the following foods, which contain salicylate naturally:

almonds
apricots
blackberries
boysenberries
raspberries
peaches
prunes
grapes
cucumbers
tomatoes
cloves

apples
apple cider
currants
gooseberries
strawberries
plums
oranges
raisins
pickles
oil of wintergreen

I once treated an aspirin-sensitive youngster and thought I had eliminated salicylates entirely from his diet. Still, he continued to suffer allergic symptoms, especially swelling of the lips. Finally (and often this necessary detective work is like chasing your shadow around a bush), I discovered that the problem was the oil of wintergreen flavoring in his toothpaste!

There are other constituents of food that can cause trouble. For instance, certain amines (one of a group of organic compounds, derivitives of ammonia containing nitrogen) are found naturally in such things as cheese, tomatoes, bananas, pineapples and animal flesh and have been implicated in migraine headaches. These amines appear to dilate the blood vessels so that fluid leakage (edema) occurs in the cranial area. A special villain is tyramine, and foods containing it in good measure are:

aged or strong cheese
chicken livers
pods of broad beans
canned figs
pickled herring

The role of allergy and the amines is not clear, but it is probably safe to say that sensitivity to the amines is one of a number of causes of headaches. For a more complete list of foods to avoid if you suffer from chronic headaches, see Appendix F.

An interesting example of built-in sensitivity is a disease called favism. It is thought generally to be an allergy and is often severe. It is a somewhat common disease in Sicily and Sardinia where a good many residents react to a particular bean, the Vicia Fava. Victims may suffer symptoms—abdominal pain, anemia, jaundice and prostration—from inhaling the pollen of the bean plant as well as from ingesting the bean itself.

So all that comes from Nature firsthand is not without allergy hazards. Still, there is growing concern that man is his own worst enemy.

Let us admit at once that man has been tinkering with his food for centuries. Nor are additives new. Animals other than man search eagerly for a salt lick and sometimes trade their lives for a chance at it. Perhaps by observing all this activity at a salt lick, man discovered that salt did improve the taste of things and, more importantly, could preserve his meat so that he could stave off starvation when times were lean. Once he had made this vital discovery, man was off and running. He has reached the point now where he is using several thousand additives, some natural, some synthetic, to pep up, color, flavor, fill out and preserve foods and even to manufacture foods from scratch. To compound the problem, residues of drugs and pesticides and chemical wastes from polluted air and water are also now incorporated into the modern diet.

There are substances in food that were not there thirty years ago, or twenty, or even ten. And there are substances missing, for a good deal of what was once in food has been refined out of existence or lost because the soils in which much of our food is grown have been depleted. A growing number of doctors are concerned about the role of both of these factors in the rising incidence of degenerative diseases such as cancer, heart problems and diabetes. A good many allergists are coming to believe that the increasing number of allergic individuals may be due, in part, to the increased use of additives in food plus the widespread use of detergents, pesticides, plastics and drugs that become incorporated in one way or another into food.

Well, just what is an intentional food additive?

Defined by the Food and Drug Administration, that arm of the government that tries to protect our food from filth, adulteration and poisons, additives are "substances added directly to food or substances which may reasonably be expected to become components of food through surface contact with equipment or packaging materials or even substances that may otherwise affect the food without becoming a part of it" (such as various forms of radiation used in food processing).

Are they necessary?

This depends a good deal upon your point of view. Food manufacturers obviously think they are. A good many doctors believe a good many, if not most of them, are not. Housewives (many of whom hold down full-time jobs as well as take care of families and homes) may feel convenience foods are a boon and a blessing. Health addicts may find them the devil's fare. A growing number of allergy sufferers probably curse the day additives ever saw light in man's fertile imagination.

A controversial out-with-'em diet that excludes artificial colors, flavors and the preservative BHT has been developed by Dr. Benjamin Feingold, chief emeritus, Department of Allergy of the Kaiser-Permanente Medical Center in San Francisco. Dr. Feingold and proponents of his program claim that it helps at least half of the hyperactive population. Other physicians dispute this claim, while recent studies indicate that perhaps some hyperactive patients are improved by the diet but that the success figure is far lower than 50 percent. At present, the middle ground, once again, is the safest place for me to stand, so I shall only say, "Try it, you might like it. But don't place all your bets upon it." Certainly it is worth trying for a few weeks when all else fails and the problem is drastic in nature. Remember, though, that judgments of behavior problems tend to be subjective, depending to a large degree upon parental and teacher capacity for patience. Still, a distinctly hyperactive child (and adult also, for that matter) can be an affliction for all around him. Anything that can mute his problem will mute the problems of those who must deal with him.

For some idea of what could be added to various foods to cause hyperactivity, see Appendix C.

Let's go back to the problem of the aspirin sensitive. Symptoms can range from localized swelling and hives to gastrointestinal distress with extensive bleeding and shock. Being sensitive to aspirin in this day and age is more hazardous than most of us might suppose. It is no longer simply a matter of avoiding those foods that contain salicylate naturally or even of refraining from reaching for the aspirin bottle when your head begins to throb. The aspirin sensitive may also react to chemically different but closely related compounds such as tartrazine, a yellow dye. Tartrazine is only one of the tribe of synthetic colors, flavors and other additives that are now thought to be responsible for allergic reactions.

A San Francisco research team reports recently that they seemed to be able to turn peculiar behavior problems on and off, even as one might pull the cord on a light bulb, in some hyperactive (hyperkinesia) children. They achieved this by restricting the children's intake of the salicylates, then releasing the restrictions. Hyperactive children have long been a mystery. Their treatment with such drugs as the amphetamines or Retalin has created a minor medical uproar. The incident of children suffering hyperkinesia—short attention span, restlessness, tension of motor nerves, inability to learn, clumsiness—appears to be rising rather sharply in our land. An Oakland study indicates that this odd syndrome has risen from some 2 percent of the school population to 20 or 25 percent in the last decade or so. The study suggests the possibility that this rising figure is correlated with the increasing use of chemicals in foods, especially such things as soft drinks, colored cereals, drink syrups, hot dogs, lunch meats, ice cream, and even children's vitamins.

Dr. Stephen Lockey recommends that anyone allergic to aspirin would do well to avoid the following, especially if they are known to be artificially flavored or colored:

ice cream	cider and cider beverages
oleomargarine	wine and wine vinegars
gin and all distilled beverages except vodka	Kool Aid and similar beverages
cake mixes	birch beer
bakery goods (except plain bread)	diet drinks and supplements
	toothpaste and toothpowder
Jell-O	oil of wintergreen
candies	mint flavors
gum	lozenges
frankfurters	mouthwash
lunch meats (salami, bologna and the like)	jam or jelly
	all soft drinks
cloves	beer
all tea	

And probably the aspirin sensitive should avoid the preservative sodium benzoate as well, since there may sometimes be an associated sensitivity. The trouble is that "salicylate" or "sodium benzoate" may not be always on the labels. When a label simply states "artificial coloring" or "artificial flavoring," how is one to know? Must the aspirin sensitive avoid everything that is artificially colored or flavored?

The answer now seems to be yes, they must.

To add to the problem, there are many additives used in food that do not turn up in any form on labels. These are the "generally recognized as safe" additives, or GRAS, which often need not be acknowledged specifically in packaging. They have been in use for so long that the FDA does not consider them harmful, at the moment anyway. It is unsettling when the FDA snatches this or that GRAS additive off the list after testing has shown hazard to laboratory animals and thus, by inference, possible hazard to humans.

Are some additives a hazard to human health?

Actually, when we examine the problem of risk from food additives, particularly synthetic chemicals, we are dealing somewhat with the unknown. No one can be quite sure what their low-level, long-term effect may be on those who consume them. Most, no doubt, will have no adverse effect. However, probably just as certainly, some will adversely affect some people. One authority, for instance, has suggested that iodized salt, long employed by vast numbers of people to thwart goiter, may so sensitize some individuals as to pose a distinct threat to their health upon a later dosage of medicinal iodides.

Monosodium glutamate, employed rather widely in a variety of foods, may enhance flavor, but it may also enhance one's allergy. Americans annually consume tons of MSG, a non-nutritional substance. Anyone who has suffered from Chinese resturant syndrome can attest to its potency. The headache it can produce far outweighs its initial effect on flavor. Once prevalent in baby food and still a member of the FDA's GRAS list, MSG, while a naturally occurring substance, can act as a toxic substance when synthesized within our bodies. It has been estimated that as many as 30 percent of us are affected unpleasantly by it.

Although no longer included in baby food, MSG can be found in some TV dinners, gravies, meat bouillons, salad dressings, mayonnaise and, of course, Chinese food, both in resturants and in frozen packages. Its presence may not be announced on the label.

Another problem additive that has received considerable attention recently is that of the sulfites. The relationship of sulfites to asthma has been of special concern since they can produce bronchospasm as well as anaphylaxis. Dr. Ronald Simon of the Scripps Clinic in La Jolla, California, has estimated that one in twenty asthmatics react allergically to sulfite. Others have estimated that at least one million Americans are affected by these additives.

Sulfites are employed to preserve the freshness and color of foods and can turn up not only in such foods as fresh fruits and vegetables in supermarket produce sections to maintain that straight-off-the-farm look, in shrimp, dried fruits and potato chips, but also in beer and wine. Sulfites are liberally employed in restaurants also, especially at the salad bar to keep the lettuce and other fresh stuff crispy, green and crunchy through a long day. A partial list of foods which could contain sulfites is given in Appendix D.

What is an "acceptably small level"? Will it remain "acceptably small," as more and more people become sensitized to the chemicals laced into their food?

Finally, how can the allergic practice the one cure for his symptoms, avoidance, when food labels do not always list all ingredients?

For labels fall very short of doing that. For instance, there are several hundred foods the FDA lists as "standards of identity." These foods need not list their ingredients even though they may contain some twenty or thirty different substances to color, preserve, flavor and fill out—you name it. Such a nonlisting was to blame, in part, for the death of the young Boston boy who ate ice cream containing the unlikely ingredient peanut butter. Dr. Lockey also details the case of a man who almost died of an allergic reaction to artificial strawberry and chocolate flavoring in ice cream when he was not allergic to either strawberries or chocolate!

Another example of a food that may be more than it seems is butter. Since, supposedly, everyone knows what butter is, its ingredients need not be listed on the package. Yet, not only is a good deal of butter on the market artificially dyed to a brighter shade of yellow than any cow can make it, but it is sometimes artificially flavored to a more buttery than butter taste with diacetyl. Again, Dr. Lockey documents the case of a youngster who had to receive emergency treatment because he ate flavored butter. To risk the life of a child, or of anyone else, simply to make butter more buttery or yellower than nature intended, or to avoid using real strawberries and real chocolate, or to fill out ice cream with something cheaper than heavy cream, does not seem fair. At the very least, if food is not what it seems, the feaster should be so notified. It is his allergy and his life that are at stake.

Am I overstating the case?

I don't think so.

For example, to the highly aspirin sensitive, there is considerable danger in ingesting more than one or two milligrams of tartrazine. Yet it has been estimated that it is quite possible to consume this and much more in one day's ordinary fare. And that does not take into account the cross reactivity (fortunately, rare) to the benzoates used widely as a preservative.

However, it must be said that the FDA has finally gotten the word from both consumers' groups and the medical profession. Better labeling has been forthcoming, although the GRAS list still exists. For a while it even seemed possible that distilleries and breweries might have to list ingredients on their labels, but lobbying pressures against such a requirement were so intense that the possibility has been moved out of the hands of government and into the courts. Thus, it may be some time before such labeling will come to pass. The allergic will have to remain wary.

These days, about 90 percent of all food color is produced from synthetic dyes—aniline or coal tar products, which seem to cause the most trouble for the allergic. Why have the synthetics become so popular with food producers? Because they are the least expensive to use and are more stable and more uniform than natural dyes. Yellow is not the only color the allergic must view with suspicion. Phenolphthalein, a coal tar derivative, often colors candy, cake icing and toothpaste a pretty pink. It, too, can bring on allergic symptoms in those sensitive to it. It is also, incidentally, an ingredient of many laxatives. However, it seems easier to avoid pink than yellow in food, perhaps because we ascribe some mystical benefit to yellow, the sunshine color of good health and wholesomeness.

One sobering aspect of all this artificial coloring and flavoring is the soft drink industry. American youngsters come close to being addicted to soda pop of one kind or another. Aside from the possible adverse effects of the sugar they consume, they are also ingesting a good bit of synthetic coloring matter.

"Caramel color" on the labels of such soft drinks as root beer and cola (and of other foods) can be produced from a variety of things, some of which may be allergenic for a good many persons. Caramel coloring results from the heat treatment of any of the following:

> sucrose from cane or beets (used in cake icings)
> dextrose or glucose from corn (used in soft drinks, gravies, rye bread, baked goods)
> molasses derived from any of the sugars
> lactose (milk sugar)

In most ice cream, sherbets, ice cream cones, gelatin puddings and most candy, food colors of one hue or another or caramel coloring is used. For some reason, the goodies seem to sell better if gaudy.

The World Health Organization (WHO) tested its way through a list of some one hundred and forty coloring agents and found a good many of them to be downright unsafe. In the end, they certified only a handful. In the United States, the FDA-approved colors number around a dozen, give or take a few that are dropped suddenly or are added to replace those that get lost. For instance, not long ago the FDA banned violet #1, a dye long used by the government to stamp inspected meat carcasses. What was perfectly harmless yesterday has an unsettling way of turning up not quite so innocuous today. An increasing segment of the medical profession wishes the United States would follow the stringent lead of Denmark, which bans all additives unless they are absolutely necessary to the food. This would seem to squeeze most, if not all, the artificial colors out of the picture. As a result of the ban, there are virtually no additives in Danish food (preservatives may sometimes be vital). No one can fault Danish culinary art. Nor the state of their national health.

Even medicine is colored with these dyes, and it is sometimes difficult for a doctor to know whether his patient is reacting to the drug itself or to its coloring.

Flavoring, like coloring, has been incorporated into human food just about as long as humans have been around to enjoy eating. Human slaves were once eagerly traded for spices and condiments. As with coloring, flavorings started off by being wholly natural ingredients, but by now a good many are as synthetic as the colors. Some flavors are even more flavorful than the original food's flavor, some are used simply to replace the original flavor that has been processed out and some are enhancers that bring out the food's own shy flavor to a greater degree. There are probably well over a thousand different natural and artificial flavoring agents for food processors to choose from.

Again, why use synthetic flavors in food?

Because they are cheaper and more stable than the natural.

Do we need them?

The Danes would undoubtedly say no.

For the allergic, flavoring, like coloring, can pose a problem, for the label term, "artificial flavor," can cover a multitude of chemicals. It may be very important for the sensitive to know whether the delicious caramel flavor in his cookies or pudding is due to burnt cane sugar or to phenylethyl. It may mean the difference between good health and illness. On the other hand, it must be admitted that sometimes the allergic come off better with the synthetic rather than the real thing, since natural spices and condiments are apt to be potent allergens.

The real crux of the flavoring matter is that the allergic (and everyone else, for that matter) must be protected by knowing exactly what sort of flavoring agent has been incorporated into the food he buys, especially since often more than one chemical or compound is used to simulate a specific flavor. To say merely "artificial flavor" on the label is not enough. For instance, the taste of citrus fruits, especially orange, can be simulated in soft drinks and "ades" by such things as C9 nonylaldehyde or C11 undecylaldehyde or yara yara. For the allergic person, these three names may make as much sense to him as Greek. But his doctor would be able to make sense of them by giving him a list of flavoring agents to avoid —for by any long and complicated name, they still may taste as sweet and cause as much trouble.

Probably the bulk of the additives we consume consists of fillers and binders, emulsifiers, stabilizers and thickeners. A good bit of your loaf of bread or quart of ice cream is filled out by such things, either in natural form (the gums) or synthetic. A cotton by-product, carboxymethyl, for instance, is frequently employed as a stabilizer in ice cream and candy. But you, the consumer, are never given a hint that it is there.

The most justifiable of all additives are the preservatives, since they prevent spoilage and lengthen the shelf life of foods. This is a necessity in an era of increasing population and massive food consumption, where vast numbers of people are divorced from the land. Spoilage is a serious problem in food distribution. WHO has come up with the grim estimate that one fifth of the world's food supplies spoil before they can be consumed. In a time of extensive food shortages, malnutrition and even famine in some parts of the world, such waste is intolerable. Old-time methods of preserving with salt, sugar, vinegar and smoke, while still used extensively, cannot begin to cope with the problem, especially with prepackaged foods. Even so, it must be admitted that some preservatives have recently come into bad odor.

For instance, sodium nitrite, widely used to preserve meats and fish, is suspected these days of being a cancer agent. Some allergists have suggested that it may also be responsible for a kind of rheumatic allergic reaction, with severe joint pains.

Several antioxidants that have been especially useful in preserving fatty foods have been indicted as the cause of severe and bizarre allergic symptoms in some persons. We turn to Dr. Stephen Lockey again, who cites (in private correspondence) an interesting case involving BHA (butylated hydroxyanisole) and BHT (butylated hydroxytoluene), both used as preservatives not only in foods themselves but in their packaging materials.

> A twenty-year-old woman ingested a spoonful of crisp corn flakes. After she had placed the corn flakes in her mouth, her uvula, the small piece of flesh that hangs down in the back of everyone's throat, swelled. She also developed shortness of breath. It took great effort for her to move her limbs and she felt extremely fatigued.
>
> An allergist skin tested her for sensitivity to corn, cow's milk and cow's milk lactalbumin but she failed to react. The source of her severe spell of illness remained in doubt until one day she sat down to dinner and ingested a couple of bites of reconstituted dehydrated potatoes. She suffered the same type of attack as previously—the swelling of her throat, extreme weakness and fatigue. She was again tested for sensitivity to potato extract. The results were negative.
>
> Puzzled by the young women's symptoms, her physician examined the labels of the box of corn flakes and also the box of dehydrated potatoes. The corn flakes had been treated with Butylated Hydroxyanisole Food Additive (BHA) and the dehydrated potatoes that the young woman had eaten contained Butylated Hydroxytoluene Food Additive (BHT), a relative to BHA—a preservative and an antimold agent.
>
> All symptoms disappeared when she stopped ingesting foods that contained BHA and BHT.

Dr. Lockey has compiled the following list of foods that may contain BHA and BHT:

beverages and desserts prepared from dry mixes
active dry yeast
lard and shortening
unsmoked dry sausage
chewing gum base
dry breakfast cereals
emulsion stabilizers for shortenings
sweet potato flakes
mixed, diced glacéed fruits
potato granules
defoaming agent component as an antioxidant (used in processing beet sugar and yeast)
enriched rice

You may also often find this notation on package labels: "BHT added to packaging material to preserve freshness."

Double exposure can also occur when a potent additive is both contacted and ingested. For example, propylene glycol is incorporated in household cleaning products and in toothpaste, medications and foods such as soft drinks, frozen cakes and cheesecakes, whipped toppings, salad dressings and grated coconut. Those who are allergic to it usually react with dermatitis.

The potential problems that intentional additives pose for human health could take up the rest of the book. But we will touch only on one more aspect of the subject—the great mystery of synergism, a process in which two chemicals may interact to produce a result neither one alone could produce. Thus, if a person consumes a synthetic dye in one food plus a synthetic flavor in another, the result may be quite different than if he had ingested only one or other synthetic substance. What by itself may be harmless can interact with something else to pose a real hazard. It seems logical that we run an increasing danger of syngeristic effects the more chemicals we add, intentionally or unintentionally, to our foods. Not only that, but body chemistry may interact in a synergistic fashion to various additives.

The whole business is complex and hazardous. Most unsettling of all, we don't know a great deal about what some additives conceivably could do to us. The low-level, long-term effects are wrapped in uncertainty. So are the possibilities of synergism.

With intentional additives, at least the food producers know what they have put into their products, even if the consumers do not. However, with unintentional additives, the problem, for the most part, is one of ignorance all around, ignorance by producer and consumer alike. Human error and heedlessness has always had a frightening quality.

As most of us are probably aware, a good bit of our food does not arrive upon our tables in pristine purity. It may contain what the FDA has determined is a reasonable amount of dirt and dust, insect debris and rodent hairs and pellets, residues of herbicides, pesticides and rodenticides. Ordinarily, we give little thought to this flotsam and jetsam. However, when these limits are broached, particularly by toxic substances, we, the consumers, are made ill; the FDA condemns; there is a flurry of recall; and bottles, boxes and cans are removed from supermarket shelves. In the end, a harried food products company probably has to up its advertising budget to counter all the adverse publicity such a situation can create.

But there is more to unintentional additives than this. Even when we are not being exposed to toxic amounts of these things, there is a good deal of concern being voiced these days that continuous exposure, even at the legal limits set by the FDA, may be responsible for less dramatic but equally disabling diseases, especially the so-called degenerative diseases—cancer, heart disease, diabetes and allergy. The 1970 Report of the Task Force on Research Planning in Environmental Health (U.S. Department of Health, Education and Welfare) said:

> Little is known either from the laboratory or from epidemiologic studies of the possible role that our daily food plays in man's neoplastic (new, abnormal tissue growth) and degenerative diseases. New foods, new processes, new methods of preservation, new packaging, new industrial chemical wastes, increasing use of fertilizers and pesticides and deteriorating water quality make increased research efforts imperative to assure the safety of food and water.

We are apt to serenely assume that the FDA will protect us from such residues of chemicals and drugs. So it is a shock to read announcements of the seizure of thousands of cases of lettuce contaminated by high levels of residues of an organophosphate insecticide, Monitor 4, chemically related to nerve gas. Yet, the residual problem need not be so singular. Chemicals used to bleach flour or chlorine used in high concentrations to purify drinking and cooking water can possibly cause allergy in the sensitive. Perhaps even more difficult to deal with is the problem of soil pollution, whether by an overabundance of artificial fertilizers or chemical and bacterial wastes spewed into the water and air by industry. Vegetables have an unhandy way of taking some of these undesirable elements unto themselves and passing them on to us. Thus, one researcher found that carrots grown without the use of artificial fertilizer contained 19 parts per million of iodine, whereas carrots grown with artificial fertilizers contained 2,100 parts per million, an increase that conceivably might affect the iodine sensitive and even lead to sensitization of others.

Add to all this the various chemical residues of pesticides and herbicides that do not wash off easily—a regular witch's brew is dished up. WHO estimates that this "brew" may now be a significant human health hazard in the industrialized nations of the world. And what this "brew" may mean for the especially susceptible, the allergic, is anyone's guess.

But we haven't exhausted the problem yet. The medical profession has been particularly concerned about the widespread and increasing use of antibiotics and antibacterials in animal feeds. There is reason to believe that residues of these drugs in meat, eggs and dairy products may be strong enough to affect the already allergic (and for those allergic to penicillin, for instance, this can be serious). Such abundant usage can also sensitize great numbers of people over a period of time, even as it leads to the breeding of new strains of drug-resistant bacteria. This concern has been voiced so strongly that recently the FDA gave drug companies promoting such feed additives two years to prove that they presented no such hazard to human health.

Why use such drugs in feed in the first place?

Because they promote faster growth in meat animals and prevent disease in crowded conditions such as cattle feed lots or, in the case of chickens, jampacked broiler houses.

Use of such drugs in feeds has increased some 600 percent in the last decade. No doubt, the residues in meat as well as the reservoirs of resistant bacteria have increased proportionately.

Once again, the most unsettling factor is the great unknown of synergism and long-term, low-level exposure. To quote again from the report of 1970 Task Force on Research Planning in Environmental Health: "There is particular concern over the possibility of formation of substances that induce or modify carcinogenicity, substances capable of bringing about sensitization, or those causing other forms of intolerance."

Thus, all that you heap upon your platter is not, strictly speaking, food. Some of it may be bad news for you if you happen to be allergic. It may be bad news for you even if you are as healthy as an ox!

Checklist

Additives, or nonfood components of food, can be classified into two categories: the intentional and the unintentional.

Intentional additives are those natural and synthetic substances incorporated into foods to color, flavor, fill, bind, thicken, preserve and the like.

Unintentional additives are traces or residues of such substances as pesticides, herbicides, artificial fertilizers, pollution wastes, drugs and so on that are accidentally incorporated into foods.

Some 12 percent of the American population may be sensitive in some degree to food additives.

Some substances or their derivatives often incorporated into foods as additives also appear naturally in some foods.

The aspirin sensitive must be wary of a number of foods that either contain the salicylates naturally or to which salicylates have been added.

It is important, especially for the allergic, that foods be completely labeled and additive ingredients specifically listed.

No one can really be sure what the long-term, low-level effect of both intentional and unintentional additives is on human health.

Chemicals from various sources—pollution, artificial fertilizers, additives and Nature herself—may interact with each other or with the body's own chemicals to form hazardous substances in a process known as synergism.

The use of antibiotics and antibacterials in animal feeds may be hazardous to humans because (1) they may be creating a reservoir of resistant bacteria strains; (2) they may be sensitizing large segments of the population to drugs important in the treatment of human diseases; and (3) they may be affecting the already drug sensitive.

Ten

The Food Allergic's Special Problems

Allergy to anything—food, inhalants, drugs or insects—creates special problems for its victims. The magnitude of these problems depends on the magnitude of the individual's allergic condition and the measures he takes to avoid or prevent his allergic symptoms. If an individual is allergic to a good many foods, then his troubles are likely to be many, his life complex. In this chapter, we consider the problems of the hard up.

Those allergic to the basic foods of eggs, milk, wheat and corn have a real dietary problem. Neither avoidance nor substitution is easy to handle. Yet, it is not impossible to live without these fundamentals of the American diet. A good many people in the rest of the world rarely, if ever, consume eggs, milk, wheat or corn. Dietary deprivation, then, is relative.

Still, if avoidance and dietary restrictions were all the food allergic had to contend with, life might run along smoothly enough, with only an occasional squeak in the machinery. But sensitivity to food can present some peculiar problems for its "first class" victims.

At the beginning of this book, we noted that a good many people are inclined to dismiss allergy as being all in the victim's head, a figment of his imagination or even an indication of hypochondria. For a long time (and there still may be plenty of persons around today who believe this), allergy symptoms were considered a result of emotional disorder. An individual broke out into hives because he was emotionally distressed. He developed asthma because he was a nervous person and easily upset. And so on. (Conversely, symptoms of allergy can be used to avoid responsibility or to get your own way or to gain special attention and concern.) A good many parents even now are inclined to view their allergic children's symptoms with skepticism—this in spite of a doctor's careful explanation of the problem. Many people similarly view their allergic fellow adults with more suspicion than sympathy.

All this doubt and disbelief in what for the sufferer is very real can be mighty hard on the allergic person. He knows that he is ill. He feels his symptoms keenly. He can be especially distressed when others find his inability to tolerate certain foods amusing or a matter for ridicule. All this may only increase his problems, emotional as well as physical.

And such skepticism can be dangerous. I have seen sad results where allergy was not taken seriously. During my allergy residency, a boy in his teens, son of an athletic coach, came into the hospital. He had the barrel chest indicative of asthma of long duration. It was a severe attack of asthma that brought him to the hospital, where he died two weeks later. The father, thinking his son's illness was emotional, had ignored it and had made the boy participate in all sports.

Are they correct or mistaken, these individuals who believe allergy is all in the mind, a product of one's emotional distress?

This is the old, old mind-over-matter question, and it still circulates in modern medicine like a ghost at the feast. There is probably no definitive answer. It is not yet possible to separate the mind from the body and assign them absolutely separate roles in disease. Since we are products of our genetic inheritance, interacting constantly with our environment, we surely cannot help but be affected by not only what goes on around us but also by what goes on inside us. Comprehension of this fact has led to the concept of "holism," a concept that dictates that the patient be approached as an entity rather than divided into segments—mind and body, emotional problems versus physical symptoms. Holism suggests that the well individual can be considered to be in balance. But when he is ill, one adaptive force or another is out of balance with the whole. Adaptation to stress, whether emotional stress or physical, is the key to health. An adaption that allows the individual to still remain in balance with himself and his world is health, whereas an adaption that throws him out of kilter with himself or his world results in illness. And we would do well to constantly remind ourselves that each individual reacts to stress in an individual way, both physically and mentally. One man's balance is not the same as another's.

And because we all react differently, it is very difficult to find cut and dried answers, specific rules, definitive causes and effects. So let us just explore possibilities.

We have likened the tolerance threshold of the allergic individual to the balancing action of a child's seesaw. Not only is that balance upset by allergens, but it can also be knocked out of whack by the presence of infection. In a like manner, emotional stress may tip the seesaw and trigger allergic reaction. It, too, can be a factor in overwhelming the individual's level of tolerance to allergens. Thus, there are three general elements of stress—emotional, infectious and allergenic—which pose a threat to the body's adaptive and protective mechanisms. Often enough, especially when they work in combination, they can overcome these mechanisms. The result is imbalance and illness.

In this way, emotional stress can be a potent factor in allergy, although it is not generally considered a "cause" as such but rather a "trigger." This is probably the most accepted view. In other words, a case of asthma may not be the result of emotions. But the emotions may trigger an underlying allergic condition, which in turn sets off the asthmatic attack. Thus a person mildly allergic to a food may consume it without symptoms until beset by emotional stress. Then he may react. He is thrown out of balance, at least momentarily, and wheezing and breathing difficulties may be the result.

But this not the whole story by any means. Allergy symptoms, especially if severe, may bring on emotional distress. We can understand this easily when we realize how upset and distressed is a person beset by oozing eczema, for instance; or how continually terrorized is he by the suffocating symptoms of asthma. Fear, embarrassment, torment—all may combine to bring about symptoms of emotional stress—nervousness, sleeplessness, depression, a whole gamut of problems.

Thus, like circus elephants tramping around the main ring, we go head to tail in an endless circle of allergy-emotions, emotions-allergy.

Holism, then, emphasizes that mind and body work together so closely in health and in illness that it is not possible to treat the one without taking the other also into consideration. When any part of the organism breaks down or is disturbed, the whole is also affected.

Fair enough. Now let us try to be more specific.

Since, as Wordsworth said, "the Child is father of the Man," we start with the emotional problems that can crop up in youngsters allergic to food. We acknowledge that underlying allergy to food may be triggered by the various emotional stresses of childhood. But our main concern is the emotional responses to the allergic condition.

When a child's diet is limited by his allergy he may become resentful about the need to avoid the foods that make him ill and even hostile toward other members of the family spared this necessity. A child may interpret such dietary restrictions as punishment or believe that he is being singled out unfairly, especially if his siblings are able to enjoy unrestricted goodies. It is no easy matter to arrange an elimination and avoidance diet in a family of several children so that the allergic child does not feel discriminated against and the other, non-allergic children do not resent being bound by his illness. The parents must walk an uneasy tightrope here and remain as inhumanly patient as possible when besieged by resentment from all quarters.

Whoever cooks for such a family will need to be unusually creative and ingenious to come up with goodies that fit within the allergic child's restricted diet, yet are considered a treat by his siblings on a normal diet (see the Candy and Ice Cream recipes in Chapter Thirteen). Such goodies act to dissipate resentment and to unite, at least temporarily, the warring parties in a common pleasure.

The parents, but especially the mother of a severely sensitive child carries a continual and heavy burden of anxiety, especially when the child is too young to understand the consequences of eating a forbidden food. There is always the chance that a young chum will share with him the food he is allergic to—a hard-boiled egg or a handful of peanuts or a candy bar. Well-meaning neighbors and mothers of the child's playmates are very apt to offer goodies. And then there are those people who don't believe in allergy and can't imagine that a little egg or a peanut or chocolate could possibly hurt the allergic child. For instance, when I was an intern, we had a patient in our hospital whose chart commanded "no aspirin." A doctor who didn't believe in such things prescribed aspirin. The patient nearly died.

How to combat such possibilities?

One ingenious mother of a small, allergic child met this danger by pinning a plastic name tag, the kind one sees at conventions and large gatherings, on the child, stating:

ALLERGIC CHILD
NO FOOD OR DRINK
COULD BE DANGEROUS

But labeling is recommended only for a very small child. Older children not only would suffer by being so labeled but should be taught responsibility for their problem in any case. However, I recommend that a severely allergic person of any age wear a warning tag or some type of warning bracelet at all times.

There is a more subtle and devastating anxiety—that the mother herself, by accident or forgetfulness, might incorporate the forbidden food into the child's diet. For instance, she might break an egg into something she was cooking for the family's meal and forgetfully allow the allergic child to eat the dish. We can comprehend rather easily the load of guilt she could carry if she did not follow his diet strictly and the child's symptoms flared anew. Or he became dangerously ill. We can also understand how her guilt may be increased a hundredfold if the father should add his censor to her self-blame.

Censoriousness and blame can often crop up between divorced parents, as though the child's allergy is a handy excuse for a flareup of the parents' animosity and resentment against each other. If the allergy should flare up when the child is visiting one parent, the other seems very ready to cast blame. I hear such remarks as "He doesn't believe in allergy, so he doesn't pay any attention" or "He took the child to his mother's, and she always lets him eat what he wants"—all said bitterly and accusingly. Sometimes I get trapped in the middle; one parent wants me to write a letter prohibiting the child from visiting the other parent for health reasons. I refuse to accommodate such a request. An allergist is entangled in enough problems without becoming the middleman in other people's divorces.

The parents of an allergic child have more problems than guilt and bickering to cope with. Frequently, allergic children indulge in that universal emotion—self-pity. "They'll be sorry when I'm dead" is a response that should be understood but not catered to, for some children may be inclined to use their illness as a weapon against both authority and responsibility. All they need to do is break their diet to bring on their symptoms and then enjoy seeing their parents upset and anxious and themselves the center of attention, extra parental care and concern. They are not slow to learn this maneuver.

I have discovered that adults are not above self-pitying tactics, either.

There is another side of the coin, however. The parents may develop an entirely human resentment against the allergic child, especially if his allergy is severe and their anxiety a burden. His illness may be a tremendous drain on their energy and the time they can devote to themselves and the rest of the family. If the child is allergic to the three basic foods—milk, eggs and wheat—there must be a good deal of home baking and cooking and far less reliance on the so-called convenience foods. Dining out in restaurants with the family may be just too difficult to be practical.

Though the parents try to hide their resentment, children are very quick to sense such things. This can be emotionally damaging to the allergic child, and perhaps to the parents as well, for guilt is a concomitant of resentment. What can be done? Accept the resentment as natural and be as matter of fact with the child as possible. Put it down to being "one of those days" and say so to the child. Acknowledge the feeling of resentment as being temporary and only human. Occasional resentment of heavy burden is not rejection, by any means. Nor will the child whose parents love him well feel that it is. The parents have enough of a load to carry without adding the weight of an undeserved guilt for an occasional feeling of resentment or rebellion.

In addition to the extra effort they must make to see that the allergic child has a nutritionally sound and pleasant diet, the parents have another duty. They must teach the child to accept responsibility for his own illness and its avoidance measures. This is not an easy task but it is a vital one. As the child grows older, the parents have less and less chance to protect him themselves. He must look after himself. Yet, again, parents walk a difficult tightrope, because they do not wish to make their child feel different, set apart from his peers, or crippled and somehow not whole.

Again, matter-of-factness is the key. After all, most of us enter life with some sort of handicap, or develop one soon after our entry. Allergy is just one of a number of possible handicaps, and that is the way the allergic child must accept his own special problem. He is a normal child and should be treated as such. He has limitations to his diet. But his sister has limitations in her vision and must wear glasses. His brother, in order to walk and run in comfort, must wear corrective shoes. And so it goes. We are normal, but we do have our little imperfections. Allergy is such an imperfection. Insofar as it is humanly possible, parents should place no special emphasis on either the child's allergy illness or his limited diet. If they are to avoid making him feel different, punished or dependent, if they are to avoid spoiling him even as the family is disrupted, they must simply treat him as a normal child and as matter-of-factly accept his allergy as they do his sister's glasses or his brother's special shoes.

Simple? No, not really. But vital.

And the allergic child must learn to manage his own diet and his own brand of imperfection, even as his sister must accept responsibility for her glasses and his brother for wearing his special shoes. He may have to learn it the hard way with illness when he "forgets" or cheats a little. The results of indiscretion have a marvelous way of maturing one's ability to make hard decisions. As he grows older, the choice between what is proscribed and the symptoms those proscriptions can evoke must be his. And he must know this.

Not that it will always be pleasant or simple for him. Other children are quick to discover the imperfections of their peers and are eager to taunt them. His sister may find herself called "four eyes," his brother "clod feet" and he himself may be dubbed "Allergy Al" or "Egghead Eddie" or "Cautious Claude." He may find himself tempted to go ahead and eat the proscribed food to escape the teasing, just as his sister might take off her glasses and hide them to avoid being called "Four Eyes" and his brother leave his special shoes at home in the closet. Yet, the resulting discomfort of his allergic symptoms probably sooner or later will teach him the truth of that old sing-song, "Sticks and stones may break my bones, but names will never harm me."

As he grows older, life does not necessarily become any easier for the allergic individual. The teens are a time of great uncertainty, both as to one's future and one's personal worth and place in the scheme of things. Allergic symptoms such as eczema or hives or asthma can engender acute emotional stress at this exceedingly stressful age. I have treated a number of young patients, especially girls whose eczema has apparently made them shy and withdrawn and resentful that they have been so singled out by misfortune. I treated one very beautiful young girl who had no sign of a rash except on her hands, which were very rough, almost like sandpaper. She constantly wore gloves, hiding her hands and keeping the boys from knowing how rough they were.

Nor does adulthood bring relief from emotional problems created by allergy. It is possible that a good many marriages may have foundered on the rock of food allergy. Special diets can breed resentment. The relationship of an allergic wife and her nonallergic husband is so familiar a pattern that I have ceased to be surprised at my fellow males, although I have not lost my desire to scold them. Husbands are usually more resentful of their wives' need for a restricted diet (or to have no smoking or pets in the house) than vice versa. Usually, the wife of an allergic husband on a limited diet is less likely to complain. Since it is extra work for her to prepare two separate diets, she prepares one—his—and eats it without fuss. Perhaps women are simply a little less rigid about food preferences and customs than men.

A good many adults have difficulty accepting their allergies, especially if they have not grown up with them and learned to live with them. These skeptical folk will have trouble sticking to a limited diet. "Too much trouble," they say. Or "Don't believe it helps." Or it may just plain be too difficult for them. Perhaps they are traveling salesmen or college students where they have little chance to arrange their meals themselves. These are the folk who, when symptoms result, feel very much put upon. They often don't and won't make an effort to understand either their illness or the measures necessary to avoid it. They seem to feel that the doctor should step into their lives, lead them by the hand, do everything for them. They take little or no responsibility for measures to combat their problem and are unwilling to make any special efforts when they are necessary. Consequently, their allergies will abide with them. They will have wasted their money and their allergist's time. Maturity, unfortunately, is not an automatic concomitant of adulthood.

The allergic woman, both during pregnancy and when nursing her baby, could run into a few special problems. It is essential that she consult her physician in the matter of her allergy medications and to be certain that he or she is aware of all such medications. If her allergy symptoms are mild, the safest course is to forswear medication—to grin and bear it, as it were. However, if her allergy is severe—let us say that she suffers from severe asthma—studies indicate that theophylline is probably quite safe and perhaps far less risky for the fetus during pregnancy than loss of oxygen that could occur in the mother's asthmatic attacks. While many of the corticosteroids have not been known to cause fetal damage, it has been suggested that inhaled steroids offer less exposure to the fetus than those taken orally. Some of the antihistamines are best avoided during pregnancy, however, but others appear to be safe. When the mother-to-be's allergy is severe, the following antihistamines appear to offer little risk to the fetus:

chlorpheniramine	methapyrilene
pyrilamine	pheniramine
tripelennamine	

Breast-feeding also requires a careful assessment of the possible effects of medications upon the nursing infant. For example, in order to minimize the amount of a necessary medication in her breast milk, the mother should take it immediately after nursing the baby. Long-acting antihistamines are best avoided, and iodide-containing drugs and some antibiotics are contraindicated. For instance, there is some risk of the infant developing jaundice if a nursing mother takes the antibiotic, erythromycin, or of altering the baby's thyroid function if she takes drugs containing iodide. As far as we know, broncodilators can be used safely by the nursing mother. Probably cromolyn sodium is also safe, but since the drug has been employed relatively recently we cannot be entirely certain of its long-term effects.

The holidays can present a special problem for food allergic children and adults alike, but especially for the parents of the allergic children, who know how much importance children set upon these special and exciting times. Holidays are the highlights of childhood. But for the food sensitive they become traps, since they are so often celebrated with special and traditional things to eat. Even adults who cannot partake of this traditional fare are likely to feel forlorn.

Easter, with its special myth of rebirth, is a virtual cornucopia of eggs (chocolate-covered, hard-boiled and dyed) and jelly beans. All are taboo for those allergic to eggs and usually for those allergic to milk, wheat and the artificial dyes. Even the black jelly bean coveted by old and young alike may be proscribed to those allergic to peanuts, for licorice belongs to the legume family. Adults may be able to smile bravely and help themselves to an extra portion of lamb and mint sauce, but children are apt to find their exclusion from this egg feast a minor tragedy.

What can be done to ensure that this will not be so?

The child allergic to the food colors may have to forego the pleasure of a good many of the jelly beans, but the traditional candy Easter egg can be duplicated (See the recipes on pp. 282 and 283). And the egg sensitive child can still share in the pleasure of dyeing the eggs he dare not eat.

For adults, Halloween is no special problem other than the constant ringing of the doorbell and the occasional prank. For children, Halloween is an orgy of goodies, but not for the allergic. Most candies are highly colored. Even the traditional candied apples are heavily spiced with cinnamon, a potent allergen. And of course gingerbread and gingerbread men and pumpkin-faced cookies all contain wheat, eggs, milk and more spices.

Can Mother make Halloween less dismal for the allergic child?

Yes, thanks again to the Allergy Information Association's recipes—try the spice and raisin cake on p. 261 or the icebox cookies on p. 276 decorated with drip chocolate or, if the child is allergic to chocolate, the white frosting on p. 284. Halloween need not be a hopeless holiday.

Thanksgiving has its pitfalls for the allergic young and old alike in the form of turkey stuffing, cranberries and nuts, especially peanuts. Can these dangers be skirted?

Of course. After all, the big bird need not be stuffed with bread stuffing. There are excellent rice or potato stuffings or a gourmet's wild rice stuffing. Or a soya bread (see p. 212) stuffing can replace the traditional bread. The turkey itself can be basted with suet or melted meat drippings instead of butter, for the milk allergic. Nuts, naturally, can be avoided. However, even an adult gets carried away by the general permissiveness of the holiday spirit, and I shall myself be the bad example. A few Christmases ago I spent the holidays at home. My Dad always gets English walnuts for the occasion, and I, who am exceedingly allergic to walnuts, threw caution to the winds and ate and ate. Either I was sensitive to walnuts all along without realizing it or I simply ate myself into it by gorging. In any case, I developed a beaut of a reaction. Needless to say, walnuts are now prominent on my list of foods to avoid.

If peanuts alone present the allergic with a problem, it is wise to simply keep them in a separate dish so that he can enjoy the other nuts uncontaminated. The nut sensitive must also be wary of holiday cookies and cakes, since they so frequently contain nuts of one kind of another, including peanuts.

Finally comes the biggest and best of all holidays—Christmas. Even adults can be saddened by a limited diet at this time of year. Do not despair. Sugar plums and eggnog may be out, but the Allergy Information Association has come up with a Christmas menu of good cheer. They recommend that the chief cook of the household (and all her assistants, hopefully) bake up a storm, using the recipes in Chapter Thirteen for cookies and cakes (especially the Christmas Cake on p. 251). Thus, plenty of goodies will be on hand that everyone can eat without regret or worse. Their holiday menu follows:

Appetizer:
    Juice or soup as allowed.
Entree: Turkey
    Be sure it is not a butter-basted one if you have milk allergy. Stuff with rice for gluten or wheat allergies. Cook one cup of long grained rice (makes four cups). Mix amount needed with your usual spices, onion, butter (or milkless margarine) and celery. One part of wild rice and three parts regular rice is really special.

Dessert:
> The mincemeat in *The Joy of Cooking* is eggfree, milkfree and gluten and wheatfree. Make a crust (pp. 244–245). Try the St. Nicholas pudding on p. 236.

Beverage:
> Ginger ale and grape juice or soybean milk and cranberry juice.

Even the allergic child's birthday party can be made festive with Pink Ice Cream or Pink 'N Pretty Parfait (see pp. 240–241). These should surely help color his day—if he does not happen to be allergic to pink food coloring. If he is sensitive to the phenolphthalein in pink food coloring, try one of the other cake recipes in Chapter Thirteen. And by all means try ice cream made with soybean milk (see p. 238). It is served at allergy medical meetings, and I can tell you from personal experience that it's really good.

Parties for allergic children and dining out for allergic adults pose awkward problems. No child wishes to be unable to eat or do what his peers can eat or do, and, in a way, neither do adults. Once out in company, it is not easy to decline a hostess's fervent offerings, especially when she makes it plain that she has gone to some trouble to whip up this little dish.

The child is somewhat more fortunate than the adult, for his parents can prepare the way for him. One or the other parent can call the child's prospective hostess and explain the problem ahead of time. Probably the worst thing a parent can do is arrive with child in tow at the party and give the hostess instructions. This will instantly rivet the attention of the other small partygoers upon the allergic child, with all that that may mean for him in the way of unrelenting curiosity and unmerciful teasing. Best to discuss the matter ahead of time and even possibly supply the child's non-allergenic foods in as close a substitution of the proposed party fare as possible.

The parents (or the mother, to be realistic) of an allergic child who throw a party for him have a different sort of problem. They will, no doubt, wish to stay within the limits of his diet, yet make the party food appealing to his nonallergic guests. If there is any reason to suspect that the food will not be appealing, don't serve it, for the party is sure to be a flop. It usually takes time to become accustomed to the taste of soybean milk, for instance. To serve it to guests, even disguised by choloate syrup, is to risk dismayed reactions. Thus, matter of factly, serve regular milk to the guests, soybean as usual to the allergic child. No comment necessary. Popsicles can replace ice cream. Or soybean milk ice cream can be served. A good eggless and milkless cake can be made, although substituting other flours for wheat does create a different product. Or, rather than risk a crumbling wheatless masterpiece, serve cupcakes, most of which can be made with regular flour, but a few made with substitute flours can be quietly palmed to wheat sensitive offspring. Again, if the allergic child is forewarned, no comment is necessary. If sandwiches are to be the party fare, serve them on individual plates and give the allergic child his special brand. The chances are that no one will even notice that his is not exactly like everyone else's.

The best bet in all this is to plan with the youngster, so that he accepts the responsibility of seeing to it that his guests have a pleasant time even as he sticks to his own regime.

As the child grows older, his parents, of course, must bow out of the picture. He steps out into the social whirl under his own recognizance, as the lawyers say. However, when he gives a party for his teenage friends, his parents can still be helpful. Teenagers are often snack lovers, which makes things easier for the allergic. The food can be arranged so that everyone can "do his own thing," including the allergic host. Thus, without fuss, he can pick his own party refreshment within his diet limitations (see the Party Pleasers recipes in Chapter Thirteen).

Adults allergic to food are apt to find themselves in embarrassing predicaments on occasion, especially when they neglect to forewarn their hostess. There is nothing more guaranteed to raise the hackles of a hostess than to decline the dish she spent hours preparing and is serving up with quiet pride to her little group of social lions. It is surely better to explain, briefly and matter of factly, one's dietary problem when accepting the invitation. Then at the party, avoid the food presented as unobtrusively as possible or accept the hostesses's quiet substitution with gratitude. It is surprising how many unusual occurrences can be camouflaged by a matter-of-fact attitude, or conversely, how many everyday events can be jazzed up by a secretive approach. What is open, frank and casual often goes unnoticed or scarcely noticed. But the opposite is true of the embarrassed and the furtive.

In the course of human history all kinds of myths and symbolisms have grown up around foods. Different cultures view different foods from very different viewpoints. Many an emissary to foreign lands has had to eat his chicken complete with entrails or had to down a sheep's eye without a blink of his own, all in order not to offend his hosts. Psychologically, it is not easy to decline food that is proffered. This difficulty may have its roots in prehistory, when to refuse food offerings, a man's only claim to riches and importance, was to mortally insult. Many an allergic person has found himself uncomfortably on the spot simply because he lacked the courage to discuss the problem with his hostess or the restaurant waiter. Come now, face up to it like the hero that you are! And if you are calm and matter of fact, how can you offend? Your alternative, of course, is to gulp down the stuff and be sick. And such a result would also be offensive. What hostess wishes to see a sudden indisposition on the part of a guest who has just consumed her cooking? Or to learn later that immediately following her party said guest was laid up for a week?

Last (and deliberately least, for one can live without liquor, probably to one's great benefit), there is the problem posed by that popular American custom, the cocktail hour. It is astonishing how many people find that alcoholic beverages not only go to their heads but also to their skin and gastrointestinal and respiratory systems. A number of substances contained in these beverages can cause a variety of allergic reactions. Grains, yeast, fruit, malt, molasses, spices, even the egg white and fish glue used to clarify wine, may be the offenders. In Appendix E, I summarize the possible allergenic ingredients of various drinks. To paraphrase a bit of Edward Fitzgerald, Be cautious when you pick up your Jug of Wine and Loaf of Bread to go singing into the Wilderness, lest Paradise enow fall a bit short of your expectations.

There is a special problem when some other illness strikes or when a visit to the hospital is indicated. It is imperative that the diet of the allergic person go with him, for when he is beset by other health problems, he can least afford to deal with his allergic symptoms. Thus, the parents of an allergic child who must be hospitalized, for instance, should be absolutely certain that the child's special diet is fully understood, not only by the attending physician but also by the hospital dietician as well. To this end, it might be well to furnish the hospital dietician with a copy of the child's list of excluded foods. For the same reasons, adults allergic to foods, especially if severely so, would do well to carry a typed list of forbidden foods in their wallets, lest they be hauled off to the hospital following an accident of some sort and not in the greatest shape to give directions or instructions.

Nor should the hospitalized succumb to the succulent gifts of candy and the like brought by well-wishers to restore morale. A body weakened by illness is no excuse for a weakened will.

Before we conclude with special problems, let us go back to children. Allergic children do encounter more problems than allergic adults—or, better, parents of such children do. School lunches for the food sensitive child, for instance, can be difficult, perhaps because there have to be so many of them. One solution is to use a wide mouthed thermos for soups and salads. And plastic containers. All sorts of things can be substituted for the regular sandwich, including stews and casseroles. One ingenious mother uses taco shells (made with corn) as a substitute for bread and fills them with meat and other allowable fillings. Commercial shells may contain wheat, so these may have to be homemade. Crispy no doubt, but good! Rye bread, banana bread and other wheatless baked goods can also be bread substitutes. School lunches can be rounded out with fruit or vegetables such as carrot sticks. Beverages can be fruit juice, soybean milk or goat's milk.

Camping trips and picnics require the same ingenuity. Extended camping trips or travel means careful menu planning of the family's diet for the allergic member. It is wise to stash away enough of his special foods (substitute flours, milk, egg replacers, what-have-you) to last in case there are no stores that would carry the required items. Picnics, hikes and outdoor living generally call for a higher protein diet since these are the best fuel foods for an active body. Fruit is a number-one provider of sugar for quick energy. And meat and potatoes not only provide protein but fill the empty void so much activity engenders.

While there are some very definite and on occasion delicate problems that can arise for the food allergic, none is insurmountable. They simply require two things—a little forethought and a matter-of-fact attitude.

I conclude this chapter with some good advice to families with allergic children offered by Mrs. Hilary Clark ("Meal Planning for the Allergic Child," distributed by the Allergy Information Association):

> Something I have had fair success with is to give the child his nutritively most important meal when he has his biggest appetite. So, if your child is raving hungry first thing in the morning and he is on an exceedingly limited diet, give him meat and potatoes and vegetables first thing in the morning. If he is hungriest at lunch time that will be the biggest meal for him. The tradition of our meal patterns dies awfully hard. They don't matter, as long as you get his daily requirement into the child and he enjoys eating. And along with following the child's lead and giving him his most important meal when his appetite is keenest, don't dull his appetite the rest of the day. So, whenever he comes to a meal he is right ready—he is not overtired or overhungry, he is really hungry and he is going to sit down and eat the food that you have prepared for him. Besides eliminating candy and soft drinks and other trivia as much as you can from the child's diet, or only allowing him, if he can have it, to have these things after a meal, try not to dull his appetite in other ways. If your child is having snacks in the morning or snacks in the afternoon, time them so he doesn't have a snack any later than, say, 3:30 if you eat at 5:30. And make the snack something that is not going to fill him up but something that is going to give him a source of energy in the middle of the afternoon, like fruit juice. Try to keep the sugar content of the desserts down as low as possible so that the child never gets used to having something really sweet or really rich at the end of the meal. Give him fresh fruit for dessert and if you and your husband like sweet, rich desserts, save them for later on in the evening after the child has gone to bed or is doing his homework. And never, never use dessert

as a bribe. Dessert is not something that is a bonus for eating something horrible. It is just a part of the meal and, hopefully, nutritively it is just as good as part of the main course. My system is this. Both our children know that they have a certain pattern: main course, dessert, two cookies, and their beverage. Now, they can eat any portion of any of this that they want to. In other words if they say "no main course," I give them their dessert and cookies and beverage. They eat that and say "I'm still hungry," and I say, "That's fine, before you get extras you have something to eat here. If you aren't hungry enough to eat that, then you're finished." Since they are normal children, a dish of apricots, a couple of rice-and-rye cookies and a glass of Sobee just isn't enough to keep them going and usually they come back and eat their main course. Try to prevent the developing of "food games" by talking about everything except food and table manners at the table.

Checklist

It is possible for emotional stress to "trigger" allergy symptoms, but probably the emotions do not directly cause allergy.

Allergy symptoms, on the other hand, can cause emotional stress.

The parents must walk a tightrope between the allergic child and his needs and the needs of the rest of the family.

The allergic child is a normal child who has limitations, just as a child with nearsightedness or fallen arches may have limitations. The allergic child's limitations should be treated matter of factly. Spoiling him by allowing him to escape responsibility or to gain attention because of his illness could affect him adversely for the rest of his life. His limitations must be recognized and because of them he may need extra care, but it is important not to allow those limitations to become a barrier to maturity and independence nor as a tool to allow him to wield power over others.

It is vital to teach the allergic child responsibility for his illness and its avoidance measures.

A warning tag or bracelet, such as Medic Alert, is an excellent idea for severely allergic individuals, child and adult alike.

One menu can be worked out for family meals so that the allergic member can stay within his diet limitations while the nonallergic members enjoy nutritious and tasteful foods.

Child or adult, it is better that hostesses be advised of diet limitations when their invitations are accepted.

Eleven

Better Safe Than Sorry or Can Allergy Be Prevented?

Opposite camps and battle lines are drawn up on most questions about allergy but perhaps none more forcefully than on the question—Can allergy to foods be prevented? Battle streamers go up, flags unfurl and physicians get ready to do battle. It is enough to make a less cautious man than I hesitate.

What do we really know?

We know that allergy diseases are the leading chronic diseases of childhood, that about one in five school children suffers from a major allergy such as asthma, eczema or gastrointestinal disorders and that it is generally believed among allergists that the incidence of allergy is on the increase among the young.

But can allergy be prevented?

I'll put it this way: If I had a child who was considered allergy prone (children with a history of allergy in the family, especially on both the mother's and father's sides), I would operate on the theory that it is better to be safe than sorry. I would definitely take measures that, hopefully, might keep that child from becoming sensitized in the first place. Allergy can be severe; it can be chronic; it can last a lifetime. And since I am myself allergic and, therefore, my experience with allergy firsthand, I would do my best not to wish allergy upon my child.

Nobly said, perhaps; but how would I accomplish this?

I would employ, without quibble, the prophylactic measures described in this chapter. I recommend them, although I do not guarantee anything, to all parents, prospective as well as in fact, whose family history includes allergy. These measures may not be 100 percent effective in preventing the development of allergy in children. But even if they do not prevent allergy, they may well lessen its load.

144

And there flies my battle streamer, there my flag unfurled. Let's take a look at the ramparts on which I have chosen to take my stand.

Prophylaxis, as this regime of prevention of allergy is called, begins with the fetus. We remarked in Chapter Two on the controversial theory that fetal hiccoughs may be a response by the fetus to foreign protein (allergens) passed from the mother's blood stream through the placenta into the blood stream of the child. Research has so far failed to show that skin-sensitizing antibodies are passed through the placenta from the maternal blood stream to the fetus. However, some studies with guinea pigs have seemed to demonstrate that pregnant guinea pigs fed foods not normally a part of their diet often produce offspring who suffer allergic reactions when they first come into contact with such non-guinea-pig fare after birth. In other studies, guinea pig mothers-to-be, when injected with protein substances, also produced allergic guinea pig babies.

Still, the research to date is inconclusive.

Yet, if we are going to play the game of "better safe than sorry"— and this is my game—we must give due consideration to the theory that one of two things may happen to sensitize the fetus: (1) allergens may pass into the mother's blood stream and through the placenta to the blood stream of the fetus, where they induce the production of antibodies; or (2) the mother forms antibodies herself against allergens and these may pass through the placenta to sensitize the fetus. This latter possibility is known as passive sensitization. Its effects are not likely to be very long-lasting.

But I am compelled to play the devil's advocate and so must mention that there is a theory that, in order to develop tolerance to potent allergens, the fetus must be deliberately exposed to them early in the game. If one were to test this hypothesis, a mother-to-be would dine richly on milk, eggs, wheat, corn and the like, especially during the first trimester of her pregnancy. However pleasant this might be for her, I do not recommend it for the infant who may come into this world heir to allergic tendencies.

But, despite the uncertainties and unknowns, I stand firmly on my operating principle of "better safe than sorry." I advise mothers-to-be, when there is history of allergy in the family and especially if it occurs on both sides, to follow the dietary suggestions of the proponents of the theory that the fetus may be sensitized in the womb. Dr. Jerome Glaser is an early and ardent advocate of the value of prophylaxis, both during pregnancy and for the newborn. In brief his regime for mothers-to-be is as follows:

1. Probably the most important tenet is that the mother-to-be should not eat great quantities of a single or a few foods. She should eat a variety of foods and not too much of any one thing at a time or over a period of time. Thus, for instance,

spinach now and again may be a very fine thing, but spinach, spinach, spinach might be too much of a good thing for the fetus with built-in allergic tendencies. A mother-to-be often thinks she will do her baby a favor by drinking great quantities of milk. Unfortunately, the infant may arrive unable to tolerate cow's milk without colic or eczema or both. Nor should the mother-to-be give into her legendary odd cravings lest she sensitize her child. He may not thank her if, for instance, he cannot touch chocolate without reaction.

2. Stern advocates of the prophylaxis theory believe the mother-to-be should eat no eggs during her pregnancy, although they do not mean total avoidance but caution. Thus, she should not eat eggs per se nor angel food cake. But she need not worry about traces of eggs in baked goods.

3. Stern advocates of the prophylaxis theory also believe that the mother-to-be should drink no more than a pint of milk a day and then only after it has been boiled for ten minutes to denature the protein. The longer milk is heated and the higher the temperature, the less likely it is to sensitize. Of course, the flavor is likely to suffer a little in the process.

4. Nor should the mother-to-be eat cheese or much in the way of fish, nuts or spices, since these are all potent allergens.

5. Nor should she eat foods that she, herself, is allergic to, a natural enough proscription.

6. She should take all possible steps to ensure that she will be able to breast-feed the baby when it arrives. This last commandment is subscribed to by all sides of the question of the value of prophylaxis and for nonallergic infants as well as for the allergy prone. Most allergists recommend breast feeding as the best hope of preventing the development of allergy in the newborn. Thus, the clash of controversy stops here, and we are all agreed —breast-feed.

A good deal of help for the mother-to-be on this score can be obtained either from her local branch of the La Leche League (and a good many of the larger cities have such branches) or by writing to the La Leche League International, Inc. at 9616 Minneapolis Avenue, Franklin Park, Illinois   60131.

The above regime, or any part of it, is no do-it-yourself program, nor is it a rigid affair to be rigidly followed. It should only be attempted upon the recommendation and under the supervision of the mother-to-be's own doctor, for her own health may conceivably make parts of the regime unwise. Also, her doctor is very likely to wish to supplement her diet with such things as calcium, phosphorus and vitamins.

As a regime, it may be helpful in preventing allergy in the child. Or, it may do no good at all. No one knows with any great degree of certainty. Thus, the mother must realize this and not blame herself for real or supposed lapses if the result is less than expected. It is offered here as a hopeful possibility not as positive prevention, and it should be accepted as such.

There are even sterner (leaner might be a better word) regimes that have the mother-to-be cut out all citrus fruits, chocolate, tomatoes and just about all allergenic foods of any consequence. And there are more moderate regimes that simply have her eat in moderation and try not to give into those cravings that so frequently accompany pregnancy. Her own doctor is the best source of advice in any case, so let us leave the specifics up to him. I, myself, tell my expectant mothers to dine in moderation, rotate their fare and stay away from milk and eggs, and I do believe that such a regime may be helpful.

But after the allergy-prone child is born—What then?

If the mother can breast-feed and keep it up for the first four to six months, also following the above dietary regime (for allergens may pass to the infant via the mother's milk), the infant should have it made. With the exception of mineral or vitamin supplements as the doctor may prescribe, he needs little or nothing else. Nature intended it this way, which may be why cow's milk is such a potent allergen for some human babies while calves thrive on it.

It should be noted that the nursing mother must be wary of passing allergens as well as such toxic substances as caffeine to her baby via her breast milk. As we mentioned earlier, the nursing mother should consume cow's milk only moderately, if at all, when allergy runs strongly in the family. Some physicians recommend that if cow's milk is drunk that it should be cut with water (1 part water to 1 part milk) and boiled for 10 minutes, which will not make it very palatable, I should think. If the baby exhibits colic or eczema, the nursing mother should put cow's milk aside until the baby is eating on his own.

The nursing mother should also be exceedingly moderate in her consumption of eggs, peanuts, orange juice, wheat and corn. She should avoid entirely chocolate, nuts and fish.

But if, for one reason or another, the mother cannot breast-feed her newborn infant, the strict proponents of prophylactic measures against allergy argue that he should still receive no cow's milk in any form. They state that soybean milk or meat-base substitute formulas be used instead. Some babies, of course, may become sensitive to soybean. Soybean milk may on occasion cause diarrhea and sore buttocks, in which case meat-base formula can be used. This sturdy "no cow's milk" stand for the first months of life goes back to Dr. Jerome Glaser's long-term study to determine the role of cow's milk in the development of allergy in children.

Dr. Glaser studied an experimental group of potentially allergic children born of families with a history of allergy. He divided them into one group of 96 children who were fed no cow's milk for the first few months to one year of age and whose diet was free of eggs, wheat, fish, chicken, beef, veal, cheese and chocolate. Those who were not breast-fed received soybean or meat-base milk substitutes. The other group of 65 allergy-prone children, siblings of the first 96, were given cow's milk during infancy. He also studied a third group of 175 youngsters who were unrelated to the allergy-prone groups and were fed a regular diet, including cow's milk in infancy. All three groups were followed approximately six years. The following table gives a rough idea of Dr. Glaser's results:

	Fed cow's milk?	Number who developed major allergies by five years of age
Allergy prone (96)	no	1*
Siblings of allergy prone group (65)	yes	15
Unrelated children (175)	yes	30

* *One child in the allergy-prone group developed asthma by three years of age.*

Not only did the youngsters following Dr. Glaser's prophylactic regime have 25 percent less allergy than their siblings but they also seemed to develop only a fourth as many major allergies as the control group of unrelated children.

In a more recent Finnish study (1979), results indicated that the longer an infant with a family history of allergy was breast-fed, the less the occurrence of allergy. The authors of this study recommended that allergy-prone infants be nursed for six months at a minimum and longer if possible. They also recommended that the more highly allergenic foods (fish, nuts, citrus fruits, eggs, chocolate, peanuts, honey, tomatoes) be withheld until the child was at least a year old.

Again, I must play the devil's advocate and report that a recent study at the University of Texas tends to refute the belief that cow's milk affects the incidence of allergy in infants. A group of 1,753 children, followed for periods ranging up to seven years, were fed breast, soybean and cow's milk. No significant difference in the incidence of allergy diseases among the three groups were found, with the exception that those children fed cow's milk did develop allergy, if they developed it, at an earlier age than those who were breast-fed.

This is the uneasy see-saw of science. Invariably just when we'd like to make a firm pronouncement, along comes a brand new study to turn things upside down. This tends to teach us to keep our minds open and our spirits cautious. Yet, when a child has developed allergy, particularly a severe one, women pregnant with a sibling-to-be will probably want to join Dr. Glaser's camp and play the "better-safe-than-sorry" game.

In any case, the prophylactic diet is a safe and nutritious one, and while it may not totally guarantee that a child will not develop allergy, it can do no harm. It may do a great deal of good.

When cow's milk is first given to the allergy-prone infant, it should be in a heat-treated form. Heat breaks down the protein and makes it more digestible.

Eggs should not be introduced into the allergy-prone infant's diet until he is nine months to a year old. Again, there are pro's and con's. Another recent series of studies at the University of Texas discount the role of early egg yolk in the development of allergy.

If the parents and their doctor are going the better-safe-than-sorry route, however, it's best to withhold egg yolk until, preferably, the infant is a year old. When egg yolk is first brought into his life, it should be as a little hard-boiled yolk, perhaps mixed with his cereal. The amount probably can be doubled each day until the baby is eating the whole yolk. When he is at three yolks a week with no signs of trouble, the parents and doctor alike can heave a sigh of relief and add a little hard-boiled egg white. Again, start with a tiny amount and double it until he is eating a whole egg. If he can down three hard-boiled eggs a week for three weeks without the appearance of allergy symptoms, he will be able to tolerate eggs cooked in any fashion, and parents, doctor and the baby have sailed over that particular allergenic hurdle.

The introduction of cereals poses a real problem in our culture, since we are conditioned to the notion that infants need solid foods early in the game. Cereals seem to us to have the best staying power. But, unless the doctor recommends otherwise, it is best to delay cereals and other solid foods until the infant is at least three months old. Some doctors recommend that he be at least six months old. The younger the infant, the less efficient his digestive equipment. If he is not an allergic baby, he will simply waste a good deal of the protein that cereals and other solid foods contain. If he is allergy prone, such protein may pass through his immature intestinal walls and into his blood stream to sensitize him. It is well to remember that the older he grows the better he becomes at handling solids and allergenic foods, which is why many allergists recommend that he not be given solids early and that potent allergens such as cow's milk, eggs, fish, chocolate, corn, wheat and cheese not be fed him at all until his digestive system can handle them. And that's not until he's nine months or a year old.

Social pressure is an odd rationale for determining a baby's diet. Yet, parents who are given to comparing every move their baby makes with that of others are often pressured into keeping their baby up with the Jones' little tyke. The parents of an allergy-prone child must resist this kind of pressure. They must keep firmly in mind that their baby does not need solids at a month or six weeks or even two or three months. They must not let friends or relatives "egg" them on.

One study divided newborn babies into two groups. In the first group, solids were introduced during the first month of life, and in the second group not until the ninth to twelfth week. By the end of a year, there was no significant difference in the growth or health of the infants. Thus, the early introduction of solids may not be of any value to the nonallergic baby. But it may be harmful to the allergy prone.

So, at three months or, preferably, even later, begin with cereals, starting with an unmixed or single cereal, preferably oats, barley or rice since they are the least allergenic. Since wheat (and corn) is the most allergenic, it should not be introduced until the child is nine months old.

Fruits and vegetables should arrive a little later than cereals in the allergy-prone infants' life, preferably when he is four to six months old. Start small with a teaspoon and double it the next time around until the baby is eating a baby-sized helping. Be cautious! Don't give too much at one feeding. And avoid mixtures until the baby can handle all the component parts. Start all new foods as separate items and see how they go.

The least allergenic fruits are pears and apricots. If these cause no problems, then move on to mashed bananas. Apples and peaches and orange juice should wait until the first birthday rolls around for the allergy prone. And berries should wait until he is two years old.

As for vegetables, start with carrots, soon followed by beets, squash and sweet potatoes. White potatoes may come a bit later, but the legumes (peas and beans) and spinach should wait for that first birthday. Tomatoes should not arrive in the child's life until he is at least a year and a half.

Again, all of this should be discussed with your doctor and implemented only upon his recommendation. He will have his own ideas about the baby's diet and he will fit that diet to the infant's very individual needs.

Meats can be started when the infant is six to nine months old, although some doctors recommend starting them at the same time fruits and vegetables are introduced. Begin first with lamb or veal, since they are least allergenic, then move on to beef and pork. Many allergists recommend leaving chicken and liver until last.

There it is, the better-safe-than-sorry regime. I do not guarantee it. No one does. But I do recommend it as a program to be discussed with your doctor if your infant is allergy prone. And I reiterate, this is no do-it-yourself program. It is, rather, a regime to be planned and plotted with your own doctor every step of the way.

There are other preventive steps that can be taken, not only for infants but for older children and adults as well. For instance, when a child has been ill with an acute gastrointestinal upset, he may become sensitized by foods that he has previously tolerated. Thus, it is a good idea during such an illness and throughout the convalescent period following it to feed him a nonallergic diet with no uncooked foods and with as little change in diet as possible.

The allergic and nonallergic alike would do well to avoid food fads. The consumption of a great amount of a few foods can sensitize. Some diet experts, for instance, recommend as a weight control diet a wide variety of low caloric foods with none of this "eat nothing but grapefruit or swordfish" sort of commandment. They are wise to do so. In the same vein, pie-eating contestants and goldfish swallowers may be setting themselves up for allergy, depending, I suppose, on how competitive they get.

It would be pleasant to end this chapter on this light note, but perhaps it would be well here to review the early signs of allergy. They are:

> colic
> sniffles that persist
> abdominal pain
> diarrhea and/or constipation
> excessive vomiting
> skin rashes and eczema
> canker sores
> need for formula changes and refusal of food in infants
> fretfulness
> failure to thrive

These are not solely symptoms of allergy, but when your doctor has ruled out other possibilities, then allergy to food should be considered. Let us hope that the prophylactic measures in this chapter have kept such symptoms at bay.

Checklist

There is no guarantee that allergy can be prevented, but there are prophylactic measures that seem well worth taking in the hope of preventing the development of allergy in the allergy-prone newborn.

If the hypothesis that a fetus may be sensitized in the womb is correct, then a mother-to-be should eat moderately of a variety of foods during her pregnancy, avoid potently allergenic foods whenever possible and drink no more than a pint of milk daily that has been boiled for ten minutes—if all of this has been approved of by her own doctor.

Most important of all, she should do everything possible to ensure that she can breast-feed the baby, a measure equally important for the nonallergy-prone infant as it is for the allergy prone.

If the baby is not breast-fed, then under the prophylactic hypothesis he should receive no cow's milk but should have soybean or meat-base milk substitute formulas.

Eggs should not be introduced until the baby is nine months or a year old and should then be given as hard-boiled yolk to begin with.

Always begin new foods unmixed with any other food and one single food at a time.

Cereals should not be introduced until the baby is at least three months old.

Fruits and vegetables may be introduced at four to six months.

Meat should wait until the baby is six to nine months old.

Diet during an illness and convalescence should be as free of allergenic foods as possible with as little changing about as possible.

The allergy prone should avoid food fads and an immoderate consumption of a single or a few foods.

All of this is relatively uncertain, not wholly proved and not absolute, but it is a better-safe-than-sorry approach to the problem.

Each child is an individual and must be treated as such, nonallergic and allergy prone alike.

Twelve

Menus To Manipulate

I proudly lay claim to being an allergist but not to being a dietitian. I can fry a reasonably good egg and operate the toaster to good effect, and that is about the limit of my cooking skills. So I have turned to more knowledgeable people for these final two chapters.

Alberta Boyce Wall of Edwardsville, Illinois, whose excellent advice I quoted in Chapter Eight, has supplied the following menus, which she developed in almost forty years of cooking for her allergic husband. The menus are for a milkfree and wheatfree diet. Recipes for selected dishes are given in Chapter Thirteen. (Specific page references are given in parentheses.)

Milkfree and Wheatfree Menu Suggestions

Breakfast

Fruit, fresh or canned as allowed.

Muffins, pancakes or coffeecake. Mixes can be bought at Health Food Stores with various combinations of grains to fit a particular diet. However, a satisfactory mix may be homemade by buying the different flours and mixing as you like (see p. 106).

Cornmeal pancakes or muffins, corn if allowed (see pp. 220, 228).

Fried mush or hominy grits, if not allergic to corn.

Potatoes

Oatmeal

Dry cereal, if carefully chosen, for many apparently innocent items have an unallowed ingredient. Read labels carefully. Dry cereals do not give the "satisfied" feeling that hot foods give. There is also the problem of liquid to pour over them. Syrup from canned fruits is good. Liquid coffee creamer is good but high in saturated fats. There is also an unsaturated liquid coffee creamer.

Jam, jelly or syrup as allowed

Eggs, if allowed

Beef sausage or beef bacon.

Milkfree margarine, if milk is not allowed. Diet Imperial imitation margarine and Diet Parkay imitation margarine are safe. Otherwise read labels to be sure "nonfat milk solids" are not included. A firm margarine, in quarters, is made by Hain Pure Food (Los Angeles, California 90012). It is made of safflower oil and comes salted or unsalted. It is especially useful in frying or sautéing, as it has a higher percentage of fat than the soft margarine.

Fruit juice, if coffee or tea are not allowed. A good hot drink can be made from Cara-Coa. This is made from a material called carob, or "St. John's Bread." Carob is a powder made from the pod of a tree of the locust family. It does not contain the fat the chocolate does nor the caffeinelike stimulant but does contain valuable minerals and nature's own sugar (see p. 281).

Luncheon

Kosher lunch meats and frankfurters are always all beef and milkfree. Oscar Mayer makes "All Beef" lunch meats and frankfurters. But read the labels, for milk or wheat ingredients may be included.

Very satisfactory sandwiches can be made with whole rye crackers and a little salad dressing. Note that mayonnaise contains eggs.

Salad mixtures of diced chicken, fish, veal, with either cooked or uncooked vegetables, moistened with salad dressing (see p. 173).

Homemade soup or bouillon cubes, with or without salt. Wyler is available in supermarkets; Cellu, which is saltless, in health food stores. Lipton makes a green pea soup that has no pork or onion or wheat.

Dinner

1 Chopped beef Stroganoff (p. 183)
  Butter beans
  Lettuce salad
  Pineapple chunks

2 Oven fried chicken (p. 193)
   Creamed potatoes (p. 199 for milkless cream sauce)
   Mixed vegetables
   Lettuce salad
   Apricots
3 Swiss steak (p. 190)
   Potato cooked in meat gravy
   Eggplant (p. 203)
   Gelatin dessert, either plain or with fruit
4 Tuna soufflé (p. 195)
   Creamed peas (p. 199 for milkless cream sauce)
   Lettuce salad
   Lemon meringue pie (pp. 244–245 for crusts)
5 Beef patties (p. 183)
   Hot potato salad (p. 173)
   Braised celery (p. 204)
   Pears
6 Poached fish fillet (p. 194)
   Baked potatoes
   Green beans
   Fruit cocktail
7 Beef roast
   Potatoes cooked in gravy
   Harvard beets (p. 204)
   Tapioca cream (p. 233)
8 Beef patties (p. 183)
   Fried potatoes
   Creamed corn with green pepper and pimiento
   Lettuce salad
   Applesauce
9 Oven fried fish fillets (p. 194)
   Hollandaise sauce (p. 200)
   Boiled potatoes
   Cooked romaine (p. 172)
   Pineapple slices
10 Baked hash (p. 190)
    Creamed celery (p. 199 for milkless cream sauce)
    Three-bean salad (p. 174)
    Coconut cream pie (pp. 244–245 for crusts)
11 Meat loaf (p. 183)
    Scalloped potatoes (p. 202)
    Zucchini or summer squash (p. 204)
    Lettuce salad
    Blueberry pie (pp. 244–245 for crusts)
12 Baked chicken dinner (p. 193)
    Jellied cranberry salad (p. 175)
13 Beef patties with mushrooms and celery sauce (p. 199 for sauce)

    Potato puffs (p. 203)
    Lettuce salad
    Fruit cocktail
14 Vegetable soup
    Hot muffins (pp. 218–227)
    Lemon-pineapple sherbet (p. 243)
15 Corned beef
    Baked beans (p. 205)
    Hot muffins (pp. 218–227)
    Pears
16 Tuna fish or chicken salad (p. 173)
    Hot muffins (pp. 218–227)
    Zucchini (p. 204)
17 Beef steak
    Potatoes and green beans in imitation sour cream
    Lettuce salad
    Peaches
18 Kosher weiners or frankfurters
    Cold potato salad (p. 173)
    Green beans
    Pineapple chunks
19 Beef stew (p. 190)
    Lettuce salad
    Hot muffins (pp. 218–227)
    Gelatin dessert
20 Acorn squash with meat balls (p. 184)
    Braised celery (p. 204)
    Baked apples
21 Tuna-corn casserole (p. 195)
    Waldorf salad
22 Sliced roast beef warmed in gravy (no wheat flour for
      thickener)
    Potatoes and peas
    Gelatin dessert
23 Beef patties with yellow hominy (p. 183)
    Green beans
    Grapefruit soufflé salad (p. 172)
24 Chicken à la king (p. 194)
    Hot muffins (pp. 218–227)
    Jellied fruit salad (p. 174)
25 Meatballs in creamed vegetable sauce (p. 199 for milkless cream
      sauce)
    Potato puffs (p. 203)
    Lettuce salad
    Pears
26 Beef franks and beans in savory sauce (p. 191)
    Lettuce salad

Junket dessert, plain or with eggless custard sauce (p. 237 for sauce)
27 Tuna-stuffed zucchini cases (p. 196)
Baked potatoes
Fruit cocktail
28 Hashed-brown hamburgers (p. 182)
Harvard beets (p. 204)
Pears
29 Dinner in a skillet (p. 191)
Lettuce salad
30 Oven fried chicken (p. 193)
Cold potato salad (p. 173)
Green beans
Apricots

There you are, ideas for just about every dinner in the month. Mrs. Wall suggests that

It helps the patient's morale if the family eats the same diet and it can be done quite comfortably—items can be added for unrestricted members. Several years ago, in an emergency, we kept house for our daughter's family for seven weeks. I cooked Jim's (her allergic husband) diet the whole time and our ten-year-old grandson remarked that he couldn't tell if something was "real" or "diet"!

She also offers the following advice about her menus and recipes:

These menus and recipes are designed for two people, reasonably active, 70 years old; the man 5′ 9½″, 160 lb.; the woman 4′ 9″, 103 lb. The menus furnish approximately 2000 to 2200 calories for the man, 1600 to 1700 for the woman. They're designed for a low-fat, low-salt diet.

Meat servings—7-8 oz. for the man and 4-5 oz. for woman. Chicken and fish—8-10 oz. for the man, 6-8 oz. for the woman. All visible fat is removed from the meat, and skin and fat from the chicken before cooking.

Potatoes—5-6 oz. for the man, 4-5 oz. for the woman.

Frozen vegetables are used for the most part because they can be cooked without salt. An entire package of 9 oz. is usually eaten for one meal. Small leftovers are saved for stew, hash, soup or salads. One pound of fresh vegetables such as eggplant, zucchini or romaine lettuce is usually eaten at one meal, and leftovers saved. Canned vegetables are all right where salt is not a problem.

I consider lettuce salad essential, and we have one almost every day. Different greens make for variety (cabbage is excluded).

Various herbs indicated in recipes may be omitted if they are troublemakers, or varied to taste.

No salt is added to any meat or vegetable dish, but I do put a "shake," probably ⅛ teaspoon, of monosodium glutamate in almost every pot. People with a gluten problem should avoid this. Of course, if salt is not a problem, it may be added to taste, or a sprinkle of salt substitute on the helping on the plate is sometimes palatable for low-salt diets. However, we have found saltless food acceptable and have discovered flavors in food hitherto unnoticed.

Jell-O puddings and pie fillings (vanilla and lemon) are wheat-free and eggfree. If made with milk substitute, they are safe for milkfree diets also. Be sure to get the kind you cook, not instant.

Marion L. Conrad of Davis, California, has sent me menus arranged by seasons, which I will include here with her kind permission. Mrs. Conrad is a consulting dietitian specializing in diet plans for people with allergy problems. First, her explanation of the allergy diet, then the menus.

An allergy diet . . . is as individual as people, their allergies, their families and friends can make them.

The following is the allergy diet followed successfully for nearly forty years by a man whose tests . . . showed definite allergies to egg, milk products in any form, wheat and all the cereals such as rye, corn, rice, barley, etc. He has very few minor allergies, but they are important—especially citrus, tomato, most raw fruits and berries. It is suited to him individually and may or may not be suited to other individuals.

These menus are for a man 6′ 1″ tall, weight 205 to 210 lb., and 80 years old. All his medical and panel tests done [in] 1973 show nothing off normal. He keeps active and well.

His list of foods includes all the meats, fish, fowl, variety meats such as liver, heart, etc.—with beef his major meat; potatoes, sweet potatoes as the major starch; almost all of the vegetables and cooked fruits. He can use tea, coffee or "Decaf," sugar, salt, spices, olive and Wesson oil, vinegar, pecans and almonds. Vitamins are in his foods. Hard water and foods supply needed calcium.

Milkfree, Eggfree, and Wheatfree Menu Suggestions

SPRING

Breakfast
Small beef patty (water and salt added to loosen texture)
Small cooked sausages (all meat)
Browned potato patty
Homemade jam or jelly (no corn syrup)

Lunch (Eating out)
    Cold meats with tomato and cucumber salad
    French fried potatoes
    Fruit cup

Dinner
    Standing rib roast
    Browned potatoes
    String beans and peas with sliced water chestnuts or bacon
    Tossed salad with oil and vinegar dressing
    Strawberry pie with ground almond crust

Breakfast
    Apricot juice (made without corn syrup)
    Ham and finely diced boiled potatoes
    Sweet pickle relish

Lunch
    Fish loaf or cakes with potatoes
    Cucumber salad with sliced radishes
    Frozen green peas with chopped mint
    Cherry gelatin

Dinner
    Lamb or beef shish kabobs
    Scalloped potatoes
    Mixed vegetable salad
    Pineapple ice with a dash of crème de menthe
    Almond cookie

Breakfast
    Pear and pineapple juice
    Buckwheat waffles with maple syrup
    Bacon

Lunch
    Boiled beef tongue with chopped pickle sauce
    Mashed potatoes
    Tossed vegetable salad
    Apricot sauce with slivered almonds
    Cookie

Dinner
    Baked chicken, cranberry sauce
    Pickled apricots
    Baked sweet potato
    Jellied vegetable salad
    Fruit cup
    Cookies

Breakfast
    Mixed Grill—Lightly pan fried calves' liver, rolled in potato
        meal; bacon and sausages; diced boiled potato with dash of
        paprika
    Relishes

Lunch
    Baked halibut, red currant jelly
    Baked potato with bacon
    Cabbage salad with pickle juice (wine vinegar, salt, and sugar to
        taste)
    Fruit cup (strawberry, pineapple, and pear)

Dinner
    Broiled flank steak
    Bread and butter pickles
    New potatoes and peas
    Green gelatin (lime with crème de menthe and pear nectar)
    Cookie

Breakfast
    Leftover chicken and potato hash (or casserole)
    Cranberry juice
    Sweet and sour relishes

Lunch
    Shrimp and/or crab salad in artichokes
    French dressing
    French fried potatoes
    Pears (canned) with cooked strawberry sauce

Dinner
    Roast beef
    Browned potato

Carrots and peas
Tossed romaine and vegetable salad
Warm candy cake with peach sauce or upside-down cake

Breakfast
Peach nectar
Fish and chips (trout and French fries)
Tart jelly or green relish

Lunch
Chicken salad
Potato chips or French fries
Fruit cup with sherry flavor
White sugar cookie

Dinner
Swedish meatballs with gravy
Riced potato nests or potato dumplings
Peas and string beans
Mixed salad with French dressing
Peach crisp with ground almonds

Breakfast
Fruit cup
Fresh ground round (or small can of corned beef) and potato
hash
Sweet and sour relish

Lunch
Beef heart stew with spring vegetables
Fruit cup with a strawberry on top

Company Dinner
French onion soup or clear soup (with optional dash of sherry)
Relishes—carrot sticks, olives, cucumber sticks, and radishes
White wine
Baked fresh lobster or salmon or trout
Baked potato, stuffed and lightly browned
Peas with a dash of chopped mint
Tossed green salad with oil and vinegar dressing
Pineapple slice with apricot ice
Caramel cookie

SUMMER

Breakfast
 Apricot nectar
 Fresh ground round and potato hash
 Chopped pickle or jam or jelly

Lunch
 Potato soup with dried beef
 Mixed vegetable salad
 Cooked pears with preserved ginger
 Candy cake cupcake

Dinner
 Roast eye of round beef
 Browned potato
 Zucchini
 Fruit salad
 Carrots and cucumber sticks, olives optional
 Frozen brown sugar pudding

Breakfast
 Small breakfast steak and bacon
 Hashed-brown potato
 Green tomato and cucumber relish

Lunch
 Leftover cold roast beef
 Browned potato
 String beans
 Apricots and cherries (cooked)

Dinner
 Baked chicken
 Baked potato
 Zucchini and crookneck squash
 Carrots and pineapple salad with French dressing
 Strawberry ice or crème de menthe ice with almond cookies

Breakfast
    Apricot nectar
    Broiled ham
    Cooked sweet potato, lightly browned

Lunch
    Beef stew with fresh vegetables
    Peach crisp

Dinner
    Pan broiled steak with string beans
    Mashed potato (no milk) with steak juice from pan drippings as
        gravy
    Mixed fruit and almond cookie

Breakfast
    Ground beef patty (¼ t. calcium carbonate added when mixing
        with water or soup stock)
    Riced potato, lightly browned in patty drippings
    Chopped green tomato or cherry jam or relish

Lunch
    Chef's salad—Ham or chicken strips and vegetables with French
        dressing
    French fried potatoes
    Freestone peaches (canned) with slivered almonds

Dinner
    Lamb chops
    Diced boiled potato with dash of paprika
    Peas with chopped mint
    Cabbage salad with chopped pickle or cucumber and string bean
        salad
    Apricot freeze with apricots (canned)
    Cookies

Breakfast
    Peach and apricot nectar
    Corned beef hash circles
    Bacon

Lunch

Pork chops on scalloped potatoes
Cabbage salad with pickle juice dressing, salt, and sugar to taste
Peach halves (cooked) with chopped almonds

Dinner

Sirloin steak
German fried potatoes
Broccoli
Tossed green salad with oil and vinegar dressing
Fruit cup with rum flavoring

Breakfast

Apricot nectar
All pork cooked sausages and small beef balls
Hashed-brown potato (using beef drippings from a roast)

Lunch

Minute steak
Riced potato with meat juice gravy
Vegetable salad
Cherries and pear half (cooked)

Dinner

Baked trout and homemade chili sauce
Baked potato with bacon
Summer squash
Tossed salad
Pickles
Fruit cup and cookies

Early Morning

Snack of coffee and a plain sugar cookie

Brunch

Fruit cup with strawberry on top
Swedish meatballs and ham
French fried potatoes or sweet potato puff
Relishes

Company Dinner
>   Seafood cocktail
>   Sirloin tip roast
>   Browned potatoes
>   Carrots and banana squash
>   Jellied vegetable salad
>   Tossed lettuce with French dressing
>   Pineapple ice

FALL

Breakfast
>   Mixed fruit juice
>   Scandinavian fish and potato balls
>   Bacon

Lunch
>   Shepherd's pie with riced potatoes, lightly browned in oven
>   Mixed vegetable salad
>   Baked pears

Dinner
>   Clear soup
>   Flank steak (broiled and cut diagonally)
>   Diced potatoes with chives
>   String beans with slivered almonds
>   Southern pudding with brandy-flavored sauce

Breakfast
>   Pear nectar
>   Roast beef hash
>   Pickle or jam

Lunch
>   Beef stew with potato dumplings
>   Hot mixed fruit pudding (thickened with potato starch)

Dinner
>   Baked pork chops
>   Baked potatoes (split lengthwise and baked face down on greased pan)

Mixed string beans and peas
Tossed salad with French dressing
Baked peaches or fruit cup
Almond cookies

Breakfast
Peach nectar
Cooked potato flakes with dried beef (made into cakes and lightly browned, or in casserole)

Lunch
Relishes
Meat loaf
Baked potatoes
String beans or Swiss chard
Fruit cup with slivered almonds

Dinner
Bread and butter pickles
Baked white fish
Riced potato with bacon
Mixed vegetable salad
Hot peach halves with pecans or dash of cinnamon on top
Cookie

Breakfast
Pear nectar
Ham and hashed-brown potatoes

Lunch
Lamb chops
Diced boiled potatoes with chopped chives
Grated carrot and pineapple salad with French dressing
Fruit gelatin

Dinner (Eating out)
Clear soup
Sirloin steak
French fried potatoes
Tossed salad
Dessert at home: Royal Anne and Bing cherries with warm candy cake

---

Breakfast
> Tomato juice
> Pan broiled liver (rolled in potato flour)
> Pan broiled potatoes
> Jelly

Lunch
> Sausages and boiled diced potatoes
> Banana squash with brown sugar on top
> Sliced tomatoes and cucumber
> Baked peach crisp

Dinner
> Cranberry sauce
> Baked chicken
> Baked potatoes with parsley
> String beans with bacon
> Fruit ice and caramel cookie

Breakfast
> Small pork sausages and beef patties
> Browned riced potatoes
> Jam

Lunch
> Artichoke and shrimp salad—Fill artichokes with shrimp and
> peas, cover with French dressing
> Baked pear and a cookie

Dinner
> Baked skirt steak
> Stuffed baked potato (use bouillon to whip potato)
> Steamed crookneck squash, carrots, and string beans
> Vegetable salad
> Swedish fruit soup

Breakfast
> Fresh ground round (or small can of corned beef) and potato
> hash
> Sweet and sour relish

Lunch
>   Potato soup with chives
>   Jellied chicken salad
>   Squash with peas
>   Pear halves (cooked) with apricot sauce

Dinner
>   Broiled salmon steaks
>   Baked potato and fresh peas
>   Tossed salad with vegetables
>   Strawberry ice
>   Cookie

WINTER

Breakfast
>   Peach nectar
>   Beef patties and hashed-brown potatoes
>   Bacon

Lunch
>   Pork chops with scalloped potatoes
>   Apple or cranberry sauce
>   Peas and carrots
>   Cherry gelatin and brown sugar cookie

Dinner
>   Baked ham
>   Baked yams or sweet potato
>   String beans
>   Vegetable salad
>   Baked pear with cookies

Breakfast
>   Apricot nectar with lemon juice
>   Chicken hash
>   Strawberry jam

Lunch (To carry)
    Bread and butter pickles
    Cold roast veal
    Vegetable and potato salad
    Peach and pear sauce (cooked) with almond cookies

Dinner
    Steak
    Broccoli or squash
    Baked potato
    Jellied vegetable salad
    Fruit ice and cookies

Breakfast
    Peach nectar
    Potato pancakes with maple syrup
    Bacon and small sausages

Lunch
    Corned beef hash in bell peppers
    Cabbage salad or spinach
    Apricot sauce and cookies

Dinner
    Pot roast
    Browned potatoes with gravy (use potato flour)
    Carrot, peas and string beans
    Artichoke with French dressing
    Baked peach with cherries

Breakfast
    Tomato or pineapple juice
    Ham
    Fried raw potatoes
    Jam or jelly

Lunch
    Leftover pot roast and potato
    String beans with slivered almonds

Mixed vegetable salad
Baked apple with cookie

Dinner
Roast pork
Browned potato
Baked acorn squash with brown sugar
Carrots or mixed vegetables
Baked pumpkin pudding

Breakfast
Pear nectar
Canadian bacon
Browned riced potatoes
Jam
Coffee

Lunch
Beef stew with potato and vegetables
Small vegetable salad
Gelatin dessert with fruit and cupcake

Dinner
Meat loaf
Whipped potatoes
Baked banana squash with brown sugar
Vegetable salad
Peach sauce and cookies

Breakfast
Bacon and fried raw potatoes
Cooked sausages
Fruit juice
Jelly or jam
Coffee

Lunch
Baked lamb chops
Cooked potatoes and beans (grated together and broiled))
Hot lightly cooked cabbage with vinegar, sugar and salt
Southern pudding with hot cherry sauce

Dinner
Beef roast
Baked potatoes (split lengthwise and baked face down on
greased pan)
Broccoli
Mixed green salad with French dressing
Peach crisp or tarts

Breakfast
Buckwheat hot cakes
Maple syrup
Canadian bacon
Coffee

Dinner
Pickles and olives
Roast chicken or turkey with sausage dressing
Cranberry jelly and pickled peaches
Sweet potato with grated pineapple
Tossed salad with oil and vinegar dressing
Southern pudding with hot cherry sauce or
pumpkin pie with almond crust
Coffee

Supper
Cold roast beef and ham slices
Potato chips
Jellied vegetable salad
Cookies or fruitcake
Tea

Thirteen

Recipes To Keep the Allergic Together and Allergyfree

The recipes in this chapter are supplied courtesy of Mrs. Alberta Boyce Wall and the Canadian Allergy Information Association. Mrs. Wall's recipes are all designed for a milkfree and wheatfree diet; in the recipes that call for eggs she gives specific instructions on how to make them eggfree.

Salads

Cooked Salad Greens (Romaine, Endive, Escarole)

Wash and cut into 1-inch pieces 2 cups of greens, pressed down.
Cook 20 minutes using ¼ cup water and 1 tablespoon margarine.
Cover at first, then let water boil away.
Serve like spinach.
Use romaine alone or with mixtures of the other greens, as you like.

Wall

Grapefruit Soufflé Salad
Dissolve ½ package lime Jell-O in 1 cup boiling water.
Add

    ¼ cup grapefruit juice
    1 tablespoon vinegar
    ¼ cup salad dressing

Blend with rotary beater.
Chill until almost set, then beat with beater until light and fluffy.
Fold in

½ cup grapefruit sections broken in pieces
¼ cup finely diced celery

Chill until firm. Serve on shredded lettuce and top with grapefruit sections.

Wall

Tuna Fish or Chicken Salad

Flake 7-oz. can drained, waterpack tuna fish or ½ cooked chicken, diced
Add

> 1 stalk celery, chopped fine
> 2 oz. jar sliced pimiento
> ½ cup salad dressing
> 1 tablespoon lemon juice
> 2 diced hard-cooked eggs (if eggs are not allowed, substitute a second stalk of diced celery)

Wall

Hot Potato Salad

Cook 2 medium potatoes in skins.
While they cook, cut 2 slices beef bacon in ½-inch pieces and sauté until crisp.

Remove bacon from pan and pour off all but 2 tablespoons fat.
Add 2 tablespoons oat flour and brown over moderate heat.
Remove from burner and add

> ⅓ cup vinegar plus 2 tablespoons water
> 2 teaspoons sugar
> ½ teaspoon celery seed

Return to burner, add bacon pieces and cook until thick and smooth.
Skin potatoes and slice hot into sauce in skillet, turning gently so each slice is coated but not too broken. Serve hot.

Wall

Cold Potato Salad

Cook 2 medium potatoes in skins
Peel and dice.
Marinate with a mixture of

> 2 tablespoons vinegar
> 2 tablespoons salad oil
> 1 teaspoon sugar

Allow to cool.
Add

> 1 stalk celery, chopped fine
> ¼ cup green pepper, chopped fine
> 2 oz. jar sliced pimiento
> ½ cup salad dressing
> 2 hard-cooked eggs (omit if eggs are not allowed)

Toss gently until thoroughly mixed. Chill and serve.

Wall

Three-Bean Salad

Cook ½ package each frozen beans and wax beans.
Drain and save liquid for soup or gravy.
Chill beans and add

> 1 stalk celery, chopped fine
> 1 can (#1) red kidney beans

Marinate with mixture of

> 2 tablespoons wine vinegar
> 2 tablespoons salad oil
> 1 teaspoon sugar
> ¼ teaspoon paprika

Chill for several hours or overnight.
Serve on shredded lettuce, to be eaten with the salad.

Wall

Basic Recipe for Gelatin Salad

Add ½ cup boiling water to ½ package lemon Jell-O. Stir until dissolved.
Add

> 2 tablespoons vinegar
> 1 teaspoon lemon juice
> pinch of salt

Chill until syrupy but not firm.
Stir in chopped vegetables, raw or cooked, to taste.
Chill until firm.

Wall

Jellied Fruit Salad

Dissolve ½ package lemon Jell-O in ½ cup boiling water.
Add ¼ cup cold water and ¼ cup pineapple juice.
Chill until syrupy.

Add

> 4 sections grapefruit, broken in pieces
> ½ apple, peeled and coarsely chopped
> 2 tablespoons finely chopped celery

Stir to mix and chill until firm.

Wall

Jellied Cranberry Salad

Dissolve ½ package strawberry Jell-O in ½ cup boiling water.
Add

> ¼ cup cold water
> 1 tablespoon lemon juice
> ¼ cup finely chopped celery

Chill until syrupy.
Add a 4-oz. can of jellied cranberry sauce that has been beaten in fine pieces.
Chill until firm and serve on shredded lettuce, to be eaten with the salad.

Wall

Uncooked Salad Dressings

Glutenfree, Milkfree, Wheatfree

Corn Oil Mayonnaise

> ½ teaspoon sugar
> ½ teaspoon dry mustard
> ¼ teaspoon salt
> pinch of cayenne pepper
> 1 egg white
> 1 cup corn oil
> 4½ teaspoons vinegar

Mix egg white, sugar, dry mustard, salt and cayenne and beat until foamy. While beating constantly, pour in ½ cup oil, 2 teaspoons vinegar, then remaining oil and vinegar. Chill and keep covered. Makes about 1 cup.

AIA

Eggfree, Glutenfree, Milkfree, Wheatfree

French Tomato Dressing

¼ cup catsup
¼ cup vinegar
½ cup salad oil
5 teaspoons sugar
2 teaspoons salt
1 small grated onion

Mix all ingredients and shake well. Keep in covered jar in re-frigerator.

AIA

Eggfree, Glutenfree, Milkfree, Wheatfree

Salad Dressing

¼ to ⅓ cup vinegar
¾ to ⅔ cup light corn syrup
1 teaspoon salt

Mix all ingredients and shake well. Keep in covered jar in re-frigerator.
Variations: Add onions, spices, salad herbs or catsup for a French-type dressing.

AIA

Salad Dressing

Mix

1 part vinegar
2 parts safflower oil

Add sugar and paprika to taste.
This can be used as a base for many mixtures by adding a little commercial salad dressing, some sesame seeds and some honey for a sweet salad dressing. Or use plain.

Wall

Eggfree, Glutenfree, Milkfree, Wheatfree

Sweet-Sour Dressing

    1 cup oil
    1 cup red wine vinegar
    ¼ cup minced chives
    ¼ cup minced celery
    2 tablespoons each minced fresh green and red peppers
    2 tablespoons minced watercress
    2 teaspoons dry mustard
    1 tablespoon Worcestershire sauce
    2 teaspoons salt

Mix all ingredients and shake well. Store in refrigerator.

AIA

Eggfree, Glutenfree, Milkfree, Wheatfree

French Fruit Dressing

    ½ cup salad oil
    2 tablespoons lemon juice
    juice of ½ orange
    1 teaspoon sugar
    ½ teaspoon paprika
    salt and pepper

Mix oil and juices together and beat well. Add remaining ingredients and mix well. Stir before serving.

AIA

Eggfree, Glutenfree, Milkfree, Wheatfree

Fruit Dressing

    ¼ to ⅓ cup frozen lemonade concentrate
    ¾ to ⅔ cup corn syrup
    1 teaspoon salt
    poppy seeds

Pour undiluted fruit concentrate into 1 cup measure, fill to top with corn syrup. Add salt and poppy seeds and shake well. Store in covered jar in refrigerator.

Variations: Substitute lime juice, limeade, apricot nectar or pineapple juice for the frozen lemonade concentrate. When the sweeter juices are used, add a little lime or lemon.

AIA

Glutenfree, Wheatfree

Fruit Dressing

1 cup sweetened condensed milk
3 oz. frozen lime juice
2 egg yolks
¼ teaspoon dry mustard

Mix all ingredients and beat until well blended. Refrigerate in covered jar.

AIA

Cooked Salad Dressings

Eggfree, Glutenfree, Milkfree, Wheatfree

Rice Flour Salad Dressing

2 tablespoons rice flour
½ teaspoon salt
2 tablespoons sugar
1 teaspoon citric acid crystals (or 1 tablespoon lemon juice)
½ cup water
½ cup olive oil
¼ cup caramel sugar syrup (below)

Mix together dry ingredients. Stir in water. Cook, stirring over low heat 2 minutes or until thickened. Cool. Beat in syrup. Makes 1 cup.
Caramel Sugar Syrup: Sprinkle ¼ cup sugar into small skillet over low heat. Stir until sugar melts and turns golden brown. Add ¾ cup sugar and 1 cup boiling water. Cook until smooth, stirring constantly. Boil 10 minutes longer without stirring. Makes ¾ cup.

AIA

Eggfree, Glutenfree, Milkfree, Wheatfree

Potato Flour Mayonnaise

1½ tablespoons potato flour
¼ teaspoon dry mustard
½ teaspoon salt
2 teaspoons sugar
¼ cup cold water
¾ cup boiling water
2 tablespoons lemon juice
1 tablespoon white vinegar
½ cup salad oil
salt and pepper

Mix dry ingredients in saucepan, then stir in cold water and mix well. Add hot water and cook just until mixture is clear. Cool to lukewarm, then gradually add remaining ingredients, beating constantly.

AIA

Eggfree, Glutenfree, Milkfree, Wheatfree

1000 Island Dressing

1 cup mayonnaise (your own diet type)
4 tablespoons chili sauce
1 tablespoon chopped chives (or onion)
3 tablespoons catsup
1 teaspoon vinegar (or pickle juice, if suited to diet)
2 tablespoons chopped green pepper
1 tablespoon chopped red pepper
1 teaspoon paprika

Mix ingredients well and chill in refrigerator.

AIA

Glutenfree, Milkfree, Wheatfree

Salad Dressing

  1 cup vinegar
  1 heaping tablespoon cornstarch
  1 teaspoon salt
  ⅔ cup sugar
  2 eggs
  1 teaspoon prepared mustard

Boil vinegar. To beaten eggs, add sugar, salt, cornstarch and mustard. Add a little hot vinegar to the egg mixture. Add egg mixture to the vinegar and bring to a full rolling boil.

AIA

Glutenfree, Wheatfree

Salad Dressing

  ½ teaspoon salt
  1 teaspoon prepared mustard
  2 tablespoons cornstarch
  ¾ cup milk
  ½ cup vinegar
  1 egg or 2 egg yolks, slightly beaten
  2 tablespoons butter

Sift together into top of double boiler the salt, sugar and mustard, and add cornstarch Add egg and milk and mix well. Add vinegar very slowly. Cook and stir mixture over boiling water until it begins to thicken. Remove from heat and stir in butter. Strain and cool.

AIA

Eggfree, Milkfree

Fruit Salad Dressing

2 tablespoons milkfree margarine
2 tablespoons all-purpose flour
1½ cups pineapple juice
½ cup orange juice
2 tablespoons lemon juice
1 cup marshmallows
½ cup nondairy product such as Coffee Rich

Heat butter and blend in flour. Add juices and stir until thickened. Add marshmallows. When cold, whip nondairy product such as Coffee Rich and fold into mixture. Refrigerate in covered jar.

AIA

Eggfree, Milkfree

Paprika Salad Dressing

1 cup sugar
2 tablespoons all-purpose flour
2 teaspoons thyme
1 tablespoon paprika
½ cup vinegar
½ cup water
½ cup oil
parsley

Combine dry ingredients. Gradually stir in vinegar and water. Cook 8 minutes, stirring frequently. Beat oil slowly into mixture. Add parsley when serving.
Delicious over greens; good also as a spread for hamburgers when one can't have mustard, catsup, mayonnaise, onions, and the like.

AIA

Eggfree, Milkfree

Macaroni or Potato Dressing

> 3 tablespoons all-purpose flour
> 3 tablespoons sugar
> 1 teaspoon salt
> 1 teaspoon thyme
> ¾ cup Coffee Rich
> ¾ cup water
> ¼ cup vinegar

Mix dry ingredients in pan. Add Coffee Rich and water gradually and stir until thick. Add vinegar and mix well.

AIA

Main Dishes

Meatballs in Creamed Vegetable Sauce

Make meatballs with meat loaf recipe (p. 183).
Sauté until brown.
Melt 1 tablespoon margarine in skillet and add

> 1 stalk celery cut in ½-inch pieces slantwise
> 2-oz. can mushroom stems and pieces with liquid plus any other reserved mushroom liquid
> ½ package frozen green peas

Cover and cook over low heat until vegetables are done.
Heat and pour milkless cream sauce (p. 199) over meatballs.

AIA

Hashed-Brown Hamburgers

Grind

> 1 medium potato
> 1 stalk celery
> 1 inch strip green pepper

Mix with 9 oz. ground beef. Add dash of monosodium glutamate if gluten is not a problem.
Shape into 3 thick cakes.
Sauté on one side until brown over medium heat.

Pour off fat, turn cakes carefully, reduce heat to low, cover and cook
about 15 minutes or until potatoes are done.

Wall

Beef Patties with Yellow Hominy

Make meat loaf recipe (below) into 4 patties and saute until done.
Cook 1 can hominy in its liquid until liquid is almost gone.
Pour off fat from beef patties and add hominy.
Allow to boil up, stirring to incorporate all browned bits from
meat.

Wall

Chopped Beef Stroganoff

Crumble ¾ pound ground beef into 8 or 9-inch skillet.
Cook over medium heat, stirring constantly until red color disap-
pears. Pour off fat.
Add

> 2-oz. can mushroom stems and pieces with liquid
> pinch of grated nutmeg
> pinch of sweet basil

Stir and heat.
Add ¾ cup imitation sour cream.*
Stir and heat until blended. Do not boil.

* Note: Make sure the imitation sour cream does not contain
sodium caseinate, if you are hypersensitive to milk.

Wall

Meat Loaf (or Beef Patties)

Soak 2 crumbled rye crackers in ¼ cup water until soft.
Add

> ½ pound ground beef
> 1 teaspoon Worcestershire sauce
> pinch of thyme
> pinch of marjoram
> pinch of savory
> 1 teaspoon parsley flakes
> 1 egg (1 tablespoon Egg Replacer* beaten into 2 tablespoons
> water may be substituted)

Mix well with fork. Mold into loaf and bake in greased pan at 375° for 30 minutes.

* Note: Egg Replacer and Imitation Egg Powder are not the same product. The latter usually contains egg white.

Wall

Acorn Squash with Meatballs

Cut ½ pound acorn squash in half and remove seeds.
Place cut side down in baking pan with ¼ cup water.
Bake at 350° until done.
Make balls of Meat Loaf recipe. Saute in 1 tablespoon margarine until brown.
Set acorn squash halves in baking dish, sprinkle with nutmeg. Score inside of squash with fork so it can be eaten from the shell. Fill with meatballs and serve.

Wall

Glutenfree, Milkfree, Wheatfree

Shepherd's Meat Loaf

    1 pound chopped lean chuck beef
    2 tablespoons diced onion
    1 teaspoon salt
    1 hot cooked medium potato, mashed (no milk)
    ½ teaspoon garlic powder
    1 egg
    ½ pound fresh mushrooms sliced (or 1 can sliced mushrooms, drained)

In 8-inch loaf pan, thoroughly mix together meat, onion, salt, potato, garlic powder and egg and form loaf about 7 by 1 by 1½ inches. Firmly press mushroom slices over entire surface of loaf. Bake at 350° for about 1 hour. Slice and serve with catsup.
Yield: 4 servings.

AIA

Glutenfree, Milkfree, Wheatfree

Rice-Burger Casserole

1 pound ground beef	1 teaspoon seasoning salt
1/4 pound ground pork	1/2 teaspoon salt
1/4 cup diced bacon (4 slices)	1/4 teaspoon pepper
2 tablespoons parsley flakes	4 cups seasoned, cooked,
1 tablespoon finely chopped	long grain rice
onion	1 tablespoon glutenfree soya
1 tablespoon chopped celery	sauce
1 tablespoon chopped green	2 tablespoons tomato catsup
pepper	1/4 cup water
1 egg, unbeaten	2 tablespoons margarine

Mix thoroughly the beef, pork, bacon, parsley flakes, onion, celery, green pepper, egg, seasoning salt, salt and pepper.*

* Note: Recipes such as casseroles (or cookies) can be made up to the point where the allergic person's allergenic food is added. Then take out a portion for the allergic person, add any touches necessary to finish the portion according to his diet restrictions, and bake in a separate container. The rest of the casserole can be finished according to the normal recipe and baked for the family.

Butter a large casserole dish and spread warm cooked rice over the bottom, making a layer with approximately 3 cups of the rice. Cover rice with meat mixture, flattening it fairly well. On top of meat, sprinkle soya sauce, catsup and water mixed. Make another layer on top of meat with remaining rice. Cover and bake in moderate oven at 375° for 30 minutes. Remove casserole dish from oven, spread margarine over top layer of rice and replace the cover. Allow casserole to bake for 10 minutes longer at 350°.
Yield: 6 to 8 servings.

AIA

Glutenfree, Milkfree, Wheatfree

Salisbury Steak Casserole

2 pounds lean ground beef
1 1/2 teaspoons salt

pepper to taste
2 tablespoons finely chopped onion
1 egg
2 tablespoons melted milkfree margarine

Mix beef, salt, pepper, onion and egg thoroughly but lightly. Grease a shallow casserole, mold the meat mixture into an oval resembling a small loaf of French bread, and put in center of casserole. Brush with margarine and bake in a 450° oven for 10 minutes. Reduce heat to 325° and bake 25 to 35 minutes longer. Brush with melted margarine at least twice during baking.
Serve with sautéed mushrooms and buttered little white onions.
Yield: 6 servings.

AIA

Eggfree, Glutenfree, Milkfree, Wheatfree

Beef-Rice Casserole

1 pound ground beef	1 can water
⅓ cup chopped green pepper	1 teaspoon salt
½ cup chopped onion	¼ teaspoon pepper
1 cup chopped celery	¼ teaspoon Tabasco
1 cup uncooked rice	Chinese noodles (omit for gluten-
1 can Vegetable Beef soup *	free, wheatfree diets)

Brown beef. Add vegetables and rice. Cook until rice is golden, stirring constantly. Add soup and seasonings. Heat to boiling, stir well. Pour into 2-quart casserole, cover and bake at 350° for 20 to 25 minutes. Chinese noodles may be sprinkled on top after baking if not on glutenfree and wheatfree diet.

* If allergic to tomatoes, substitute Old Fashioned Vegetable soup (contains wheat), and add 2 or 3 beef bouillon cubes.

AIA

Eggfree, Glutenfree, Milkfree, Wheatfree

Beef Casserole

1½ pounds ground chuck
¾ pound sliced mushrooms (or 10-oz. can)
1 green pepper, chopped

1 cup celery, chopped
1 package dried onion soup
1 teaspoon Worcestershire sauce
6 oz. fine noodles (use rice vermicelli for glutenfree diets)
Grated cheese (omit for milkfree diets)
½ teaspoon salt
pinch of thyme
28-oz. can of tomatoes

Saute beef, mushrooms, pepper and celery in oil. Add tomatoes, soup mix, Worcestershire sauce, salt and thyme. Cook until excess moisture has gone. Cook rice vermicelli or noodles, drain well, and add to meat mixture. Put in casserole, adding grated cheese if allowed. Heat in 350° over for 30 to 45 minutes. If desired, omit mushrooms, celery and tomatoes, and substitute stuffed olives, canned corn niblets and your favorite soup.
Yield: 12 servings.

AIA

Eggfree, Glutenfree, Milkfree, Wheatfree

Jambalaya

2 slices chopped bacon
2 tablespoons chopped onion
2 cups tomatoes
1 cup water
Grated Parmesan or Cheddar cheese (omit for milkfree diets)
½ teaspoon salt
¼ teaspoon pepper
¾ cup uncooked rice
2 cups cooked ham, chicken or turkey

Cook bacon slowly, add onion and cook until clear. Add tomatoes, water and seasonings. Bring to boil. Add rice to boiling liquid, lightly stir with fork until mixtures come to boil. Cover tightly, reduce heat and let simmer 20 minutes. When rice is tender and dry, add diced meat. Heat to serving temperature. Add cheese if allowed.

AIA

Eggfree, Glutenfree, Milkfree, Wheatfree

Potato and Meat Scallop

    3 large potatoes, pared and thinly sliced
    ¾ or 1 pound round steak, minced
    salt, pepper, parsley and minced onion to taste
    chicken broth

Alternate layers of potato and chunks of beef in a deep casserole.
Season each layer. Pour broth over mixture. Bake at 350° for 1½
hours.
Yield: 3 servings

                                                                    AIA

Glutenfree, Milkfree, Wheatfree

Meatza Pizza Pie

    1 pound ground beef
    ½ cup instant mashed potatoes (dry)
    ¼ cup canned milk (or substitute)
    ½ onion
    mozzarella cheese, mushrooms, salami and olives
    1 egg
    1 teaspoon oregano
    1 teaspoon garlic salt
    salt and pepper
    1 package dried tomato soup*

Prepare the tomato soup for sauce (use only 10 oz. of this mixture).
Mix meat, potatoes, milk, onion, egg and spices with 5 oz. of tomato
sauce. Place in a 9-inch glass pie plate or two 8-inch glass pie plates
and work out in the shape of a pie crust until it is about ¾ inch thick.
Fill center with remaining 5 oz. of tomato sauce.
Top with mozzarella cheese slices, mushrooms, salami and olives and
sprinkle with oregano. Bake at 450° for 20 minutes or until brown; or
at 350° for 30 minutes or until brown.

* Substitute: 1 can of tomato soup (but will not be glutenfree or
  wheatfree) or 10-oz. mixture of tomato catsup and tomato juice or
  10-oz. mixture of tomato paste and tomato juice. Any of these three
  substitutes can be seasoned with such spices as dried onion, celery
  salt, seasoning salt or parsley.

Glutenfree, Milkfree, Wheatfree

Pizza Rice Pie

> 2⅔ cups cooked rice
> ½ cup minced onion
> 2 eggs, slightly beaten
> 3 tablespoons butter (or substitute)
> 8-oz. can tomato sauce
> ¼ teaspoon oregano
> ¼ teaspoon basil
> 1 cup shredded mozzarella cheese
> 4½ oz. pepperoni
> ¼ cup stuffed olives

Mix together rice, onion, eggs, and melted butter. Line a 12-inch pizza pan with rice mixture. Bake 12 minutes until set.

Spread tomato sauce over rice crust. Sprinkle with oregano, basil, and shredded cheese. Top with pepperoni and olives.

Bake at 350° for 20 minutes. After removing from oven allow to stand a few minutes before serving.

AIA

Glutenfree, Milkfree, Wheatfree

Stuffed Cabbage in Tomato Sauce

> 1 pound lean ground beef
> 1 cup cooked rice
> 1 small chopped onion
> 1 teaspoon caraway seeds (optional)
> 1 teaspoon salt
> ¼ teaspoon pepper
> 1 egg
> 2 cups tomato sauce (canned)
> ¼ cup water

Trim off thickest part of stem from 12 cabbage leaves. Mix beef, rice, onion, egg and seasonings and divide into 12 portions. Wrap each in a leaf; fasten with wooden picks. Brown cabbage rolls in cooking oil. Add tomato sauce and water. Cover, cook slowly about 40 minutes.

Yield: 6 servings.

AIA

Swiss Steak

Cut ½ pound round steak into serving pieces.
Dredge with corn flakes and pound with edge of heavy plate or mallet, adding as much flour (nonwheat) as steak will hold.
Melt 2 tablespoons margarine in heavy, covered skillet.
Sear steak.
Add

> 1 teaspoon parsley
> pinch of savory

Cover closely and bake in slow oven (275°) for 2 hours. Or may be cooked on top of stove on lowest heat, but must be watched to avoid burning. Add water as needed.

Wall

Beef Stew

Melt 1 tablespoon margarine * in skillet.
Add

> 1 stalk celery cut in pieces slantwise
> 2-oz. can mushroom stems and pieces
> ¼ cup diced green pepper

Cook over low heat until celery is done, adding water if necessary.
Cut leftover meat in bite-sized pieces and add to skillet with any leftover gravy. If there is no gravy, use 1 bouillon cube, 1 tablespoon cornstarch and 1 cup water.
Add leftover vegetables. If not enough add:

> ½ package frozen mixed vegetables
> 1 tablespoon wine vinegar
> ⅛ teaspoon monosodium glutamate (omit if gluten is not allowed)
> pinch of savory and marjoram

Simmer 15 minutes.

* Note: Make sure the margarine used does not contain cow's milk in any form, if you are hypersensitive to milk.

Wall

Baked Hash

Grind together

> leftover meat and vegetables
> 1 medium raw potato

    1 stalk celery
    2 inch slice of green pepper
    1 bouillon cube

Add

    2 tablespoons dry coffee creamer *
    1 teaspoon Worcestershire sauce
    1 teaspoon parsley
    leftover gravy to make a moist mixture

Pat into 8-inch cake pan or any shallow baking dish.
Bake at 400° for 30 minutes.

* Note: Make sure the brand of dry coffee creamer used does not
      contain caseinate.

Beef Franks and Beans in Savory Sauce

Cook ½ package (5 franks) in boiling water for 10 minutes.
Make beans in savory sauce (p. 205)
Cut franks in thirds and arrange in same skillet.

Wall

Dinner in a Skillet

Slice 1-pound can all beef lunch meat (Wilson's "BIF" or some other
brand) in four slices and brown on each side in skillet.
Add

    1-pound can yams or sweet potatoes, drained
    15-oz. can cling peach halves, drained (save syrup to use in fruit
      Jell-O)

Brown peaches along with yams and meat slices.
Push meat, yams and peaches to one side in skillet.
Add

    ¼ cup apricot nectar
    1 tablespoon lemon juice

Stir with juices in skillet. Baste meat, yams and peaches with this
until glazed. Heat and serve.

Wall

Lamb Stew

    ½ pound lamb, cut for stew
    1 tablespoon rice flour
    ¾ teaspoon salt
    1 tablespoon lamb drippings
    1¼ cups hot water
    1½ cups sweet potatoes, diced and pared
    1 tablespoon rice flour

Dust lamb with mixture of flour and salt. Brown in hot drippings. Add water. Cover; simmer 1 hour. Add potatoes; cover and cook 25 minutes longer or until tender. Make gravy with liquid and 1 tablespoon rice flour.
Yield: 3 servings.

AIA

Lamb with Rice

    3 tablespoons rice flour
    2 tablespoons lamb drippings
    1 cup hot water
    ½ teaspoon salt
    1 cup diced cooked lamb
    1½ cups hot cooked rice

Brown rice flour in drippings. Add water and salt. Cook and stir until thick and smooth. Add lamb and heat thoroughly. Serve over rice.
Yield: 3 servings.

AIA

Lamb Liver Slices with Spiced Prune Sauce

    ⅔ cup dried prunes
    1½ cups water

¼ cup sugar
½ teaspoon citric acid crystals (or 2 teaspoons lemon juice)
1 tablespoon rice flour
1 pound sliced lamb liver
1 teaspoon salt
2 tablespoons lamb drippings

Cover and simmer prunes in water until tender. Drain and cut up prunes, reserving liquid. Combine sugar, citric acid crystals and rice flour. Gradually stir in liquid from prunes (about ½ cup). Cook and stir until slightly thickened. Add cut up prunes and heat thoroughly. Sprinkle liver with salt. Brown on both sides in lamb drippings (about 2 minutes on each side). Serve with prune sauce.
Yield: 3 servings.

AIA

Oven Fried Chicken

Remove skin from chicken pieces. Marinate 2 hours at room temperature in 1 teaspoon wine vinegar and 2 teaspoons safflower oil. Roll in corn flake crumbs to coat.
Sprinkle with parsley and paprika.
Bake 1 hour at 350° on ungreased piece of foil in baking pan.
If you don't want it quite so crisp, cover with foil the last 15 minutes.

Wall

Baked Chicken Dinner

1½ pounds chicken parts
2 stalks celery
2 carrots
2 medium potatoes (8 or 9 oz.)
2-oz. can mushroom stems and pieces
2 cups milkless cream sauce (p. 199)

Arrange chicken in shallow baking dish (9 by 13 inches).
Cut celery and carrots into 1-inch chunks.
Cut potatoes into eighths and arrange vegetables around chicken.
Drain mushrooms, reserving liquid to use in gravy or soup.
Grind mushrooms, add to cream sauce and pour over chicken.
Sprinkle with parsley and bake at 350° for 1 hour and 15 minutes.
Cover baking dish tightly with foil.

Wall

Chicken à la King

Melt 1 tablespoon margarine in skillet.
Add

> 2-oz. can mushroom stems and pieces
> 1 stalk celery cut in ½-inch pieces slantwise

Cook until celery is done.
Add

> 1½ cups cooked chicken cut into bite-sized pieces
> 1 tablespoon parsley flakes
> 2-oz. jar sliced pimiento
> 2 hard-cooked eggs (if eggs are not allowed, substitute ½ cup more chicken)
> 1½ cups water

Heat over moderate heat.
Add

> ½ cup dry coffee creamer
> ½ cup cold water into which 4 tablespoons cornstarch have been stirred

Cook, stirring constantly, until thickened.

Wall

Oven Fried Fish Fillets

Stir 1 tablespoon dry coffee creamer into 2 tablespoons hot water.
Cool.
Dip fish serving pieces in this, then in corn flake crumbs.
Place on foil.
Bake at 400° for 20 minutes or until fish flakes.

Wall

Poached Fish Fillets

Melt 1 tablespoon margarine in skillet.
Add 2 tablespoons sherry wine or 2 tablespoons cider
Lay fish fillets in this sauce and heat over low heat.
Turn pieces once before they are done, then spoon sauce over them until done.
Remove to warm platter.
Thicken sauce with 1 teaspoon cornstarch in 1 tablespoon cold water.
Pour over fish and sprinkle with parsley and paprika.

Tuna-Corn Casserole

1 can cream style corn
7-oz. can tuna fish (waterpack), drained and flaked
3-oz. jar pimiento
2-oz. can mushroom stems and pieces (do not drain)
¼ cup diced green pepper
1 stalk celery, chopped fine

Put all ingredients in casserole. Cover with corn flake crumbs.
Dot with 1 tablespoon margarine and bake at 350° for 45 minutes.

Wall

Tuna Soufflé

Dissolve ¼ cup dry coffee creamer in 1 cup hot water in top of double boiler.
Add ¼ cup quick hominy grits. Cook until thick.
Separate 2 eggs. Beat yolks and add to grits, first spooning a little of the hot mixture into the egg yolks before adding to grits.
Drain one 7-oz. can tuna fish (waterpack).
Flake and stir into grits mixture.
Add 1 tablespoon margarine and ½ teaspoon baking powder.
Beat egg whites stiff but not dry. Fold into tuna mixture.
Bake in greased casserole 45 minutes at 350° or until knife inserted comes out clean.

Wall

Glutenfree, Milkfree, Wheatfree

Salmon Bake

1½ cups precooked rice
1½ cups boiling water
1 can salmon (drained, flaked)
2 teaspoons salt
¼ teaspoon black pepper
2 tablespoons minced onion
2 egg whites
1 egg
2 tablespoons melted butter

Add rice to boiling water; cover; remove from heat; let stand 5 minutes.
Set oven at moderate 375°.

Combine salmon, rice, salt, pepper and onion.
Beat egg whites and egg; add to salmon mixture; blend well.
Press into buttered 8 by 1½-inch baking dish or loaf pan. Brush top with melted butter.
Bake at 375° for 30 minutes, or until firm and golden. Garnish with lemon wedges and parsley.

AIA

Tuna-Stuffed Zucchini Cases

Scrape 2 medium size zucchini but do not peel. Remove stem.
Cook whole in salted water for five minutes.
Cut in half lengthwise and place in shallow baking dish.
Scoop out centers to make boats or cases.
Melt 1 tablespoon margarine in skillet.
Add

> chopped zucchini centers
> 1 stalk celery, chopped fine

Cook over low heat until celery is done. Flake and drain 7-oz. can tuna fish (waterpack).
Add to skillet along with

> 1 tablespoon lemon juice
> 1 teaspoon parsley flakes
> pinch of grated nutmeg
> 2 tablespoons mayonnaise

Fill cases with this mixture.
Cover with corn flake crumbs that have been mixed with 1 tablespoon margarine.
Put 2 tablespoons water in bottom of baking dish.
Bake at 350° for 30 minutes. This mixture is also good in baked potato cases.

Wall

Eggs Benedict

Toast a slice of whatever bread is allowed for the base. If no bread is available, use hot hominy grits spread in a circle on warm plate.
Heat slices of corned beef lunch meat in a little hot water.
Lay these on hominy grits.
Top with poached eggs and Hollandaise sauce (p. 200).

Wall

Fish and Meat Sauces

Eggfree, Glutenfree, Milkfree, Wheatfree

Oriental Sweet-Sour Sauce

Combine in saucepan and bring to boil:

¾ cup water
3 tablespoons brown sugar
2 tablespoons vinegar

Stir in 1 tablespoon cornstarch mixed with ¼ cup water. Cook until thickened.
Add

¼ cup diced canned pineapple chunks and diced sweet pickles
2 tablespoons chopped pimientos
¼ teaspoon soy sauce (AIA recipe; optional)

Serve over pork, chicken or shrimp.

AIA

Eggfree, Glutenfree, Milkfree, Wheatfree

Hot Barbecue Sauce

2 teaspoons Tabasco sauce
2½ cups chili sauce
1 teaspoon chili powder
¾ cup oil
½ cup lemon juice
2 tablespoons tarragon vinegar
1 tablespoon brown sugar
1 bay leaf
1 teaspoon prepared mustard
1 teaspoon salt

Combine and cook for 15 minutes.

AIA

Eggfree, Glutenfree, Milkfree, Wheatfree

Tomato Sauce

2½ cups canned tomatoes
2 stalks celery, diced
1 small onion, diced
2 tablespoons catsup
1 tablespoon brown sugar
1 tablespoon vinegar

Add celery and onions to tomatoes and simmer 10 minutes. Add catsup, sugar and vinegar. Simmer until vegetables are cooked. This may be thickened with a glutenfree flour, if desired.

AIA

Eggfree, Glutenfree, Milkfree, Wheatfree

Sweet-Sour Sauce for Spareribs

Chop and fry:

1 onion
1 green pepper

1 cup (14 oz.) pineapple chunks
2 teaspoons cornstarch
3 tablespoons vinegar
½ teaspoon ground ginger

Drain pineapple juice into saucepan. Stir together a little syrup with cornstarch and pour into syrup in pan. Cook, stirring until thick and clear. Stir in vinegar and ginger. Add onions and peppers and use to bake spareribs in for 45 minutes.

AIA

Eggfree, Glutenfree, Milkfree, Wheatfree

Sauce Piquante

3 tablespoons white wine
1½ tablespoons vinegar

1 teaspoon onion, chopped
1 cup beef broth or juice
1½ tablespoons each chopped pickle and parsley

Cook together wine, vinegar and onion for 5 minutes. Stir in beef broth or juice and let it come to a boil. Add pickle and parsley. Serve with any meat. Thicken with 1 tablespoon cornstarch, if desired.

AIA

Eggfree, Glutenfree, Milkfree, Wheatfree

White Sauce

1 tablespoon milkfree margarine
1½ teaspoons potato flour (or any other glutenfree flour)
¼ teaspoon salt
½ cup soybean milk
1 teaspoon dried parsley (optional)

Melt margarine in saucepan. Add flour and salt and stir until well mixed. Add milk and parsley and continue stirring until mixture thickens.

AIA

Mushroom and Celery Sauce

Drain liquid from 2 oz. can of mushroom stems and pieces into saucepan.
Grind mushrooms and 1 stalk celery.
Add to liquid along with

2 tablespoons brown sugar
1 tablespoon wine vinegar
1 teaspoon Worcestershire sauce

Cook until celery is done.
Set aside to be added to skillet after sauteing beef patties (or what you will).
Thicken slightly with 1 teaspoon cornstarch in 1 tablespoon water.

Wall

Milkless Cream Sauce

Add ½ cup dry coffee creamer* to 1 cup hot water.
Stir 3 tablespoons cornstarch into ½ cup cold water.

Add to hot mixture with 1 tablespoon margarine.
Cook until thickened.
For variation, add ½ cup imitation sour cream.
Use with potatoes, vegetables, beef patties and the like.

* Note: Make sure the dry coffee creamer does not contain caseinate, if that's what you're sensitive to in milk.

Wall

Eggless Hollandaise Sauce

Whip until fluffy 2 tablespoons Egg Replacer and ¼ cup water.
Heat

>   juice of half a lemon
>   ¼ cup water
>   3 tablespoons firm margarine

Pour Egg Replacer mixture into hot mixture.
Beat while heating until thick.
Good with fish, eggs Benedict or vegetables.

Wall

Spaghetti Sauces

Eggfree, Glutenfree, Milkfree, Wheatfree

Wine Spaghetti Sauce

>   1 pound ground beef
>   celery
>   green pepper
>   zucchini squash
>   ¼ teaspoon thyme
>   1 tablespoon paprika
>   ¼-½ cup dry red wine

Place a little salt in skillet and fry ground beef (no oil is used). Drain
fat. Add chopped vegetables. (The amounts may be suited to your
own preference.) Add enough water to cover, then wine, thyme and
paprika. Simmer 1 hour. Add more water if necessary. Thicken if
desired.

AIA

Eggfree, Glutenfree, Wheatfree

Bacon and Green Pepper Spaghetti Sauce

½ cup chopped bacon
2 tablespoons chopped onion
3 tablespoons chopped green pepper
1 tablespoon olive oil
pepper to taste
2 drops Tabasco sauce
¼ teaspoon salt
grated cheese (optional)

Fry bacon, onion, green pepper and Tabasco sauce until golden brown. Add oil, salt and pepper. Simmer a few minutes. Put rice vermicelli (or spaghetti if allowed) in heated bowl. Add sauce. Mix well. Serve with grated cheese if milk is tolerated.

Note: These spaghetti sauces can also be mixed with rice.

AIA

Eggfree, Glutenfree, Milkfree, Wheatfree

Soy Sauce

Commercial soy sauce contains gluten and wheat. Ingredients are protein extracts from corn and soy beans, wheat, parts of corn and cane, with water and salt added.
The recipe for a homemade soy sauce is: salt, hot water, molasses or caramel.
The flavor changes with the heat of the water; you will have to experiment until you find the right combination of ingredients. It won't be real soy sauce but it makes a good substitute.

AIA

Vegetables

Eggfree, Glutenfree, Milkfree, Wheatfree

Chicken Fried Rice

1 can chicken with rice soup
¾ can water

1½ tablespoons milkfree margarine
1 onion, chopped fine
1 cup long grain rice
parsley

Bring soup and water to a boil. Melt 1½ tablespoon milkfree margarine in saucepan and add onion. Add 1 cup rice and fry until dark brown. Add boiling soup. Cover with tight-fitting lid and let simmer for 15 minutes. Add parsley.

AIA

Eggfree, Glutenfree, Milkfree, Wheatfree

Scalloped Potatoes

Rub milkfree margarine generously on sides and bottom of casserole. Put a thick layer of thinly sliced potatoes in casserole, pour ⅓ can of beef-vegetable soup (glutenfree variety) over potatoes. Add more potatoes and soup until casserole is filled, sprinkle salt and pepper on top.
If there is not sufficient liquid add a soup can full of water. Dot with milkfree margarine generously. Cover and bake in 350° oven until potatoes are tender.

AIA

Eggfree, Glutenfree, Milkfree, Wheatfree

Casserole Potatoes

4 medium potatoes
1 teaspoon salt
1 tablespoon chopped parsley or parsley flakes
1 cup boiling water
2 tablespoons milkfree margarine

Mix all ingredients in casserole, cover and bake in 375° oven for 1 hour.

AIA

Glutenfree, Milkfree, Wheatfree

Potato Puffs

    1 cup mashed potatoes (do not add milk)
    1 teaspoon baking powder
    3 tablespoons potato flour
    1 egg
    1 teaspoon salt
    1 teaspoon chopped onion

Mix all ingredients together. Shape into 18 fingers or drop by teaspoonfuls into deep fat. Fry until golden brown on all sides— 3 to 5 minutes.

AIA

Eggplant with Sour Cream

Slice eggplant in ½-inch slices and pare.
Soak 1 hour in salt water. Drain and pat dry on paper towels.
Spread margarine on one side of each slice and arrange on medium hot griddle with this side down.
Cover and cook until golden brown on one side.
Turn (no extra margarine), reduce heat slightly, and sprinkle each slice with

    few drops of lemon juice
    pinch of grated nutmeg
    pinch of monosodium glutamate (omit if gluten is not allowed)

Cover and cook until done through.
On top of half the slices place 1 teaspoon imitation sour cream.*
Cover with other slices. Put 1 teaspoon sour cream on top.
Serve hot.

* Note: Make sure your imitation sour cream contains no sodium
       caseinate if you are sensitive to milk.

Wall

Baked Eggplant Slices

Prepare eggplant as above.
Dip dry slices in mixture of 1 tablespoon of vinegar and 1 tablespoon salad oil.
Coat with corn flake crumbs.

Place on greased foil on cookie sheet and bake at 350° until done. Serve with Milkless Cream Sauce or Eggless Hollandaise Sauce (pp. 199–200) or serve plain.

Braised Celery

Slice 4 stalks of celery slantwise.
Cook covered over low heat in ¼ cup water and 1 tablespoon margarine until nearly done.
Remove cover and finish cooking until water disappears (don't burn!).
Add pinch of paprika and 1 tablespoon lemon juice.
Serve hot.

Wall

Harvard Beets

Reserve 2 tablespoons liquid from 15-oz. can of sliced, diced or whole beets.
Add to rest of liquid

    2 tablespoons vinegar
    1 tablespoon margarine
    1 teaspoon sugar
    pinch of tarragon

Heat beets until liquid is reduced by half.
Stir 1 tablespoon cornstarch into reserved liquid and add to hot beets.
Cook until thickened. Serve hot.

Wall

Zucchini or Summer Squash

Scrape but do not peel squash. Slice thin or dice.
Cook covered over low heat with 2 tablespoons water and 1 tablespoon margarine, shaking occasionally to keep from sticking. Add water only to prevent scorching. Ten minutes is usually long enough.
Add 1 tablespoon lemon juice or ¼ cup imitation sour cream and dash of nutmeg. Serve hot.

Wall

Baked Beans

Soak 1 cup Great Northern beans overnight. Next day simmer gently until almost done.
Drain and rinse.
Add

    1 cup hot water
    ¼ cup unsulfured West Indies molasses
    1 teaspoon Worcestershire sauce

Pour into covered baking dish.
Cut 2 slices bacon in 1-inch pieces and fry gently until crisp. Arrange over top of beans. Cover tightly.
Bake at 275° until beans are done and brown. Add water during this time if necessary.

                                        Wall

Dried Lima Beans or Black-Eyed Peas in Savory Sauce

Cut 1 slice bacon into ½-inch pieces and saute until crisp.
Remove from skillet to paper towel. Drain all but 1 tablespoon fat.
Add

    1 stalk celery, chopped fine
    ¼ cup green pepper, chopped fine
    liquid from 1 pound can dried butter beans or black-eyed peas
    or ¼ cup liquid from same if cooked from scratch

Cook over low heat until celery is done.
To beans from which liquid was drained, add

    2 tablespoons brown sugar
    2 tablespoons wine vinegar
    1 teaspoon Worcestershire sauce
    1 teaspoon parsley flakes
    2-oz. jar sliced pimiento
    the bacon pieces

Cook covered over low heat until liquid is almost gone. Add water if necessary during the cooking to keep from burning.
Serve hot.

                                          Wall

Eggfree, Milkfree, Wheatfree

Bread

Rye Bread

> 1 cake fresh yeast
> 1¼ cups lukewarm water
> 2 teaspoons salt
> 1 tablespoon brown sugar
> 4 cups rye flour

Dissolve yeast in ¼ cup lukewarm water; combine with salt, sugar, and remaining water. Stir in flour; beat till smooth. Turn out onto rye-floured board, knead, using enough additional rye flour to make firm, elastic dough. Place in greased bowl; brush top with salad oil. Cover; let rise in warm place until double in bulk. Knead as before. Place in bowl, and let rise again 1 hour.

Shape into loaf; place in greased 9 by 5 by 3-inch loaf pan. Cover with clean towel; let rise in warm place until double in bulk. Bake in hot oven (450°) 15 minutes; reduce heat to moderate oven (350°) and bake 55 minutes.

Yield: 1 loaf.

Eggfree, Milkfree, Wheatfree

Rye Bread

> 1⅓ cups water
> 1½ teaspoons salt
> 3 tablespoons sugar
> 3 tablespoons fat
> ¾ cake compressed yeast
> 4-5 cups rye flour, approximately

Dissolve the yeast in part of the water. Measure the remaining water, salt, sugar and fat into a bowl. Pour about half of the flour into this liquid mixture and stir until smooth. Continue beating for about 30 seconds. Add the remaining flour, kneading it in if necessary. A soft dough is formed. Add more flour if quite sticky. Knead about 250 strokes in a well-greased bowl if you find it hard to handle.

Let rise until double in bulk (about 1 hour) at 80°. Knead about 100 times and place in pans, which have been greased only on the bottom. This amount can best be separated into two small loaves and shaped before placing into the pans. Let rise again until double, about 30 minutes, at 80°. Bake 10 to 15 minutes until brown at 425°, then 25 to 35 minutes or until done at 350°.

AIA

Wheatfree

Rye Bread

½ cup sugar
2 tablespoons butter
½ teaspoon salt
1 egg
1 cup sour milk
1 teaspoon baking soda
1 tablespoon molasses
2 cups rye flour
¼ cup cold water

Cream butter and sugar; add egg, water, milk and molasses. Then add sifted flour, salt and soda. Put into a loaf pan. Bake 1 hour at 350°. Nut meats, raisins or dates may be added.

AIA

Glutenfree, Wheatfree

Rye-Rice Bread

1 cup plus 1⅓ tablespoons rye flour
1 cup plus 1⅓ tablespoons white rice flour
½ teaspoon salt
3 tablespoons plus 1 teaspoon baking powder
2 teaspoons cooking oil
1⅓ cups water
4 tablespoons sugar

Mix all ingredients together. Bake in greased loaf pan in moderate oven (350°) for 60 minutes.*

* Note: The batter of baked goods made from substitute flours can often be runny. Protect your oven by using pans with ample rims or by not filling pans too much.

AIA

Glutenfree, Wheatfree

Potato Starch Banana Bread

    ½ cup potato flour
    ¼ teaspoon salt
    1½ teaspoons baking powder
    2 tablespoons vegetable shortening
    2 tablespoons sugar
    1 egg yolk
    1 tablespoon plus 1 teaspoon milk
    1 egg white, well beaten
    ½ banana, mashed*

Measure flour, baking powder and salt. Combine and sift.
Cream softened shortening; then cream with sugar until well blended.
Stir in unbeaten egg yolks into the shortening mixture.
Add flour alternately with the milk and banana, beating after each addition.
Fold in the well-beaten egg white.
Spread batter into well-greased 4 by 2 by 1½-inch loaf pan
Baked at 325° for about 45 minutes until crumb is dry when tested with toothpick. If a browner loaf is desired, temperature may be raised to 450° for the last 5 minutes of baking.
Remove bread from oven. Let stand 5 minutes. Loosen loaf with spatula and turn out on a rack.

* Note: A mashed banana can be used in many mixtures in which
        there have been substitutes. It helps to hold the mixture
        together and adds flavor.

                                                                AIA

Glutenfree, Wheatfree

Batter Bread

    2 cups cornmeal
    5 teaspoons baking powder
    1½ teaspoons salt
    1 cup rice, cooked
    2 eggs, beaten
    4 tablespoons fat, melted
    2¼ cups milk

Sift together cornmeal, baking powder and salt. Mix with rice. Combine eggs, fat and milk. Add this to first mixture. Beat until smooth. Turn mixture into two well-greased 8-inch square pans. Bake at 425° for about 30 minutes.

AIA

Glutenfree, Wheatfree

Banana Bread

> 1 cup unsifted rice flour
> ½ teaspoon salt
> 3 teaspoons baking powder
> 4 tablespoons shortening
> 1 ripe banana (medium-sized)
> 4 tablespoons sugar
> 2 egg yolks
> ½ cup milk
> 2 egg whites, well beaten

Measure flour, baking powder and salt; sift. Cream softened shortening, add sugar and blend. Stir in unbeaten egg yolks. Add flour alternately with milk. Fold in with beaten egg whites. Mash banana well and fold in. Spread batter into well-greased loaf pan (8 by 4 by 3-inch) and bake at 325° oven for 45 minutes.

AIA

Glutenfree, Wheatfree

Corn Bread

> 1 cup cornmeal
> 2 tablespoons sugar
> ¼ teaspoon salt
> 2 teaspoons baking powder
> 2 eggs
> ½ cup milk
> 2 tablespoons shortening

Mix dry ingredients. Melt shortening. Add shortening, eggs and milk all at once to dry ingredients and blend well. Pour into greased 8-inch square pan. Bake at 425° for 20-25 minutes.

AIA

Milkfree, Wheatfree

Barley Bread

   1 teaspoon sugar
   1 cup barley flour
   ¼ cup rice flour
   1 tablespoon baking powder
   ¼ teaspoon baking soda
   ¼ teaspoon salt
   ⅛ cup soybean milk
   ⅛ cup corn oil
   1 cup water

Put all dry ingredients in bowl unsifted. Put all wet ingredients in at once. Mix until blended. Bake at 250° for about 45 minutes. Bread will keep for a week in refrigerator.

AIA

Milkfree, Wheatfree

Raisin Oat Bread

   1 cup rolled oats
   1 cup hot water
   2 eggs
   ¼ cup sugar
   ¼ cup molasses
   ¼ teaspoon salt
   1 cup oat flour
   ¼ teaspoon baking soda
   3 teaspoons baking powder
   ¼ cup chopped raisins

Mix oats with hot water; let stand 5 minutes. Stir in eggs, sugar, molasses and salt. Add oat flour, baking powder, baking soda and raisins; mix well. Turn into greased 9 by 5 by 3-inch loaf pan and let stand 20 minutes in warm place. Bake at 350° for 45 minutes.

AIA

Milkfree, Wheatfree

Orange Bread

Orange mixture

    peel of 2 oranges
    ½ cup sugar
    ½ cup water

    2 cups barley flour
    ½ cup sugar
    ½ teaspoon salt
    3 teaspoons baking powder
    2 eggs, beaten
    ½ cup orange juice
    3 tablespoons fat, melted

Cover orange peel with water; boil 10 minutes. Drain. Add more water; boil 10 minutes or until tender. Chop peel in food chopper. Add ½ cup water and sugar and cook until thick.
Sift dry ingredients together. Add beaten eggs, orange juice, melted fat and orange mixture. Combine well. Pour into well-greased loaf pan. Bake at 350° for 60 to 70 minutes.

AIA

Eggfree, Milkfree

Homemade White Bread

    3 cups boiling water
    1 tablespoon salt
    6 tablespoons sugar
    ¼ cup shortening

Combine and cool to lukewarm, about 20 minutes.

    1 cup lukewarm water
    2 packages dry yeast
    2 teaspoons sugar

Stir and let work for 10 minutes. Combine yeast and hot water mixtures and stir. Add 4 cups bread flour and beat with spoon. Add 4 more cups flour. Knead or stir well for 5 minutes.
Grease a very large bowl, place dough in it covered with sheet of

greased wax paper and tea towel. Let rise for 1 hour or longer until double in bulk. Punch down and divide into 4 loaves. (Meat loaf pans are a good size.) Place in greased pans, let rise at least another ½ hour until doubled. Bake ½ hour at 350°. This makes a light moist loaf that doesn't seem to dry out even after 3 days, if kept in plastic bag.

AIA

Eggfree, Milkfree

Soya Bread

¼ cup oil
½ cup brown sugar
1½ teaspoons salt
2 cups soybean milk or water

Combine.
Dissolve 1 cake yeast or 1 package dry yeast in ½ cup lukewarm water, then add to above mixture.
Combine 5¾ cups white flour and 1¼ cups soya flour. Work into mixture and knead. Place in greased bowl and let rise to double in bulk. Punch down, let rest 10 minutes. Cut in half and put in pans. Let rise to double in bulk. Bake at 350° for 40 minutes.

AIA

Eggfree, Milkfree

Whole Wheat Bread

1 package dry yeast
½ teaspoon sugar
¼ cup lukewarm water

Combine, stir and leave in warm place 10 minutes.

⅔ cup molasses or ½ cup sugar
3 tablespoons shortening
2½ teaspoons salt
2 cups hot water

Combine, stir well and cool to lukewarm. Add yeast mixture to this. Combine 3 cups whole wheat flour and 3 cups all-purpose flour. Add 3 cups of flour mixture to rest of ingredients and beat well. Add rest of flour and mix well. Cover with damp cloth, leave in warm place till double in bulk. Beat and turn into greased loaf pans, filling each pan about half full. Cover and let rise again till double in bulk. Bake in hot oven (400°) for about 50 minutes.

AIA

Glutenfree, Milkfree, Wheatfree

Soya-Rice Banana Bread

 1 cup sugar
 2 eggs
 3 ripe bananas (medium-sized)
 1 teaspoon vanilla extract
 ¼ cup margarine
 3 tablespoons water (or milk)
 1 teaspoon salt

Blend above ingredients in mixing bowl or blender.

 ½ cup carefully sifted soya flour
 1½ cups carefully sifted rice flour
 1 teaspoon baking soda

Mix wet and dry ingredients together thoroughly. Pour into 5 well greased soup tins and place on tray and into a slightly warm oven for 45 minutes. Then preheat oven at 350° and bake 25 to 30 minutes. Let stand 5 minutes and remove bread from tins. Refrigerate all but currently used loaf.

Note: If mixture seems too dry add a bit more liquid.

AIA

Glutenfree, Milkfree, Wheatfree

Caraway Sponge Bread

 6 eggs, separated
 ¾ cup potato flour
 ½ cup rice flour
 2 teaspoons baking powder
 1¼ teaspoons salt*
 ⅛ teaspoon pepper*
 6 tablespoons sugar
 caraway seeds (optional)

About 1 hour ahead, separate eggs and let stand to room temperature.

When ready to make bread, start heating oven to 350°. Line bottom of 8 by 4 by 3-inch loaf pan with wax paper. Stir together, then sift until well blended, potato flour, rice flour, baking powder, salt and pepper.

In large bowl, beat egg whites until soft mounds form; beat in sugar, a tablespoon at a time, then continue to beat until stiff peaks form.

In medium bowl, beat egg yolks until light, creamy and fluffy—at least 5 minutes at high speed.

Sprinkle about one-third flour mixture over whites; fold whites and flour together until well mixed; repeat two times; fold in 1 tablespoon caraway seeds, if desired.

Carefully fold beaten yolks into flour mixture until well blended. Pour batter into pan (it will be very full). Lightly sprinkle top of bread with caraway seeds, if desired. Bake 45 to 50 minutes or until top is golden-brown and crisp.

Cool 1 hour before removing from pan. Center of bread may shrink slightly during cooling. Let bread stand about 3 hours before slicing. This bread is excellent toasted.

* If desired, 1½ teaspoons seasoned salt may be substituted for the salt and pepper.

                                                                    AIA

Eggfree, Milkfree

Oatmeal Batter Bread

Dissolve 1 package dry yeast in 1¼ cups warm water. Let stand 10 minutes.

Stir into yeast mixture

    3 tablespoons sugar
    1½ teaspoons salt
    2 tablespoons soft shortening

Add and beat for 2 minutes

    1 cup all-purpose flour
    1 cup rolled oats

Add

    1½ cups all-purpose flour
    ½ cup golden raisins

Cover, let rise till double in bulk. Then stir hard for one minute. Put in greased loaf pan 9 by 5 by 3-inch. Cover, let rise again until one inch from top of pan. Bake at 375° for 45 minutes. Remove from oven and brush with shortening.

AIA

Biscuits

Eggfree, Glutenfree, Wheatfree

Baking Powder Biscuits

- 1¾ cups rice flour
- 5 tablespoons shortening
- ¼ teaspoon salt
- ¾ cup milk or water
- 2 tablespoons baking powder

Sift dry ingredients. Cut in shortening. Add liquid. Roll to about ½-inch thickness, shape with cutter. Bake at 400° for about 15 minutes.

Variation: Dip a cube of sugar in orange juice and then press into the biscuit before baking. *Or:* Roll the dough into a rectangular shape, sprinkle with brown sugar and cinnamon, add raisins or nuts. Roll as for cinnamon rolls, slice into ½-inch pieces, place on baking sheet and bake as for biscuits.

AIA

Eggfree, Glutenfree, Wheatfree

Baking Powder Biscuits

- ⅝ cup potato flour
- 2 teaspoons baking powder
- ¼ teaspoon salt
- 3 tablespoons shortening
- ½ cup milk

Sift together dry ingredients. Cut shortening in finely. Stir in milk to make a soft dough. Round up and knead lightly on lightly floured board. Roll out about ½ inch thick. Cut and place on ungreased baking sheet. Bake at 500° for 10 minutes or until golden brown. Serve hot.

AIA

Eggfree, Milkfree

Biscuit Mix

Sift together

    9 cups all-purpose flour
    2 tablespoons salt
    ¼ cup baking powder

Mix in 2 cups shortening, in a large bowl, until it resembles cornmeal. Store in refrigerator. To be used in various quick breads and biscuits.

AIA

Eggfree, Milkfree

Baking Powder Biscuits

    3 cups Biscuit Mix
    2 tablespoons liquid shortening, plus water to make ¾ cup.

Mix together lightly. Turn out on floured board and pat to ½-inch thickness. Cut with 2-inch cookie cutter. Bake at 450° for 15 minutes.
Yield: about 18 biscuits. Biscuits may be frozen for future use.

AIA

Eggfree, Wheatfree

Baking Powder Biscuits

    ⅝ cup rice flour
    3 teaspoons baking powder*
    ⅛ teaspoon salt
    ½ teaspoon sugar
    4 tablespoons shortening
    ¼ cup milk

* Note: Use Clabbergirl or Arm and Hammer baking powder, not Calumet. Calumet gives a metal taste to the biscuits.

AIA

Eggfree, Glutenfree, Wheatfree

Cheese Biscuits

    1 cup rice flour
    1 teaspoon sugar
    ½ teaspoon salt
    2 teaspoons baking powder
    ¼ cup butter or margarine
    1 cup grated Cheddar cheese
    ½ cup milk

Sift flour, sugar, salt and baking powder together, then sift into mixing bowl. Add butter and blend. Add grated cheese and blend. Add milk. Stir with fork and roll out to ½ inch thick on floured board. Cut with knife into 1-inch squares. Place on greased baking sheet. Bake at 375° for 15 minutes or until lightly brown.
Yield: 50.

AIA

Eggfree, Wheatfree

Rye-Soya Biscuits

    2 cups rye flour
    1 cup soya flour
    2 tablespoons baking powder
    1 teaspoon salt
    4 tablespoons shortening
    1¼ cup milk

Sift dry ingredients into a mixing bowl. Blend in shortening with pastry blender. Gradually add milk, stirring until mixture forms a soft ball. Turn onto a board floured with a little rye flour. Pat into a sheet about ½ inch thick. Cut into rounds with a biscuit cutter. Place on an ungreased baking sheet. Bake at 450° for 10 to 15 minutes.
Variation: Oat flour may be substituted for soya flour. Cornstarch may be substituted for soya flour.

Muffins

Eggfree, Wheatfree

Soya Muffins

  ½ cup boiled riced potatoes
  ½ cup potato water or milk
  2 tablespoons oil
  ½ teaspoon salt
  4 tablespoons sugar
  ⅓ cup soya flour
  ⅓ cup rice flour
  ⅓ cup potato flour
  3 teaspoons baking powder

Grease 8 muffin tins.
Sift flours, salt, sugar, baking powder together.
Mix potato, milk, and oil together.
Combine all ingredients together. Do not beat!
Fill tins ⅔ full.
Bake for 25 to 30 minutes at 400°.
Remove from pan immediately and allow muffins to cool on a rack.

AIA

Eggfree, Milkfree

Date and Nut Muffins

Mix together

  ¾ teaspoon baking soda
  8-oz. package chopped dates
  ¾ cup hot water
  ¼ cup liquid shortening

Mix together and add to date mixture

  1½ cups sifted all-purpose flour
  ½ cup sugar
  ¼ cup chopped nuts
  ½ teaspoon vanilla extract

Stir until dry ingredients are just moistened. Bake in greased muffin tins at 375° for 25 minutes.
Yield: 12 muffins.

AIA

Glutenfree, Wheatfree

Rice Muffins

    2 cups rice flour
    2 teaspoons baking powder
    ½ cup sugar
    1 teaspoon salt
    1 egg
    1½ cups milk or water
    2 tablespoons butter or margarine

Sift dry ingredients. Combine egg, milk and melted fat. Add to the dry ingredients. Stir ingredients just enough to combine. Fill greased muffin tins ⅔ full. Bake at 400° for about 25 minutes.

AIA

Cornmeal Potato Starch Muffins

    ⅔ cup white cornmeal
    ⅓ cup potato flour
    2 teaspoons baking powder
    ½ teaspoon salt
    ½ teaspoon sugar
    1 egg
    ½ cup water or milk
    1 teaspoon fat, melted

Sift dry ingredients together. Beat egg slightly, add milk and stir gently into dry ingredients. Add melted fat and stir only enough to combine. Fill greased muffin tins ⅔ full. Bake at 400° for about 30 minutes.

AIA

Glutenfree, Wheatfree

Soya Muffins

    1 egg yolk
    3 tablespoons milk
    ¼ cup water
    ¾ cup soya flour
    1 teaspoon baking powder
    ¼ teaspoon salt
    2 teaspoons butter or margarine, melted
    3 egg whites

Beat egg yolks. Add milk and water. Add sifted dry ingredients. Stir only until combined. Add melted fat. Fold in stiffly beaten egg whites Fill well-greased muffin tins ⅔ full. Bake at 375° for about 15 minutes.

AIA

Glutenfree, Wheatfree

Corn Muffins

    1 cup white or yellow cornmeal
    ¾ cup unsifted rice flour
    4 teaspoons baking powder
    ½ cup margarine, melted
    1 cup milk
    ½ teaspoon salt
    ¼ cup sugar
    1 egg yolk
    1 egg white, beaten stiff but not dry

Combine dry ingredients. Add egg yolk, melted butter and milk to dry ingredients; stir until just smooth. Fold in beaten egg white until just mixed. Fill muffin tins ⅔ full and bake in 425° oven until lightly browned. Serve warm.
Yield: 12 muffins.

AIA

Wheatfree

Barley Muffins

    4 tablespoons shortening
    ¼ cup-sugar
    ½ teaspoon salt
    1 egg
    ¾ to 1 cup milk
    1½ cup barley flour
    5 teaspoons baking powder

Mix and sift the dry ingredients, then add the well-beaten egg and liquid. Beat thoroughly and add the melted shortening. Bake in oiled muffin tins in a moderate oven (375°) for about 30 minutes.

AIA

Wheatfree

Rye Muffins with Egg

> 1 cup coarse rye flour
> ¼ teaspoon salt
> 2 teaspoons baking powder
> 2 tablespoons sugar
> 1 egg
> ½ cup milk
> 2 teaspoons fat, melted

Sift dry ingredients. Combine beaten egg, milk, and melted fat. Add to dry ingredients, stir just enough to combine (should have rough appearance). Fill greased muffin tins ⅔ full, handling the batter as little as possible. Bake at 400° for about 25 minutes.

AIA

Eggfree, Wheatfree

Rye Muffins

> ½ cup cornstarch
> ½ cup white rye flour
> 2 teaspoons baking powder
> ½ cup milk
> 2 tablespoons plus 1½ teaspoons oil
> ½ teaspoons salt *

Sift dry ingredients together. Combine oil and milk. Add liquids to sifted ingredients all at once. Stir only until combined. Drop into greased muffin tins, handling as little as possible. Bake at 450° for 15 to 20 minutes.

* Salt may be decreased to ¼ teaspoon if desired.

AIA

Eggfree, Glutenfree, Milkfree, Wheatfree

Soya-Potato Muffins

> 1 cup soya flour
> 1 cup potato flour

1 teaspoon salt
2 tablespoons baking powder
1 tablespoon sugar
1 tablespoon brown sugar
½ cup fat, melted
¾ to 1 cup water

Sift dry ingredients four times. Add fat and water. Beat well. Fill greased muffin tins ⅔ full. Bake at 350° for 25 to 30 minutes. Yield. 12 muffins.

AIA

Eggfree, Glutenfree, Milkfree, Wheatfree

Rice-Soya Muffins

1 cup rice flour
½ cup soya flour
½ teaspoon salt
3 teaspoons baking powder
1 tablespoon sugar
¾ cup water
2 tablespoons melted shortening

Mix and sift dry ingredients three times. Stir in water and the melted shortening; beat until very well blended. Bake in small greased muffin tins in 400° oven for 20 to 25 minutes.
Yield: 8 small muffins.

AIA

Eggfree, Glutenfree, Milkfree, Wheatfree

Banana Muffins

2 well-ripened bananas, mashed
⅓ cup sugar
¼ cup oil or milkfree margarine

Add and mix

2 teaspoons baking powder
½ teaspoon vanilla extract
1¼ cups rice flour
½ teaspoon baking soda
¼ teaspoon salt

Turn into greased muffin tins or a small loaf pan. Bake at 325° for 25 minutes for muffins and ¾ hour for loaf.

AIA

Glutenfree, Milkfree, Wheatfree

Potato Starch Muffins

> 5 egg whites, beaten
> 2½ teaspoons sugar
> ½ teaspoon salt
> 2½ tablespoons ice water
> 5 egg yolks, beaten slightly
> 1 cup potato flour
> 2 teaspoons baking powder

Beat the sugar and salt into the egg whites until they are stiff but not dry. Gradually add the ice water to the egg white mixture. Add the slightly beaten egg yolks to the egg white mixture. Sift together the potato flour and baking powder. Add flour to the egg mixture and mix thoroughly. Place in greased muffin tins immediately. Bake at 400° for 20 minutes.
Yield: 12 large muffins.
Variation: This recipe may be baked in a medium-sized loaf pan with cooking time increased accordingly. Very good toasted.

AIA

Glutenfree, Milkfree, Wheatfree

Potato-Soya Muffins

> ½ cup potato flour
> ½ cup soya flour
> 2 tablespoons sugar
> 2 teaspoons baking powder
> ¼ teaspoon salt
> 2 egg yolks
> 6 tablespoons cold water
> 2 tablespoons melted shortening
> 2 egg whites, beaten stiff

Mix and sift dry ingredients. Beat egg yolks with water and combine with dry ingredients. Gradually stir in the melted shorten-

ing. Fold in the beaten egg whites. Put in oiled muffin tins and bake at 400° for 25 to 30 minutes.
Yield: 8 muffins.

Note: The above procedure yields a popover-type muffin. If a more compact texture is desired, mix as follows: Mix and sift dry ingredients. Beat whole egg with water and combine with melted shortening. Make a well in dry ingredients and add liquid. Mix only to coat all the dry ingredients. Put in oiled muffin tins and bake as directed above.
Yield: 6 muffins

AIA

Glutenfree, Wheatfree

Rice Chex Muffins

1 cup Rice Chex
1 cup rice flour
½ teaspoon salt
1 or 2 eggs
1 cup milk
2½ teaspoons baking powder
2 tablespoons sugar or honey
¼ cup soft butter or margarine

Combine Rice Chex and milk and set aside. Combine rice flour, baking powder, salt and sugar. Add egg and butter to Rice Chex and mix well. Combine with dry ingredients, stirring only until mixed. Bake in greased muffin tins at 400° for about 30 minutes.

AIA

Glutenfree, Wheatfree

Southern Corn Muffins

1 cup boiling water
1 cup white cornmeal
½ cup milk
½ teaspoon salt
2 teaspoons baking powder
1 tablespoon soft butter or margarine
1 egg, well beaten

Pour boiling water over cornmeal. Beat in milk, salt, baking powder, butter and egg. Pour into very well-greased glass muffin cups. Bake 25 to 30 minutes at 475°. Serve hot.
Yield: 9 medium-sized muffins.

AIA

Glutenfree, Wheatfree

Rice Flour Muffins

    1 cup unsifted rice flour
    ½ teaspoon salt
    3 teaspoons baking powder
    ¼ cup vegetable shortening
    ¼ cup sugar
    2 egg yolks
    ¾ cup milk
    2 egg whites, well beaten
    ½ teaspoon vanilla, lemon or almond extract

Sift rice flour, baking powder and salt together twice. Cream softened shortening, add sugar and cream together. Stir in egg yolks. Add flour mixture alternately with milk, beating after each addition. Fold in well-beaten (but not dry) egg whites and extract. Spoon into well-greased muffin tins. Bake 30 minutes at 325° or until lightly browned.
Yield: 6 muffins.

AIA

Muffin-Pancake Coffee Cake Mix

    2 cups oat flour
    1 cup millet flour
    1 cup barley flour
    1 cup soya flour
    ½ cup sugar
    ⅓ cup baking powder
    1 teaspoon salt

Measure all ingredients into a bowl large enough to allow them to be stirred and turned until thoroughly mixed. Store in jars in refrigerator.

Muffins

Spoon mix into 1 cup measure. Do not sift. Pour into medium bowl.
Stir 2 tablespoons dry coffee creamer into ⅓ cup hot water.
Add ⅓ cold water.
Mix this with 1 beaten egg. If eggs are not allowed, beat 2 table-spoons Egg Replacer into ¼ cup cold water with a rotary beater until thick and foamy. Use the same as 1 egg. Pour into dry ingredients. Beat together until smooth. Spoon into greased paper muffin cups in muffin pan.
Yield: Six muffins.
Variation: Half-fill cups, add 1 teaspoon jam and fill cups.

Pancakes

Increase the liquid in the muffin recipe above to 1 cup for thinner, consistency.
Bake at 350° on electric skillet or medium hot griddle over burner.
Sprinkle few drops of oil for each pancake. Turn only once.

Coffee Cake

Use recipe for Muffins above.
In 8-inch pan spread ½ cup jam, sprinkle with 2 tablespoons brown sugar and dot with 1 tablespoon margarine.
Spread batter over this. Don't worry about complete cover, as it will spread out while baking.
Sprinkle the top with either

    cinnamon and sugar
    2 tablespoons brown sugar
    2 tablespoons margarine
    ¼ cup oatmeal rubbed together
    flaked coconut
    sesame seeds

Bake 20 minutes at 350°.
Leftovers can be frozen and reheated another time.

                                                            Wall

Waffles, Griddle Cakes and Pancakes

Glutenfree, Wheatfree

Rice Waffles

  1¾ cups rice flour
  3 teaspoons baking powder
  1 teaspoon salt
  1½ cups milk
  2 egg yolks, beaten
  3 tablespoons fat, melted
  2 egg whites, beaten

Sift dry ingredients together; add milk and egg yolks, then melted fat. Fold in stiffly beaten egg whites. Bake in hot waffle iron.

AIA

Eggfree, Glutenfree, Milkfree, Wheatfree

Rice Waffles

  2 cups rice flour
  4 teaspoons baking powder
  1 tablespoon sugar
  2 cups water
  3 tablespoons corn oil

Sift dry ingredients together, add water and oil gradually, stirring mixture constantly until smooth. Bake in hot waffle iron greased with corn oil.

AIA

Glutenfree, Wheatfree

Rice Griddle Cakes

Mix, then sift

  2 cups rice flour
  2½ teaspoons baking powder
  2 teaspoons maple sugar
  2 teaspoons salt

Beat mixture while adding 2 cups milk. Add and barely blend 1 beaten egg and 1 tablespoon melted butter. Bake on a hot griddle.

AIA

Glutenfree, Wheatfree

Rice Pancakes

2 eggs
1¼ cups buttermilk
¾ cup rice flour
1 tablespoon sugar
½ teaspoon salt
1½ teaspoons baking powder

Beat eggs and add part of buttermilk. Stir in sifted dry ingredients and add remainder of buttermilk. Bake on hot griddle.

AIA

Eggfree, Glutenfree, Milkfree, Wheatfree

Rice-Potato Pancakes

½ cup rice flour
⅓ cup potato flour
¼ teaspoon salt
4 teaspoons sugar
½ teaspoon baking powder
water (or milk if allowed)

Sift dry ingredients together. Store in airtight container. When needed, mix about ¼ cup liquid with each ½ cup of mix. Stir and cook as regular pancakes.

AIA

Glutenfree, Milkfree, Wheatfree

Cornmeal Pancakes

Mix

⅓ cup yellow cornmeal
1 tablespoon sugar
2 tablespoons dry coffee creamer

Scald with ⅓ cup boiling water and stir until thick.
Add 1 egg beaten into ⅔ cup cold water.
Add ⅓ cup corn flour (Masa Harina, if you can find it).
Beat batter smooth and bake on medium hot griddle (350°).
Sprinkle a few drops of oil on griddle for each cake. Turn only once.
Makes eight 4-inch cakes.
Leftover pancakes should be wrapped in paper towels with a towel between each cake, put into plastic bag and frozen. To use, spread on sheet of foil, still in paper towel, cover with foil and heat 15 minutes at 350°.

Wall

Eggfree, Glutenfree, Milkfree, Wheatfree

Crisp Corn Pone

    1 teaspoon bacon drippings
    ½ cup boiling water
    ½ cup cornmeal
    ½ teaspoon salt
    1 tablespoon sugar

Add drippings to boiling water. Stir in cornmeal, salt and sugar and stir over low heat until mixture thickens. Spread mixture on well-greased 9-inch pie pan. Dot with milkfree margarine. Bake at 450° for 20 minutes. Place under preheated broiler about 5 minutes until lightly browned. Serve in pie-shaped wedges with milkfree margarine.

AIA

Puddings and Desserts

Eggfree, Glutenfree, Milkfree, Wheatfree

Fruit Crisp Dessert

    1 can (16 oz.) peach halves
    1 can (16 oz.) pear halves
    1 teaspoon lemon juice
    2 cups rice cereal
    3 tablespoons brown sugar
    1 teaspoon grated lemon rind
    ½ teaspoon salt
    3 tablespoons milkfree margarine

Remove fruit from juice and place halves, alternating peach and pear, hollow side down in shallow 9-inch baking dish or pie plate. Add lemon juice to ¼ cup peach juice and ¼ cup pear juice, pour over fruit.

Crush rice cereal into coarse crumbs. Mix with brown sugar, lemon rind, nutmeg and salt. Melt margarine, pour over crumb mixture, mix well. Spoon evenly over fruit. Bake at 350° for about 1 hour. Serve warm.

AIA

Eggfree, Glutenfree, Milkfree, Wheatfree

Fruit-Rice Pudding

    1½ teaspoons gelatin
    ¼ cup cold water
    ⅓ cup hot pineapple juice
    2 tablespoons sugar
    ⅛ teaspoon salt
    ½ cup rice, cooked
    ½ cup diced pineapple and peaches

Soak gelatin in cold water. Dissolve soaked gelatin in hot pineapple juice. Add sugar and salt. Chill until slightly thickened. Add cooked rice, fruit and vanilla. Turn into molds and chill until firm.

Variation: Other combinations of fruit may be used.

AIA

Eggfree, Glutenfree, Milkfree, Wheatfree

Apple Strudel

    3½ cups corn flakes, slightly crushed
    2 cups sliced apples, sprinkled with few drops of lemon juice
    ½ cup sugar
    ½ teaspoon ground cinnamon or nutmeg
    2 tablespoons milkfree margarine

Butter baking dish. Arrange crumbs and apples in layers, sprinkle the apples with sugar and spices and dot with margarine. Cover and bake at 375° for about 40 minutes or until apples are soft.

AIA

Glutenfree, Milkfree, Wheatfree

Rice Pudding

1½ cups uncooked rice
1 cup orange juice
1 large can fruit cocktail
2 eggs
salt to taste
sugar to taste (about ½ cup)

Grease casserole, pour in mixed ingredients, sprinkle cinnamon on top. Bake at 350° for about 1 hour. If more liquid is required, add fruit cocktail juice during baking time.

AIA

Glutenfree, Milkfree, Wheatfree

Lemon Snow

1 cup sugar
juice from 2 lemons
2½ teaspoons gelatin
5 eggs
1 grated lemon rind

Dissolve gelatin in warm water. Combine egg yolks with sugar and beat until creamy and light. To this mixture add the lemon juice and grated lemon rind. Beat egg whites until stiff. Add by folding into lemon mixture. Add in the dissolved gelatin stirring slowly. Pour mixture into glass or serving bowl. Chill until time to serve. Yield: 6 servings.

AIA

Glutenfree, Milkfree, Wheatfree

Pineapple Upside-Down Cake

3 tablespoons margarine
½ cup brown sugar
⅛ teaspoon ground cinnamon
1 1-lb can pineapple slices
maraschino cherries

6 tablespoons unsifted potato flour
¼ teaspoon salt
6 tablespoons sugar
1 teaspoon baking powder
2 tablespoons salad oil
2 eggs, separated
1 teaspoon grated lemon rind
3 tablespoons syrup drained from pineapple slices
⅛ teaspoon cream of tartar

In an 8-inch-square cake pan, melt butter or margarine in oven; then sprinkle with brown sugar and cinnamon.

Arrange 7 drained pineapple slices in butter-sugar mixture, fill centers of slices with cherries. Set aside.

In medium bowl, mix together potato flour, salt, sugar, baking powder. Add, in the following order, salad oil, egg yolks, lemon rind and 3 tablespoons juice. Mix until smooth. In another bowl, beat egg whites with cream of tartar until stiff peaks form. Do not underbeat. Fold egg yolk mixture into whites until smooth. Pour cake mixture over pineapple slices; bake at 350° for 45 minutes, until very dark brown. Let stand on rack for 10 minutes, then loosen cake from sides, turn onto a flat cake plate. Serve warm or cold.

Yield: 9 servings.

AIA

Eggfree, Milkfree, Wheatfree

Peach Betty

1 can (1 pound) cling peach slices with syrup
2 tablespoons lemon juice
½ teaspoon ground cinnamon
1½ cups rolled oats, coarsely ground
½ teaspoon salt
¼ teaspoon baking soda
½ teaspoon vanilla extract
⅓ cup dark brown sugar
¼ cup melted shortening

In 2-quart casserole arrange peaches and syrup; sprinkle with lemon juice and cinnamon.

Mix together ground rolled oats, salt, baking soda and brown sugar; add melted shortening and vanilla; mix until dry ingredients are dampened. Cover peaches with crumb mixture; bake 50 min-

utes at 350°. Serve warm with Lemon Sauce (p. 238), if desired.
Yield: 6 servings.

AIA

Eggfree, Milkfree, Wheatfree

Fruit Torte

> 1 cup chopped dates, figs, cooked prunes or apricots
> ¼ cup granulated sugar
> ¼ cup fruit juice or water
> 2½ cups rolled oats, uncooked
> ½ teaspoon baking soda
> ½ teaspoon salt
> 2 teaspoons grated orange rind
> ½ cup brown sugar
> ½ cup shortening, softened
> ¼ cup water

Combine fruit, ¼ cup sugar and fruit juice. Cook until thick. Cool.
Grind oats with fine blade of food chopper. Measure 2 cups of the
ground oats.
Mix together ground oats, soda, salt, orange rind and brown sugar.
Add shortening and water. Beat until smooth. Divide dough in
half. Spread one half of dough in greased 8-inch square pan. Spread
with fruit mixture. Roll remaining dough between 2 sheets of
waxed paper; chill, remove paper and place dough over filling.
Bake at 350° for 30 minutes. Cut in squares and serve warm or
cold.
Yield: 9 servings.

AIA

Eggless Tapioca Cream

Whip 2 tablespoons Egg Replace with ¼ cup water until fluffy. Heat
in double boiler.

> 2 cups water
> ½ cup dry coffee creamer
> ⅓ cup sugar
> 3 tablespoons quick cooking tapioca

Cook 5 minutes.
Pour fluffy mixture into hot mixture.

Cook for 15 minutes over low burner, stirring so the fluffy mixture is thoroughly blended.
Chill and serve.   Wall

Eggfree, Glutenfree, Wheatfree

Rice Whip

     1½ cups cooked rice
     ¼ cup sugar
     ⅛ teaspoon salt
     ¾ cup whipping cream or nondairy product
     1 package frozen strawberries

Whip cream, add sugar and salt, and fold into cooked rice. Serve strawberries as sauce, over and under the rice whip.
Yield: 4 servings.
Variations: Any other frozen fruit or chocolate sauce made with cocoa or maple syrup may be used.

AIA

Eggfree, Glutenfree, Wheatfree

Milk Jelly

     1 envelope or 3 teaspoons gelatin
     3 tablespoons hot water
     1½ cups milk (fresh, evaporated or powdered)
     2 tablespoons sugar or artificial sweetener to taste
     Flavoring, coloring if allowed

Dissolve gelatin in hot water. Add sugar, stir gradually into milk. Flavor to taste. Chill.
Variations: Top with strawberries or other fruits or with colored mini-marshmallows. Honey may be substituted for sugar for a more nutritious dessert.

AIA

Eggfree, Glutenfree, Wheatfree

Baked Rice Pudding

     1 cup uncooked regular white rice
     1 cup (1⅔ cups) evaporated milk

1¼ cups water
¼ teaspoon salt
⅛ teaspoon grated nutmeg
1 teaspoon grated lemon peel
2 tablespoons butter or margarine
1 teaspoon vanilla extract
½ cup brown sugar or molasses

Combine all ingredients in 1½-quart casserole; mix well. Cover and bake in slow oven (325°) 1 to 1½ hours or until liquid is absorbed and rice is tender.
Yield: 6 servings.

AIA

Eggfree, Glutenfree, Milkfree, Wheatfree

Fruit Tapioca or Sago

½ cup syrup from canned peaches
1 tablespoon quick cooking tapioca or sago
½ peach, sliced
½ banana, sliced
2 tablespoons pitted cherries

Cook tapioca and peach syrup in top of double boiler until transparent, about 20 minutes. Fold in fruit and chill.

AIA

Glutenfree, Milkfree, Wheatfree

Steamed Carrot Pudding

1½ cups seedless raisins
¾ cup dates or prunes or both
⅓ cup lemon or orange peel
¾ cup suet or shortening
¾ cup brown sugar
⅓ cup molasses
2 or 3 eggs
¾ cup grated apple
⅛ teaspoon each ground cloves, ginger and allspice

1 cup grated carrot
½ cup canned cherries and juice
¾ cup soya flour
¾ cup rice flour
1½ tablespoons baking powder
½ teaspoon baking soda
¾ teaspoon salt
½ teaspoon ground cinnamon
⅜ teaspoon grated nutmeg

Sift all dry ingredients together 3 times for thorough blending. Combine all ingredients and mix thoroughly. If mixture seems too thin add more soya and rice flour in equal proportions. Turn into a greased mold or in a smaller mold and cover with aluminum foil, tying firmly with string. Steam in steamer or over boiling water on a rack for 3 to 5 hours. The longer steaming makes a lighter pudding. Allow to season for several weeks before using. Resteam until heated through before serving.

Sauce: 1 tablespoon arrowroot flour, 1 cup water, 3 tablespoons brown sugar, 1 teaspoon corn oil margarine, few grains of salt and flavoring. Cook until thickened.

AIA

Milkfree*

St. Nicholas Pudding

2 cups seedless raisins
1 cup cut up pitted prunes
¾ cup slivered mixed lemon peel and citron
½ cup of halved blanched almonds
1 cup of chopped suet
1 cup of soft bread crumbs or glutenfree or wheat-free bread crumbs
1 cup brown sugar, lightly packed
1 cup once-sifted pastry flour or ⅞ cup of once-sifted bread flour or substitute flour to suit diet

1 teaspoon baking powder
½ teaspoon baking soda
1 teaspoon salt
1 teaspoon ground cinnamon
½ teaspoon grated nutmeg
¼ teaspoon each of ground ginger, mace, allspice and cloves
¾ cup grated raw apple
1 cup grated raw carrot
½ cup grated raw potato
3 eggs, well beaten or Egg Replacer
¼ cup grape juice

Prepare and combine the raisins, prunes, peel and almonds if they are being used. Combine suet, bread crumbs and brown sugar. Measure and sift together flour, baking powder, baking soda, salt and spices. Prepare and mix apples and vegetables.
Combine these four mixtures thoroughly. Stir in well-beaten eggs and grape juice. Turn into two buttered pudding bowls. Cover bowls loosely with a scalded pudding cloth or parchment or aluminum foil. Tie in place. Steam over plenty of boiling water for 3½ hours.

* Note: Substitutions may be made as suggested in recipe to produce an eggfree, glutenfree and wheatfree pudding.

AIA

Eggfree, Glutenfree, Wheatfree

Chocolate Snowballs

Boil together 5 minutes, then cool a bit

> ¼ cup margarine
> ½ cup evaporated milk
> 2 cups sugar
> 2 tablespoons cocoa

Add

> 1 teaspoon vanilla
> 2 cups flaked coconut

Shape in balls and roll in more coconut.

AIA

Eggfree, Glutenfree, Milkfree, Wheatfree

Crunch Balls

Cook over low heat, stirring well

> ⅓ cup butter or milkfree margarine
> ½ cup brown sugar
> ½ pound chopped dates

Cool slightly and add

> 2 cups Rice Krispies
> 1 cup flaked coconut
> 1 cup drained pitted cherries

Shape into small balls with greased fingers.

AIA

Pudding Sauces

Eggless Custard Sauce

Whip ¼ cup Egg Replacer into ½ cup water.
Heat in top of double boiler

> 1 cup water
> ¼ cup sugar
> ¼ cup dry coffee creamer

Pour fluffy mixture into hot liquid and cook until thick, stirring constantly. Chill.
Use over gelatin or junket desserts.

Wall

Eggfree, Milkfree, Wheatfree

Lemon Sauce

>   3 tablespoons sugar
>   2 tablespoons cornstarch
>   ¼ teaspoon salt
>   1 teaspoon grated lemon rind
>   1 cup boiling water
>   2 tablespoons shortening
>   2 tablespoons lemon juice

In a medium saucepan combine sugar, cornstarch, salt and lemon rind, slowly stir in boiling water; simmer 5 minutes or until thickened. Add shortening and lemon juice; stir until smooth.
Yield: 6 servings.

AIA

Ice Cream

Eggfree, Glutenfree, Milkfree, Wheatfree

Similac or Isomil Imitation Ice Cream

Mechanical Freezer Method

>   4 13-oz. cans Isomil concentrate (do not dilute with water)
>   2 packets (1 tablespoon per packet) unflavored gelatin (soften in ½ cup cold water)
>   1 cup sugar (add to the gelatin and heat slowly to dissolve sugar and gelatin; cool)
>   ½ cup light corn syrup
>   ½ cup salad or cooking oil
>   2 tablespoons plus 1 teaspoon vanilla extract

Mix all ingredients and freeze in a 1-gallon or 5-quart ice cream freezer. After the mix is frozen, it may be stored in an electric freezer, but it becomes very icy.

AIA

Refrigerator Tray Method

- 1 13-oz. can Isomil concentrate, well chilled (do not dilute with water)
- 1½ teaspoons unflavored gelatin (soften in 2 tablespoons cold water)
- ¼ cup sugar (add to the gelatin and heat slowly to dissolve sugar and gelatin; cool)
- 2 tablespoons light corn syrup
- 1 tablespoon salad or cooking oil
- 2 teaspoons vanilla extract

Blend all ingredients in a blender until thick and creamy. Pour into an ice cube tray or a loaf pan and freeze until very icy. Turn into blender and blend until smooth. Return to freezer and freeze until firm. Allow to soften slightly before serving. Blender capacity for this recipe should be at least 5 cups.

Variations: Fruits such as strawberries, peaches, bananas, pineapple, oranges may be added to the recipe prior to freezing after being mashed or pureed in a blender, depending upon individual tastes and allergies.

AIA

Eggfree Glutenfree, Milkfree, Wheatfree

Imitation Ice Cream Bars

Whip lightly frozen milkless nondairy product, place in Tupperware Ice Tups, insert wooden popsicle stick and freeze. (It will not freeze hard enough to stick to the popsicle sticks when too fluffy.)

AIA

Eggfree, Glutenfree, Milkfree, Wheatfree

Fudgsicles

- ½ cup sugar
- ½ cup water
- 12 oz. semisweet chocolate chips (melt down in top of a double boiler; cool)

Add ½ cup of this mixture to one package of Rich Whip. Place in Tupperware Ice Tups, insert wooden popsicle stick and freeze.
Bars and Fudgsicles can be removed from Ice Tups and stored in

freezer. (Wooden popsicle sticks can be purchased through stationery or hobby shops.)

AIA

Eggfree, Glutenfree, Milkfree, Wheatfree

Ice Cream

Whip 1 package milkless nondairy creamer until stiff.
Add

  ¼ cup sugar
  1 teaspoon Kool-Aid powder (unsweetened) for flavor

Mix sugar and Kool-Aid into milkless nondairy creamer. Turn into a plastic freezer container and freeze.

AIA

Eggfree, Glutenfree, Wheatfree

Pink Ice Cream

  2 teaspoons unflavored gelatin
  ½ cup cold water
  1¾ cups evaporated milk
  ½ cup sugar
  1 teaspoon vanilla extract
  ¼ teaspoon almond extract
  4 drops red food coloring
  ½ cup chopped maraschino cherries
  1½ cups heavy cream, whipped

Soften gelatin in cold water. Heat evaporated milk and sugar in sauce pan, stirring until sugar is dissolved. Add softened gelatin and stir until blended. Cool, then stir in vanilla, almond extract and red food coloring. Turn into freezing tray and chill until slightly thickened. Remove to chilled bowl. Beat quickly until smooth. Fold in cherries and whipped cream. Return to cold tray and freeze.

AIA

Eggfree, Glutenfree, Wheatfree

Pink 'N Pretty Parfait

    4 cups sweetened rice (cooked)
    ½ pint whipping cream
    1 or 2 drops red food coloring
    ½ teaspoon almond extract
    4 tablespoons sugar
    1 package frozen strawberries, thawed

To sweeten the rice, add 2 tablespoons sugar to the rice after cooking. Chill. Just before serving, whip the cream, fold in food color, flavoring and remaining 2 tablespoons sugar. Then fold into the rice, reserving ½ cup for garnish. Fill clear glas serving dishes or parfait glasses with alternate layers of rice mixture and strawberries, reserve a strawberry for top of each. Top with some reserved whipped cream and a berry.

AIA

Eggfree, Glutenfree, Milkfree, Wheatfree

Ice Cream Pie

    ½ cup milkfree margarine, melted
    1 cup brown sugar, firmly packed
    3 cups corn flakes
    1 cup chopped nuts
    1 cup coconut
    1 quart ice cream, slightly softened (use one of the milkfree
        ice cream recipes in this section)

Blend margarine and sugar, mix with next three ingredients. Line bottom and sides of 9-inch pie plate with ⅔ of mixture. Fill with ice cream; sprinkle with rest of mixture, pressing lightly into ice cream. Freeze for several hours.

AIA

Ices

Glutenfree, Milkfree, Wheatfree

Fruit Ice

> 1 14-oz can apricots, plums or peaches
> 1 cup water
> ⅓ cup lemon juice
> ¾ cup light corn syrup
> 2 egg whites, stiffly beaten

Empty fruit and syrup into strainer placed over a bowl; press fruit through strainer (or blend in blender). Reserve.

Combine water, corn syrup and sugar in saucepan. Bring to boil stirring until sugar dissolves and boil 5 minutes. Cool. Add lemon juice and fruit puree. Turn into freezing tray or trays and freeze until ice crystals form.

Turn almost-frozen mixture into bowl and beat until smooth. Fold in beaten egg whites. Return to tray and continue freezing until firm.

Yield: About 1 quart.

AIA

Glutenfree, Milkfree, Wheatfree

Fruit Ice

> 1 container any strained baby fruit
> 1 tablespoon light corn syrup
> 2 tablespoons lemon juice
> 1 egg white, beaten stiff

Combine ingredients and freeze until firm. Remove to a chilled bowl, beat until free of hard lumps but still thick. Place in chilled sherbet or sauce dish (or paper soufflé cups) and finish freezing.

AIA

Eggfree, Glutenfree, Milkfree, Wheatfree

Apricot Sherbet

> 1 envelope unflavored gelatin
> ½ cup cold water

3 cups (2 12-oz. cans) apricot nectar (or orange juice)
¾ cup light corn syrup
3 tablespoons lemon juice
⅛ teaspoon salt

Sprinkle gelatin on water in saucepan. Place over low heat, stirring constantly, until gelatin is dissolved. Stir in remaining ingredients. Pour into 2 refrigerator freezing trays and freeze until firm, about 1 hour. Break up in bowl and beat until light. Return to freezing trays and freeze until firm, 2 or 3 hours. Makes 1½ quarts.

AIA

Blueberry Ice

Beat 1 16-oz. can blueberry pie filling until most of the berries are broken up.
Add

1 6-oz. can frozen lemonade concentrate
2 cans water
1 can unsweetened pineapple juice
¼ cup sugar

Stir until lemonade is melted.
Freeze 3 hours.

Wall

Lemon-Pineapple Sherbet

Boil ¾ cup sugar with 1½ cups water for 10 minutes.
Add ½ cup cold water in which 1 envelope unflavored gelatin has soaked.
Add

1 6-oz. can frozen lemonade concentrate
1 lemonade can of unsweetened pineapple juice

Stir until lemonade is thawed.
Freeze until mushy, about 4 hours.
In large bowl of electric mixer measure ⅓ cup Pillsbury Fluffy White Cake Icing. (This is the only brand I have found to be free of wheat, but this icing mix contains egg white, so if eggs are not allowed, just skip this part and whip up the mushy mixture and refreeze.)
Add ½ cup boiling water and mix at slow speed 1 minute.
Beat at highest speed until very stiff, at least 10 minutes.

Take bowl away from icing mix. Shake or scrape icing from beaters
into bowl but do not clean with water.
Beat mushy mixture with same beater at highest speed. It will
be quite light and fluffy.
Fold the two mixtures together and freeze 3 to 4 hours.

Wall

Pie Crusts

Eggfree, Glutenfree, Milkfree, Wheatfree

Coconut Crust

2 cups flaked coconut
¼ cup butter or margarine (milkfree)

Lightly brown coconut in margarine. Press mixture into bottom
and sides of an oiled 8-inch pie tin. Cool. Two tablespoons of mixture may be reserved to garnish pie.

AIA

Eggfree, Glutenfree, Milkfree, Wheatfree

Rice Crumb Crust

4½ cups rice cereal, crushed finely
¼ cup sugar
⅓ cup milkfree margarine (or butter)

Combine crumbs and sugar. Mix thoroughly. Melt fat, pour over
crumb mixture. Mix until all crumbs are coated with fat. Pack
evenly and firmly onto bottoms and sides of greased 8 or 9-inch
pie pan. Bake at 300° for 10 minutes.
Variation: If you prefer, instead of baking, refrigerate for 1 hour
before filling, then bake.

AIA

Eggfree, Glutenfree, Milkfree, Wheatfree

Crumb Crust

1⅔ cups cookie crumbs (to suit your particular diet)
¼ cup soft butter or milkfree margarine
1 tablespoon sugar

Mix cookie crumbs, soft butter and sugar together. Line 9-inch pie pan, saving some crumb mixture for topping. (This is suitable for cheese cake or cream fillings).

AIA

Eggfree, Glutenfree, Milkfree, Wheatfree

Oat Flour Piecrust

   ½ cup oat flour
   ½ cup barley flour
   1 tablespoon sugar
   ⅓ cup firm margarine
   1 egg yolk plus 1 tablespoon water

Put all ingredients in bowl and mix thoroughly with fork. If too crumbly, use another tablespoon of water. When it forms a ball, roll between two pieces of waxed paper or plastic wrap. Peel off top paper, place over 8-inch pie plate and peel off other paper. Any breaks can be pushed together and "mended." This does not get tough with handling. Press into place with fingers. If a baked shell is desired, bake at 350° for 15 minutes. You can also use this as a bottom crust for pies to be baked. Crumb toppings are best with this type of pie.

Wall

Pie Fillings

Jell-O Pudding and Pie Fillings are wheatfree, milkfree and eggfree. Get the ones you cook, not the instant type. Cool slightly before pouring into crumb crust.
Substitute ½ cup dry coffee creamer in 2 cups hot water for milk in the vanilla pudding. Sprinkle the top of the pie with coconut flakes before chilling.
If eggs are allowed, add 1 egg yolk to puddings and make meringue by whipping the egg white with 2 tablespoons sugar. Spread over the pie and bake 15 minutes at 350°.
Add Cara Coa to vanilla mixture and cook for a chocolate pie.

Wall

Wheatfree

Baked Cheese Pie

    1½ packages (8-oz.) cream cheese
    2 eggs
    sugar
    2 teaspoons vanilla extract
    2 teaspoons lemon juice
    ½ cup commercial sour cream
    ½ teaspoon vanilla extract
    1 corn flake crust

Allow cream cheese and eggs to come to room temperature. Prepare corn flake crust.

In small bowl combine cream cheese, eggs, ½ cup sugar, 2 teaspoons vanilla and lemon juice; beat at medium speed until smooth and creamy. Pour into corn flake crust and bake at 350° for 30 minutes. Meanwhile, blend sour cream, 4 teaspoons sugar and ½ teaspoon vanilla. Spread over surface of baked pie, then return to oven for 10 minutes. Cool almost to room temperature; then refrigerate. Serve cold.

Yield: 8 servings.

AIA

Cakes

The following mixture can be substituted in most recipes* calling for all-purpose flour.

    2 cups wheat flour
    ¾ cup potato flour
    ¾ cup corn flour
    ¼ cup soya flour
    1 cup rice flour
    6 tablespoons arrowroot flour
    6 tablespoons tapioca flour

* Note: With this mixture, the starch flavor is eliminated, thus
        enabling the whole family to enjoy the same foods. Our
        only recommendation is that bread, gingerbread, dough-
        nuts, fritters and shortbread not be made with this mixture,
        but only with a special glutenfree recipe. The baking re-
        sults in our tests were poor.

AIA

Eggfree, Glutenfree, Milkfree, Wheatfree

Banana Cake

> 1 cup mashed bananas
> ¼ cup corn oil
> ¾ cup sugar
> ½ teaspoon vanilla extract
> ¼ teaspoon salt
> ½ teaspoon baking soda
> 2 teaspoons baking powder
> 1¼ cups plus 2 tablespoons rice flour*

Blend bananas, shortening, sugar and vanilla. Add dry ingredients. Bake in 8 by 8-inch pan at 375° for 25 minutes. Can be used for cupcakes. Lemon-flavored icing is good on this cake.

* Note: Cakes made with substitute flours are very delicate. For easiest removal, grease pan, line it with wax paper, and then grease and flour the wax paper with some of the grease and substitute flours.

Variations

Jam Squares: Use banana cake recipe. Put ⅔ mixture in 8-inch pie pan. Cover with thick jam—mashed, cooked cherries, plums, prunes or the like. Place rest of batter on top. Bake at 375° for 25 minutes.

Coffee Cake: Place batter in pie pan and sprinkle cinnamon mixture on top. Cinnamon Mixture: ¼ cup milkfree margarine; ½ cup sugar; ¼ cup rice flour; 1 teaspoon cinnamon.

Cookies: To Banana Cake recipe, add 1 teaspoon molasses and about ½ cup coconut, oatmeal, or raisins, etc., to stiffen batter. Drop by spoonfuls on cookie sheet and flatten out. Bake in 375° oven about 10 minutes.

AIA

Eggfree, Milkfree

Banana Cake

> ¼ cup shortening
> 1 cup sugar
> ½ tablespoon oil

¼ cup water
1 cup mashed bananas
1½ cups all-purpose flour
1¼ teaspoons baking powder
1 teaspoon baking soda
1 teaspoon vanilla extract

Cream shortening and sugar. Add oil, water, vanilla and bananas. Sift and stir in dry ingredients. Bake in greased cake pan at 375° for 50 minutes.

AIA

Eggfree, Glutenfree, Milkfree, Wheatfree

Christmas Cake

1 cup brown sugar
1 cup water
1 cup raisins
2 tablespoons drippings or oil
½ teaspoon salt
1½ cups rice flour
¾ teaspoon baking soda
½ teaspoon ground ginger
1 teaspoon ground cinnamon
½ cup dates, lemon or orange peel or nuts

Sift together flour, soda, ginger and cinnamon. Stir in fruit and nuts. Add to cooked mixture. Mix well. Bake 1 hour at 350° in a greased loaf pan.

AIA

Eggfree

Chocolate or White Cake

1 cup sugar
4 tablespoons butter
4 tablespoons boiling water
3 tablespoons cocoa
1 cup sour milk
1 teaspoon vanilla extract
1¾ cups all-purpose flour

1 teaspoon baking powder
1 teaspoon baking soda

Cream together sugar and butter. Dissolve cocoa in boiling water. Sift together dry ingredients. Add dry ingredients alternately with milk to sugar-butter mixture. Bake in an 8-inch square pan for 30 minutes at 350°.

For white cake reduce milk to ¾ cup.

Variation: Bake in cupcake tins.

AIA

Eggfree

Orange Blossom Cake

½ cup butter or margarine	4 teaspoons baking powder
¾ cup sugar	1¼ teaspoons baking soda
1¾ teaspoons vanilla extract	½ cup orange juice
1 tablespoon grated orange rind	½ cup plus 2 tablespoons milk
3 cups sifted cake flour	yellow food color (optional)
1¼ teaspoons salt	

Cream butter or margarine and sugar until cream colored and light and fluffy. Do not undercream. Beat in vanilla and orange rind. Sift together flour, salt, baking powder and baking soda. Beat together dry ingredients alternately with milk and orange juice. Add yellow color, if desired. Beat batter, at medium speed, for 1 minute. Batter will be of a soft cooky dough consistency.

Divide between two 8-inch layer cake tins, lightly greased and floured. Bake 30 to 35 minutes at 350° until cake shrinks from sides. Let cool about ½ hour before turning out of pans. Handle cake carefully as it is very fragile. Fill and frost with buttercream icing.

AIA

Eggfree

Graham Cracker Brownies

24 graham crackers
1 can (15 oz.) sweetened condensed milk
1 package (6 oz.) chocolate bits

Crush graham crackers, place in bowl. Add chocolate bits and condensed milk. Mix. Spread batter in 8 by 8 by 1½-inch pan. Bake at 425° for 20 to 25 minutes. For chewy brownie, avoid overbaking. Cut in 2-inch squares and remove from pan while still warm.

AIA

Milkfree, Wheatfree

Chiffon Cake

> 1¾ cups sifted barley flour
> 1¼ cups sugar
> 4 teaspoons baking powder
> 1 teaspoon salt
> 5 egg yolks
> 1 cup egg whites (6 or 7)
> ¾ cup strained orange juice
> 3 tablespoons grated orange rind
> ½ teaspoon cream of tartar
> ½ cup salad oil

Sift together barley flour, sugar, baking powder and salt. Set aside egg yolks and egg whites, prepare orange juice, grate orange rind. In a large bowl, beat egg whites with cream of tartar until very stiff peaks form and whites are almost dry. Do not underbeat.
Make a well in center of flour mixture, then add in the following order: salad oil, egg yolks and orange juice. Beat until batter is completely mixed and smooth. Stir orange rind into flour-yolk mixture; gently fold about ½ of this mixture into stiffly beaten whites, repeat two times. Pour batter into 10-inch tube pan; smooth surface of batter. Bake at 350° for 55 to 65 minutes or until surface is well browned. Invert and suspend cake to cool.

Variation: Omit orange rind and juice and substitute ¾ cup apricot nectar or pineapple juice and 1 teaspoon vanilla.

AIA

Milkfree, Wheatfree

Banana Cake

> 2 cups sifted oat flour
> ½ cup sugar
> ½ teaspoon salt

2 teaspoons baking powder
2 tablespoons salad oil
½ cup mashed bananas
2 eggs
3 tablespoons cold water

Mix together flour, sugar, salt and baking powder. Add oil, bananas, eggs and water. Mix well. Turn into greased 8-inch square pan and bake at 350° for 25 to 30 minutes.

AIA

Milkfree, Wheatfree

Spicy Oatmeal Cake

4 beaten eggs
⅔ cup sugar
1 teaspoon vanilla extract
2 tablespoons water
½ cup melted fat
1 teaspoon baking soda
1 teaspoon salt

2 teaspoons ground cinnamon
½ teaspoon grated nutmeg
3½ cups rolled oats, un-cooked
1 cup raisins
½ cup chopped nuts

Beat eggs; add sugar, vanilla, water, fat and beat well. Grind oats with fine blade of food chopper. Measure 2¾ cups of ground oats. Mix together dry ingredients until thoroughly blended. Add dry ingredients to egg mixture and stir. Add nuts and raisins. Bake in two wax-paper-lined 8-inch round pans in moderate oven (350°) for 20 to 25 minutes. Ice with plain icing if preferred.

AIA

Glutenfree, Milkfree, Wheatfree

Christmas Cake

½ cup shortening
¾ cup sugar
1 cup raisins
⅛ pound cut mixed peel (lemon and orange)
1 cup dates, cut up
¼ cup halved glacé cherries
¼ cup nuts
½ teaspoon vanilla extract

2 or 3 eggs
½ cup crushed pineapple or ¼ cup juice and ¼ cup chunks
½ cup soya flour
¾ cup rice flour
1 tablespoon baking powder
½ teaspoon salt
½ teaspoon lemon extract

Cream sugar and shortening. Add beaten eggs. Beat until light and fluffy. Combine flours, baking powder and salt and sift together. Add about ½ crushed pineapple or the pineapple juice to the creamed mixture and some of the combined dry ingredients. Mix well, beating until smooth. Alternately add remaining dry and wet ingredients. Fold in prepared fruits and pineapple chunks. If batter is thin, add more soya and rice flour in equal parts. (Too much rice flour makes too dry a cake and too much soya will affect the taste.) Turn into greased and lined loaf pan (4 by 8 inches) and bake at 375° for about 90 minutes. Start testing cake for doneness in about 1 hour. A pan of boiling water in bottom of oven will help to avoid too dry a cake. Cool thoroughly before storing. Wrap in aluminum foil and store in refrigerator.

AIA

Glutenfree, Milkfree, Wheatfree

Potato Flour Sponge Cake

    4 eggs, separated
    ½ lemon, grated rind and juice
    ½ cup potato flour
    1 cup sugar
    1 teaspoon baking powder
    ⅛ teaspoon salt

Beat egg yolks. Add sugar, grated lemon rind and juice, continue beating. Add stiffly beaten egg whites to yolk-sugar mixture. Sift flour, baking powder, and salt and fold into batter. Pour into small ungreased tube pan. Bake at 350° for 30 minutes. Invert pan to cool.

AIA

Glutenfree, Milkfree, Wheatfree

Jelly Roll

    6 egg yolks
    1 tablespoon water
    6 tablespoons potato flour
    jelly and powdered sugar
    12 tablespoons sugar (¾ cup)
    6 egg whites, stiffly beaten

Beat yolks, sugar, and water in mixer at medium speed for 5 minutes. Add flour and mix for 2 minutes at medium speed. Fold in beaten egg whites. Bake in 12 by 16-inch pan for 15 minutes at 385°. Turn heat off and bake for 5 more minutes. Spread jelly on cooled cake. Roll. Sprinkle powdered sugar on top.

AIA

Glutenfree, Milkfree, Wheatfree

Chocolate Cake

4 eggs
4 tablespoons cocoa or 3 tablespoons melted chocolate
4 tablespoons potato flour
3½ tablespoons sugar
1 teaspoon baking powder

Beat the yolks with sugar, add cocoa or melted chocolate to egg yolk-sugar mixture and beat well. Beat the 4 egg whites until stiff, add the chocolate mixture. Sift the potato flour and baking powder together, fold into batter. Pour into a greased 8 by 8-inch pan. Bake at 350° for 30 minutes.

AIA

Eggfree, Milkfree

Chocolate Cake

Sift into bowl

1½ cups all-purpose flour
3 tablespoons cocoa
½ teaspoon salt
1 teaspoon baking soda
1 teaspoon baking powder
1 cup sugar

Make three holes in dry mixture and add

1 teaspoon white vinegar
5 tablespoons melted shortening
1 teaspoon vanilla extract

Pour over all 1 cup warm water. Mix gently. Don't beat. Bake 30 minutes in 350° oven in a greased 8 by 8-inch pan.

AIA

Wheatfree

Chocolate Cake

  2 eggs, separated
  1½ cups sugar
  1 cup sifted rye flour
  ½ cup unsifted potato flour
  ¼ teaspoon baking soda
  2½ teaspoons baking powder
  ¾ teaspoon salt
  ¼ cup salad oil
  1 cup buttermilk
  2 squares unsweetened chocolate, melted

In small bowl beat egg whites until frothy; gradually beat in ½ cup sugar; continue beating until glossy and stiff enough to stand in stiff peaks.

Using large bowl, sift together 1 cup sugar, rye and potato flours, baking soda, baking powder and salt. Make a well in dry ingredients, pour in salad oil and ½ cup buttermilk; beat 1 minute at medium speed. Add remaining buttermilk, egg yolks and melted chocolate; beat 1 minute; fold in egg white mixture.

Divide the batter between two 8-inch layer pans; bake at 375° for 30 to 35 minutes or until cake pulls away from edge of pan. Cool on cake rack about ½ hour before carefully removing from pans. Frost as desired.

AIA

Glutenfree, Milkfree, Wheatfree

Potato Flour Cake

Into one bowl, sift

  ¾ cup sifted potato flour
  1 teaspoon baking powder
  ½ teaspoon salt

Add to another bowl

  4 eggs
  ¾ cup sugar

Set egg-sugar bowl into another bowl of hot water and beat until mixture is lukewarm. Remove from hot water and continue beating 6 to 8 minutes or until it is like whipped cream.
Add

   1 teaspoon vanilla extract
   1 teaspoon lemon juice or ½ teaspoon almond extract

Gradually add dry ingredients to egg mixture and fold in flavorings. Carefully pour into ungreased tube pan (or small loaf pan). Bake at 350° about 40 minutes. Invert and suspend until cool. This can be quartered and frozen, as it dries out rapidly.

AIA

Glutenfree. Milkfree, Wheatfree

English Cake Dessert

   1 cup powdered sugar, sifted
   ⅔ cup cornstarch, sifted
   3 eggs, separated
   ⅛ teaspoon cream of tartar
   2 teaspoons water
   ½ teaspoon vanilla extract

Sift ½ cup sugar and cornstarch 3 times. Beat egg whites, water and cream of tartar to soft peaks. Beat in ½ cup sugar a little at a time until stiff peaks form. Beat yolks and vanilla till blended and add to whites. Fold in the sugar and cornstarch gradually. Bake in two 8-inch layer tins at 350° about 30 minutes.
Put layers together with drained fruits, bananas, boiled custard or other desired filling. Cake may be frozen.

AIA

Glutenfree, Wheatfree

Hot Milk Sponge Cake

   1 cup sifted rice flour
   2 teaspoons baking powder
   3 eggs

    1 cup sugar
    2 teaspoons lemon juice
    6 tablespoons hot milk

Sift flour and baking powder 3 times. Beat eggs until very thick and light and nearly white (10 minutes). Add sugar gradually, beating constantly. Add lemon juice. Fold in flour mixture, a small amount at a time. Add milk, mixing until batter is smooth. Turn at once into ungreased tube pan and bake at 350° for 25 to 30 minutes or until cake springs back when touched with fingertip. Remove from oven and invert cake until cold.
This cake may be baked in lightly greased 8 by 8 by 2-inch pan or loaf pan.

AIA

Glutenfree, Wheatfree

Italian Nut Cake

    4 oz. filberts and almonds
    ½ pound rice flour
    2 tablespoons sugar
    4 eggs
    4 oz. melted butter
    ½ teaspoon almond extract
    ½ teaspoon vanilla extract

Blanch nuts, then grind fine. Mix with rice flour and sugar. Beat eggs well and add to flour mixture. Add melted butter and stir lightly. Add almond and vanilla flavorings. Bake in a loaf pan in a moderate oven (350°) 40 to 45 minutes.

AIA

Glutenfree, Wheatfree

Cherry Bars

    1½ cups rice flour
    ½ cup brown sugar
    3 teaspoons baking powder
    ½ teaspoon ground cinnamon
    ½ teaspoon salt
    ½ teaspoon grated nutmeg
    ½ cup margarine or shortening

¼ cup skim milk
2 eggs
1 cup thick cherry jam

Grease 9-inch square pan.
Sift flour, sugar, baking powder, salt, cinnamon and nutmeg into bowl. Add margarine and cut finely with pastry blender.
Measure milk into another bowl. Add eggs and beat together with fork. Add to rice flour mixture and blend lightly with fork. Spread half of mixture in prepared pan. Spread with cherry jam evenly. Top with remaining batter and spread evenly. Bake at 400° 25 to 30 minutes. Cool in pan.
Almond Icing: Measure 2 tablespoons warm milk. Add 1 teaspoon almond extract. Add powdered sugar to thicken (not too thick). Spread on cooled pastry and cut into bars.

AIA

Eggfree, Milkfree

Spice and Raisin Cake

1 cup water	½ teaspoon ground allspice
2 cups raisins	⅛ teaspoon grated nutmeg
1 cup brown sugar	2 cups cake flour
⅓ cup fat	1 teaspoon baking powder
½ teaspoon salt	1 teaspoon baking soda
½ teaspoon ground cinnamon	1 cup nuts, finely chopped

Boil water, raisins, sugar, fat, salt and spices for 3 minutes. Cool. Sift flour, baking powder and soda. Stir flour mixture gradually into other ingredients. Beat until batter is smooth. Add nuts. Bake in a greased 9-inch tube pan at 325° for about 1 hour.

AIA

Eggfree, Milkfree

Carrot Cake

1 cup brown sugar	½ cup chopped nuts (optional)
1¼ cups water	2 teaspoons ground cinnamon
⅓ cup shortening	½ teaspoon ground cloves
½ cup raisins	1 teaspoon baking soda
1 cup grated carrots	1 teaspoon salt
½ teaspoon grated nutmeg	

2 teaspoons water
2 cups pastry flour
2½ teaspoons baking powder

Mix brown sugar, water, shortening, raisins, carrots and spices in saucepan and boil for 3 minutes. Cool to lukewarm. Add mixture of soda, salt and water. Sift flour and baking powder together and blend in. Fold in nuts. Bake in a greased 8 by 4 by 2½-inch loaf pan at 350° for 50 minutes.

AIA

Eggfree, Milkfree

Honey Cake

1 cup milkfree margarine
1 cup sugar
1 cup honey
rind of 2 oranges
1 teaspoon baking soda
3 cups sifted all-purpose flour
2 teaspoons baking powder
⅔ cup strong tea or coffee
½ cup orange juice
¾ cup light raisins, coated with some of measured flour

Cream margarine and sugar. Add honey and orange rinds, mixing well. Add sifted dry ingredients alternately with liquids. Add raisins and mix. Bake in two 4 by 8-inch loaf pans (greased and lined with greased wax paper) for 1 hour or until cakes draw away from sides. Let sit for 5 minutes to cool before removing from pans.

AIA

Eggfree, Milkfree

Dealer's Choice Cake

4½ tablespoons milkfree margarine
⅔ cup sugar
½ teaspoon vanilla extract
½ cup plus 2 tablespoons liquid (Any fruit juice such as orange
    and grated orange rind; pineapple juice and a small amount of
    crushed pineapple; or if allowed, milk.)
1½ cups sifted all-purpose flour

½ teaspoon salt
2½ teaspoons baking powder

Grease and line with greased wax paper an 8-inch cake pan. Cream margarine and sugar. Add vanilla. Sift dry ingredients together and add alternately in thirds with liquid. Bake at 325° to 350° for 30 minutes. Let stand 5 minutes to cool before removing from pan.

This recipe may be doubled and put in two layer cake pans. It also makes good cupcakes.

AIA

Eggfree, Milkfree

Pan Cake or Whackey Cake

Sift together into ungreased pan (8 by 8 inches)

1½ cups sifted all-purpose flour
1 cup sugar
3 tablespoons cocoa
1 teaspoon baking soda
1 teaspoon baking powder
½ teaspoon salt

Add to flour mixture and beat well

1 tablespoon vinegar or lemon concentrate
5 tablespoons melted butter or shortening
1 teaspoon vanilla extract
1 cup tepid water

Bake at 325° for 30 to 40 minutes. Cool, then frost in pan.

For a white cake, eliminate the cocoa and use a little more flour (¼ cup or so). The recipe can be doubled and baked in a 7 by 11-inch pan. White cake may be used for party cake by adding raspberry flavoring.

AIA

Eggfree, Milkfree

Eggless Applesauce Cake

Sift together

2 cups all-purpose flour
½ teaspoon salt

1 teaspoon ground cinnamon
½ teaspoon ground cloves

Combine ¼ cup of flour mixture with

¾ cup raisins
½ cup chopped nuts (optional)

Work ½ cup shortening with a spoon until soft.
Gradually add 1 cup packed brown sugar. Beat until soft.

Combine

2 teaspoons baking soda
1½ cups applesauce

Stir until soda is dissolved. Add applesauce mixture alternately with dry ingredients, blending well after each addition. Fold in nuts and raisins. Grease and flour 9-inch square pan. Bake at 350° for 45 minutes.

AIA

Eggfree, Milkfree

Pumpkin Cake

Cream together

¾ cup shortening
1 cup brown sugar
½ cup granulated sugar
2 cups pumpkin

Sift and add to above with ½ cup water

2 cups cake flour
3 teaspoons baking powder
1 teaspoon baking soda
¾ teaspoon ground cinnamon
½ teaspoon ground ginger
1 teaspoon salt

Beat well. Bake at 350° for 30 minutes in greased and floured cake pan. (Topped with Rich Whip, it is delicious.)

AIA

Eggfree, Milkfree

Spice and Raisin Cake

1 cup water	½ teaspoon ground allspice
2 cups raisins	⅛ teaspoon ground nutmeg
1 cup brown sugar	2 cups cake flour
⅓ cup fat	1 teaspoon baking powder
½ teaspoon salt	1 teaspoon baking soda
½ teaspoon ground cinnamon	1 cup nuts, finely chopped

Boil water, raisins, sugar, fat, salt and spices for 3 minutes. Cool.
Sift flour, baking powder and soda. Stir flour mixture gradually
into other ingredients. Beat until batter is smooth. Add nuts.
Bake in a greased 9-inch tube pan at 325° for about 1 hour.

AIA

Birthday Cake

Use your favorite cake recipe to make a three-layer cake with chocolate, white and pink layers. Flavor pink layer with raspberry flavoring
(2 heaping tablespoons raspberry Jell-O works well). Use basic marshmallow (recipe below) as a frosting and filling.

Eggfree, Glutenfree, Milkfree, Wheatfree

Basic Marshmallow

⅓ cup water
1 envelope unflavored gelatin
1 teaspoon vanilla extract
½ cup sugar
⅔ cup sugar cane syrup

Mix water, gelatin and sugar together in a saucepan. Heat until
sugar and gelatin are dissolved. Pour sugar cane syrup into a large
bowl; add hot mixture and vanilla. Beat on high speed of mixer
for 15 minutes, until mixture is thick.
Use as a garnish for jellies and other desserts in place of whipped
cream, or as a filling and frosting for cakes.

AIA

Glutenfree, Milkfree, Wheatfree

Fluffy Frosting

    2 egg whites
    1 tablespoon vinegar
    1 teaspoon lemon juice
    pinch of salt
    2 teaspoons cornstarch
    2½ cups powdered sugar

Beat egg whites until stiff but not dry. Add vinegar, lemon juice, salt and cornstarch. Continue beating. Gradually add powdered sugar until mixture can be spread. Frost cake, heaping high in center of cake. Decorate as desired.

AIA

Eggfree, Milkfree

Cookies

Shortbread Cookies

    ½ pound milkfree margarine
    2 cups all-purpose flour
    salt
    ½ cup powdered sugar
    2 teaspoons cornstarch

Cream margarine and sugar. Add dry ingredients and mix thoroughly. Roll a small amount of dough in hand to form a ball, press center with thumb and decorate with a little jam or sprinkle with colored sugar. Place on ungreased pan and bake at 350° until slightly brown.

AIA

Eggfree, Milkfree

Molasses Lace Cookies

    ⅔ cup sifted enriched flour   ½ teaspoon baking soda
    1 teaspoon baking powder   1 teaspoon salt

1 teaspoon ground cinnamon	½ cup fat
1 teaspoon grated nutmeg	¾ cup sugar
½ teaspoon ground cloves	½ cup molasses
2½ cups rolled oats	

Sift together flour, baking powder, soda, salt and spices. Mix with rolled oats. Heat fat, sugar and molasses in saucepan, stirring constantly until mixture comes to a boil. Pour hot mixture over dry ingredients, stirring constantly. Drop from a teaspoon onto a well-greased baking sheet, 2 inches apart, bake at 350° for 12 to 15 minutes. Remove from sheets immediately.
Yield: 3 dozen.

AIA

Eggfree, Glutenfree, Milkfree, Wheatfree

Marshmallow Cookies

Oil an 8-inch square pan. Add a layer of crushed dry cereal (corn flakes, crispy rice)—about 1½ cups. Spoon basic marshmallow over base. Top with another layer of crushed cereal. Chill in refrigerator until set; cut into squares.

AIA

Eggfree, Milkfree

Raspberry Squares

1¼ cups sifted all-purpose flour
1¼ cups rolled oats
1 cup brown sugar
⅞ cup melted milkfree margarine
pinch of salt
¾ cup raspberry jam

Mix all ingredients except jam together. Press half of mixture into greased 8 by 8-inch pan. Cover with jam. Spread rest of mixture over jam. Bake at 350° for 30 minutes. Cut in squares.

AIA

Eggfree, Milkfree

Cherry Squares

¾ cup milkfree margarine
⅓ cup brown sugar
1½ cups all-purpose flour
2 envelopes gelatin
½ cup cold water
2 cups granulated sugar
½ cup warm water
1 teaspoon almond extract
½ cup chopped cherries
½ cup chopped almonds (optional)

Cream margarine and brown sugar. Add flour and mix well. Put in greased 9 by 12-inch pan and bake at 325° for 25 minutes. Cool. Dissolve gelatin in cold water. Set aside. Boil granulated sugar and warm water for two minutes. Combine with gelatin mixture and beat until stiff. Add rest of ingredients and pour on top of baked mixture. Let set and cut in squares.

AIA

Eggfree, Milkfree

Chocolate Chip Cookies

½ cup milkfree margarine
¼ cup light brown sugar
½ cup sugar
1 teaspoon vanilla extract
1 cup plus 2 tablespoons all-purpose flour
¾ teaspoon baking soda
½ teaspoon baking powder
½ cup chopped nuts
6 oz. semisweet chocolate chips

Cream margarine and add sugars and vanilla. Add sifted dry ingredients and mix. Stir in nuts and chocolate chips. Drop by teaspoonfuls on greased cookie sheet. Bake at 350° for 10 minutes.
Variation: Omit chocolate chips and add ¾ cup raisins and grated rind of half an orange.

AIA

Glutenfree, Milkfree, Wheatfree

Chocolate Marshmallow Roll

> 35 colored marshmallows (cut in thirds) mixed with 1 cup
> chopped walnuts
> 3 squares unsweetened chocolate, melted
> 2 tablespoons milkfree margarine
> 1 teaspoon vanilla extract
> 1 egg, well beaten
> 1 cup powdered sugar
> ½ teaspoon lemon juice

Mix all ingredients together, form into long roll and roll in coconut, crushed nuts or crushed ready-to-eat rice cereal. Roll tightly in tin foil and chill.

AIA

Glutenfree, Milkfree, Wheatfree

Peanut Butter Cookies

> ½ cup shortening
> ½ cup granulated sugar
> 1 egg
> 1 teaspoon baking powder
> ¾ teaspoon baking soda
> ½ cup peanut butter
> ½ cup brown sugar
> 1 cup soya flour
> ½ cup potato flour
> ¼ teaspoon salt

Mix thoroughly shortening, peanut butter, sugars and egg. Sift together flours, baking powder, soda and salt. Stir sifted dry ingredients into shortening-sugar mixture. Chill dough.
Form into walnut-sized balls. Place 3 inches apart on lightly greased baking sheet and flatten with fork dipped in flour in criss-cross design. Bake at 375° for 10 to 12 minutes or until cookies are set but not hard.

AIA

Glutenfree, Milkfree, Wheatfree

Rice Flour Brownies

    2 squares unsweetened chocolate
    ⅓ cup shortening or margarine
    ⅔ cup rice flour
    ½ teaspoon salt
    1 cup sugar
    2 eggs, well beaten
    ½ teaspoon baking powder

Melt chocolate and shortening in double boiler. Remove from heat and beat in sugar and eggs. Sift together rice flour, baking powder and salt and stir into chocolate mixture. Spread in greased 8-inch square pan. Allow mixture to stand ½ hour before baking. Bake at 350° for 30 to 35 minutes. Cool slightly, cut into squares.

AIA

Glutenfree, Milkfree, Wheatfree

Chocolate Brownies

    ⅓ cup shortening or margarine
    2 squares unsweetened chocolate
    1½ cups rice baby cereal
    ¼ teaspoon salt
    1 teaspoon vanilla extract
    2 eggs, well beaten
    1 cup sugar
    ½ teaspoon baking powder
    ½ cup chopped nuts (optional)

Melt shortening and chocolate together over hot water. Blend eggs and sugar, stir in cereal and remaining ingredients. Add chocolate mixture, blend well. Spread in greased 8-inch square pan. Bake at 350° for 25 minutes or until cake tester inserted in center comes out clean. Cool thoroughly in pan. Dust with icing sugar if desired. Cut in squares.

AIA

Glutenfree, Milkfree, Wheatfree

Your Choice Squares

> 1 cup rice flour
> ¼ teaspoon baking soda
> ½ teaspoon salt
> ½ cup margarine or butter
> ½ cup chocolate chips, raisins or nuts (optional)
> 1 cup brown sugar
> 2 eggs
> 1 teaspoon vanilla extract

Cream sugar and margarine, add eggs and beat, then add dry ingredients and vanilla. Bake in oven at 375° for 20 to 25 minutes, in a greased 8-inch square pan.

AIA

Glutenfree, Milkfree, Wheatfree

Plain Cookies

> 2 cups lightly packed precooked rice baby cereal
> ⅓ cup sugar
> ¼ teaspoon salt
> 1½ teaspoons vanilla extract
> 1 tablespoon water
> 1 teaspoon baking powder
> 1 egg, slightly beaten
> 2 tablespoons soft margarine

Mix ingredients in order given. When well blended, turn out on sheet of heavy wax paper and press into flattened round. Place another sheet of wax paper over it. Pat or roll out between wax paper into a ¼ inch thick sheet. Take off top sheet of wax paper and cut dough into 16 1¼-inch squares. Lift to ungreased baking sheet, placing them 1 inch apart. Bake in center of oven at 300° for 15 minutes.
Variations: Before baking sprinkle tops with chocolate shot or color sugar or other cookie "sprinkles."

Press a whole pecan or walnut in center of each cookie before baking.

After baking, put cookies together with date filling: 1 cup chopped dates, 4 teaspoons sugar, 1 cup water, 1 teaspoon lemon juice cooked together until blended and thickened and cooled.

After baking, put cookies together with lemon frosting: 1 cup sifted powdered sugar, 2 tablespoons butter, 1 tablespoon lemon juice, mixed well.

AIA

Glutenfree, Milkfree, Wheatfree

Raisin Cookies

    2 tablespoons soft margarine
    2 cups rice baby cereal
    ½ teaspoon salt
    ¼ cup water
    1 cup brown sugar
    1 tablespoon baking powder
    1 egg, slightly beaten
    ⅓ cup raisins

Combine shortening, sugar, cereal, baking powder, salt, egg, and water and beat well. Stir in raisins. Drop by teaspoonfuls 2 inches apart on greased baking sheets. Bake at 350° for 12 to 15 minutes or until golden brown.
Yield: 3 dozen.

AIA

Glutenfree, Milkfree, Wheatfree

Rice Wafers

    ½ cup rice flour
    ¼ cup sugar
    grated lemon rind
    ¼ cup margarine
    1 egg

Mix ingredients, adding rice flour as needed to thicken dough. Roll thin and cut in desired shapes. Bake 5 to 7 minutes at 350°.

AIA

Glutenfree, Milkfree

Ginger Snaps

¼ cup plus 2 tablespoons shortening
½ cup sugar
1 egg
1 teaspoon baking soda
½ teaspoon ground ginger
2 tablespoons molasses
1 cup wheat starch flour
¼ teaspoon grated nutmeg
1 teaspoon ground cinnamon

Cream shortening and sugar. Add molasses and egg. Beat well. Add sifted dry ingredients. Beat until smooth. Chill thoroughly. Roll into small balls, dip into sugar and place 2 inches apart on greased cookie sheet. Bake at 375° for 15 minutes.

AIA

Glutenfree, Milkfree

Sugar Cookies

1 cup milkfree margarine
1 cup sugar
1 egg
1 teaspoon vanilla extract
1 tablespoon almond extract
1 cup potato flour
2 cups wheat flour

Cream margarine and sugar thoroughly. Add egg, vanilla and almond extract. Add flours, sifting them into the sugar-margarine mixture. Mix vigorously until very smooth. Drop by teaspoonfuls onto cookie sheet, press nut or cherry into center of each cookie. Bake at 375° for 12 minutes or until brown.

AIA

Glutenfree, Milkfree

Orange Cookies

> ½ cup milkfree margarine
> ½ teaspoon vanilla extract
> ½ cup fruit sugar
> ½ teaspoon grated orange rind
> 1 egg
> 1½ cups wheat flour

Cream margarine, vanilla, sugar and orange rind. Add egg, sift in wheat flour. Knead lightly to form a ball. Roll out thinly, prick all over. Cut into various shapes and place on greased cookie sheet. Bake at 350° for 15 minutes. Remove from cookie sheet while still warm. Yield: 50 small cookies.

AIA

Glutenfree, Milkfree

Butterscotch Bars

> ⅝ cup potato flour
> ½ cup wheat flour
> 1½ teaspoons baking powder
> ½ teaspoon salt
> 1¼ cups brown sugar
> ½ cup shortening
> 2 eggs, unbeaten
> ½ teaspoon vanilla extract
> ½ cup chopped nuts
> ½ cup shredded coconut

Sift together flours, baking powder and salt; set aside. Cream shortening, gradually adding sugar. Blend in unbeaten eggs and vanilla. Add dry ingredients, mixing thoroughly. Stir in chopped nuts and coconut. Spread in well-greased 9-inch square pan, bake at 350° for 25 to 30 minutes. Sprinkle with icing sugar and cut in bars while still warm.

AIA

Glutenfree, Wheatfree

Rice Flour Drop Cookies

⅔ cup rice flour, sifted twice
⅛ teaspoon salt
1 teaspoon baking powder
¼ cup shortening or margarine
½ cup sugar
¼ teaspoon vanilla extract
1 egg
2 tablespoons milk

Sift together rice flour, salt and baking powder. Cream shortening until light and fluffy. Add sugar gradually, beating thoroughly. Add vanilla and egg, beat until combined. Add rice flour mixture and milk, alternately. Allow dough to stand in refrigerator ½ hour before baking. Drop by teaspoonfuls on greased cookie sheet. Bake at 375° for 12 to 15 minutes.
Yield: 3 dozen.

AIA

Glutenfree, Wheatfree

Drop Cookies

1 cup sugar
½ cup shortening
2 eggs
2 teaspoons vanilla extract
½ teaspoon salt
1 cup rice flour
1 cup soya flour
⅝ cup potato flour
4 teaspoons baking powder
½ teaspoon baking soda
1 cup buttermilk
¾ cup pecans*

Cream together the sugar, shortening, eggs and vanilla. Sift together the salt, flours, baking powder and soda. Alternately add the buttermilk and sifted dry ingredients to the creamed mixture. Blend in pecans. Drop by teaspoonfuls on greased baking sheet. Bake at 375° for approximately 12 minutes. These may be improved by frosting with a powdered sugar icing.

* Note: Walnuts, dates, raisins, or a combination may be used.

AIA

Glutenfree, Wheatfree

Toll House Cookies

¾ cup soya flour	6 tablespoons brown sugar
¼ cup potato flour	½ teaspoon vanilla extract
½ teaspoon salt	¼ teaspoon water
½ teaspoon baking soda	1 egg
6½ tablespoons margarine	chocolate chips
6 tablespoons granulated sugar	½ cup chopped nuts

Sift together flours, salt and baking soda. Blend margarine, sugars, vanilla and water. Beat in egg. Add flour mixture and mix well. Stir in chocolate chips and chopped nuts. Drop by well-rounded teaspoonfuls on cookie sheet. Bake 10 to 12 minutes at 375°.

                                                                    AIA

Eggfree, Milkfree, Wheatfree

Oatmeal Ginger Cookies

½ cup molasses
¼ cup shortening
3 cups rolled oats (about)
¼ cup sugar
1 teaspoon ground ginger
½ teaspoon salt
¼ teaspoon baking soda

Heat molasses to boiling point. Pour over shortening in bowl. Grind oats with fine blade of food chopper, measure 3 cups rolled oats and combine with sugar, ginger, salt and soda. Stir into molasses mixture. Shape into roll about 1½ inches in diameter. Wrap in waxed paper and chill for several hours or overnight. Cut into ⅛-inch slices. Bake on oiled cookie sheets at 375° for 10 minutes.

                                                                    AIA

Eggfree, Milkfree, Wheatfree

Crunchy Cookies

⅓ cup shortening
⅓ cup brown sugar

⅓ cup granulated sugar
1 tablespoon water
1 teaspoon vanilla extract
¼ teaspoon salt
½ teaspoon baking powder
1 cup rolled oats
½ cup finely chopped nuts (optional)

Cream together shortening and sugars until fluffy; add water and vanilla; beat until smooth. Beat in salt, baking powder, oats and nuts. Drop by level tablespoons 3 inches apart on ungreased cookie sheet. Bake at 350° for 8 to 10 minutes or until light brown. Let cookies cool for 2 to 3 minutes before removing from sheet. Cookies will be thin and lacy.
Yield: 1½ to 2 dozen.

AIA

Eggfree, Milkfree, Wheatfree

Oat-Peanut Butter Cookies

½ cup sugar
1 tablespoon peanut butter
2 teaspoons salad oil
¼ cup water
1½ cups oat flour
2 teaspoons baking powder

Mix sugar, peanut butter and oil. Add water. Add oat flour and baking powder, mix thoroughly. Drop by teaspoonfuls on oiled cookie sheet; press down with tines of fork. Bake at 400° until golden brown. Remove from cookie sheet immediately.

AIA

Eggfree, Glutenfree, Milkfree, Wheatfree

Peanut Butter Chewies

½ cup light corn syrup
2 tablespoons brown sugar
½ cup peanut butter
3 cups corn flakes or rice flakes

Melt in double boiler the syrup, peanut butter and sugar. Remove from heat and mix in corn or rice flakes. Shape into small balls (with greased or wet hands) and cool.

AIA

Eggfree, Glutenfree, Milkfree, Wheatfree

Peanut Butter Balls

> 1 cup peanut butter
> 1 cup powdered sugar
> ½ cup walnuts, chopped fine
> 2 tablespoons butter or milkfree margarine
> ½ cup dates, chopped very fine

Melt peanut butter and sugar in double boiler. Remove from heat and add dates and walnuts. Form into balls, dip in icing (made with powdered sugar) and roll in coconut.

AIA

Eggfree, Glutenfree, Milkfree, Wheatfree

Chocolate Quickies

Melt 1 package semisweet chocolate pieces, 4 tablespoons corn syrup, 1 tablespoon water in double boiler. Remove from heat and stir in 2 cups of any ready-to-eat corn or rice cereal. Drop by teaspoonfuls on wax paper. Chill until firm.
Variations: Use 3 tablespoons corn syrup instead of 4. Add any of the following: 1¼ cups chopped candied fruit; 1½ cups coconut; 1½ cups raisins; 1 cup chopped nuts or chopped dates.

AIA

Eggfree, Glutenfree, Milkfree, Wheatfree

Chocolate Crunchies

> 1 package (6-oz.) chocolate chips
> 2 cups Rice Krispies
> 1 teaspoon vanilla extract
> pinch of salt

Melt chips over hot water and stir until smooth. Remove from heat and add Rice Krispies, vanilla and salt, blending until cereal is well coated. Drop from teaspoon on waxed paper. Chill.

AIA

Eggfree, Glutenfree, Milkfree, Wheatfree

Potato Flour Cookies

½ cup milkfree margarine
¼ teaspoon vanilla extract
½ cup cornstarch
⅓ cup powdered sugar
½ cup potato flour

Cream margarine until soft. Add sugar, blending well. Stir in vanilla. Sift together potato flour and cornstarch. Add to butter mixture. Mix with spoon until soft and well blended. Shape into balls about 1 inch in diameter. Place on ungreased cookie sheet, flatten with fork. Bake at 350° for 20 minutes.

AIA

Eggfree, Glutenfree, Milkfree, Wheatfree

Lace Cookies

¼ cup shortening
¼ teaspoon salt
2 cups rice baby cereal
1 can strained peaches or other strained fruit
¼ cup sugar
1½ teaspoons baking powder
1 teaspoon almond extract (optional)

Cream shortening and sugar thoroughly. Mix together salt, baking powder and cereal. Add mixture to creamed shortening and sugar, and blend until the mixture is the texture of coarse meal. Add strained fruit, mixing lightly only until mixture holds together. Form into small balls, place on lightly greased cookie sheet and press very thin with a fork. Bake at 350° for 15 minutes or until lightly brown. Remove onto a wire rack to cool thoroughly. Store in a closed container. This cookie will be translucent in appearance and of a chewy texture.
Yield. 48 1-inch cookies.

AIA

Eggfree, Glutenfree, Milkfree, Wheatfree

Ice Box Cookies

> ¼ cup shortening
> ¼ cup brown sugar (packed)
> ¼ cup granulated sugar
> ½ teaspoon vanilla extract
> 3 to 4 tablespoons water
> ½ teaspoon almond extract (optional)
> 1 cup soya flour
> ¼ teaspoon salt
> 2 teaspoons baking powder
> 3 tablespoons chopped pecans (optional)

Cream shortening and sugars together until light and fluffy. Add vanilla, almonds and water. Combine dry ingredients and add to mixture. Add pecans. Shape into 6-inch roll. Wrap in wax paper. Chill in refrigerator. Slice into ¼-inch cookies. Bake 10 to 15 minutes at 375°.

Variation: Peanut Butter Ice Box Cookies

Reduce shortening to 2 tablespoons, omit pecans, and add 3 tablespoons chunky-style peanut butter.

AIA

Eggfree, Glutenfree, Milkfree, Wheatfree

Chocolate Cookies with Variations

> ¼ cup butter or milkfree margarine
> 2 cups sugar
> ½ cup water (or milk, if allowed)
> 1 teaspoon vanilla extract

Bring to a boil.

> 3 cups instant oatmeal*
> 6 tablespoons cocoa

Mix well. Add to liquid and blend thoroughly.

Stir in 1 cup coconut and drop by spoonfuls on sheet of foil to cool.

Variations: Omit coconut and add 1 more cup instant oatmeal. Or omit cocoa and add 1 cup raisins and spices if desired. Or add 1 cup raisins to recipe or variation 1.

* Note: Substitute 8 cups Puffed Rice for oatmeal and coconut for glutenfree.

AIA

Eggfree

Graham Cracker Brownies

24 graham crackers
1 can (15 oz.) sweetened condensed milk
1 package (6 oz.) chocolate chips

Crush graham crackers, place in bowl. Add chocolate bits and condensed milk. Mix. Spread batter in 8 by 8 by 1½-inch pan. Bake at 425° for 20-25 minutes. For chewy brownie, avoid overbaking. Cut into 2-inch squares and remove from pan while still warm.

AIA

Eggfree

Neapolitan Squares

1 cup crushed graham wafers
½ cup melted margarine
½ cup brown sugar
1 heaping tablespoon all-purpose flour

Press mixture in greased 7 by 11-inch pan. Bake at 275° for 15 minutes exactly. Turn oven up to 350°.

2 cups desiccated coconut
1 tin sweetened condensed milk

Spread coconut-milk mixture on top gently. Bake at 350° for 20 minutes exactly.

4 tablespoons butter
2 cups sifted powdered sugar
2-3 tablespoons milk
vanilla extract
salt
coloring

Making icing and spread on top of cooled cake. Cut into bars.

AIA

Eggfree

Ginger Date Dainties

½ cup sweetened condensed milk
¼ pound cut marshmallows (or small)
2 cups cut up dates
1 teaspoon grated orange rind
1 tablespoon lemon juice
1 cup flaked coconut
½ cup chopped cherries
1½ cups crushed ginger cookies or graham wafers

Combine all ingredients. With wet hands, form rolls 6 inches long and 2 inches in diameter. Wrap in wax paper. Keep in refrigerator or freeze. Slice when needed.

AIA

Eggfree

Yule Logs

¾ cup butter
2 cups all-purpose flour
¼ cup powdered sugar
1 teaspoon vanilla extract
1 cup chopped peanuts

Cream butter. Add rest of ingredients. Roll out like logs, chill and bake at 350° for 10 minutes. Roll in fruit sugar.

AIA

Glutenfree

Cherry Winks

¾ cup margarine or shortening
½ cup plus 1 tablespoon
  sugar
1 egg
2 cups wheat flour
1 teaspoon baking powder
½ teaspoon baking soda
½ teaspoon salt

2 tablespoons milk
1 teaspoon vanilla extract
1½ cups chopped pecans
1 cup chopped dates
⅓ cup maraschino cherries,
  chopped and drained
2½ cups corn flakes, rolled
  fine

Cream shortening and add sugar gradually. Add egg. Sift dry ingredients. Alternately add dry ingredients and milk to creamed sugar and egg mixture. Add vanilla. Add chopped pecans, dates and cherries. Drop dough by teaspoonfuls into crushed corn flakes, roll, and garnish with quartered cherry. Bake on greased cookie sheet at 350° for 10 minutes.

AIA

Glutenfree

Wheat Starch Cookies

1¾ cups wheat flour
⅓ cup sugar
½ teaspoon salt
4 teaspoons baking powder
¼ cup shortening or butter
¾ cup milk
1 egg
1 teaspoon flavoring or grated lemon or orange rind

Mix dry ingredients together; blend in shortening. Add milk, egg and flavor and mix well. Drop from teaspoon onto greased cookie sheet 2 inches apart. Bake at 350° for 15 to 20 minutes.
Variation: Add chopped nuts, raisins or fruit.

AIA

Glutenfree

Vanilla Doughnuts

1½ cups wheat flour	1 teaspoon salt
¾ cup soya flour	1 tablespoon butter
¼ cup potato flour	2 eggs
1 cup sugar	1 teaspoon vanilla extract
2 teaspoons baking powder	¾ cup milk

Sift dry ingredients into bowl. Add softened butter, eggs, vanilla and milk. Mix quickly. Pat dough about ½ inch thick on floured board. Cut with doughnut cutter. Fry in deep fat heated to 365°. (Batter may also be dropped by spoonfuls into heated deep fat.) May be sugared or glazed if desired.

AIA

Beverages

Eggfree, Glutenfree, Milkfree, Wheatfree

Flavorings for Soybean Milk

To improve the flavor of soybean milk, one or more of the following may be added per cup of milk:

pinch of salt	2 tablespoons fruit syrup
2 teaspoons vanilla extract	2 tablespoons maple syrup
1 tablespoon molasses	2 tablespoons malt syrup
1 tablespoon honey	1 mashed banana
¾ cup frozen raspberries	chocolate syrup to taste

AIA

Eggfree, Glutenfree, Milkfree, Wheatfree

Orange Frost

¼ cup soybean milk, undiluted
¼ cup cold water
½ cup orange juice
1 tablespoon sugar

1 teaspoon lemon juice
½ cup crushed ice

Combine all ingredients in shaker with tight-fitting lid. Cover and shake well. Serve at once.

AIA

Eggfree, Glutenfree, Milkfree, Wheatfree

Pineapple Flip

¼ cup soybean milk, undiluted
¼ cup cold water
½ cup cracked ice
⅓ cup pineapple juice
1 tablespoon sugar
1 tablespoon lemon juice

Combine all ingredients in shaker with tight-fitting lid. Cover and shake well. Serve at once.

AIA

Hot "Chocolate"

Stir into 1 cup of water
2 tablespoons Cara Coa
1 tablespoon brown sugar
½ teaspoon cornstarch

Cook over moderate heat, beating slowly until it comes to a boil. Remove from burner. Add 2 tablespoons dry coffee creamer and whip vigorously for a few turns. Serve hot.

Wall

Candy

Eggfree, Glutenfree, Milkfree, Wheatfree

Ten-Minute Marshmallows

2 tablespoons gelatin
4 tablespoons cold water

½ cup boiling water
1½ cups granulated sugar
½ cup powdered sugar

After soaking gelatin in cold water, dissolve it in boiling water and stir in the granulated sugar. Stir until crystals disappear. Beat mixture until thick and foamy, takes about 10 minutes with an electric mixer. Beating is essential. Pour into large pan rinsed with ice water and let cool. When cold, cut into squares and roll in powdered sugar. Candy may be stored in plastic bags in refrigerator. It also freezes well.

AIA

Eggfree, Glutenfree, Wheatfree

Easter Eggs I

⅔ cup (½ 15-oz. can) Eagle Brand sweetened condensed milk
½ cup butter
1 teaspoon vanilla extract
1 teaspoon salt
5½ cups sifted powdered sugar (approximately 1½ pounds)

Cream together butter, salt and vanilla. Add condensed milk and blend until smooth. Gradually stir in sugar. Mixture will become very stiff. Then knead until all sugar is combined.
Place fondant on board or wax paper and continue kneading for several minutes, until mixture is very smooth and not sticky. Cut off ⅓ of the fondant and add a few drops of yellow food coloring for yolks. Knead until color is evenly blended. Cut into 10 portions and roll into balls for the center of the egg.
Cut remaining fondant into 10 equal portions and pat out flat, then mold around egg yolk and into elongated egg shape. Chill for short time, then, if necessary, remold gently. Chill for several hours or overnight.
Yield: Makes 2 pounds of fondant, enough for 10 3-oz. eggs

AIA

Eggfree, Glutenfree, Milkfree, Wheatfree

Easter Eggs II

2 tablespoons milkfree margarine
1 cup powdered sugar

½ teaspoon vanilla extract
1 teaspoon water

Cream margarine. Add sugar, vanilla and water, mixing well. Follow directions for Easter Eggs I for kneading and rolling eggs. This amount will make two large eggs.

AIA

Dipping Chocolate

½ pound semisweet chocolate
⅓ to ½ slab paraffin wax

Melt chocolate and wax in top of double boiler over hot water, stirring until blended. Remove from heat.
Dip bottom half of egg in chocolate using either kitchen tongs or fingers. Let drip for a moment, then turn it over and place on wax paper for chocolate to harden, chocolate side up. If chocolate becomes thick, reheat gently and continue dipping.
When eggs have been dipped on one side, then dip other side in chocolate; let drip a moment and place on wax paper with the soft chocolate side up to harden.
Note: Half of this recipe is sufficient to dip eggs, but it is awkward towards the end as it gets rather shallow.

AIA

Glutenfree, Milkfree, Wheatfree

Royal Frosting (for decorating)

2 egg whites (room temperature)
2¼ cups sifted powdered sugar
¼ teaspoon cream of tartar
½ teaspoon vanilla extract

Combine all ingredients. Beat with electric mixture 5 minutes or until very stiff.
While decorating, keep frosting remaining in bowl covered with damp cloth or waxed paper to prevent a crust from forming. This frosting becomes very hard and is good for making flowers and leaves and writing names. The decorations will hold their shape, and the eggs can be wrapped and boxed.

AIA

Eggfree, Milkfree

White Frosting (for decorating)

> ½ cup water
> 2 tablespoons flour (Use rice, potato or wheat flour for gluten-free diets. Use rice or potato flour for wheatfree diets.)

Blend and cook to thick paste. Cool to lukewarm.

> ⅔ cup granulated sugar
> ½ cup white shortening
> 1 cup powdered sugar

Cream sugar and shortening until light and fluffy. Add paste. Beat well. Thicken with powdered sugar.
Note: This icing works well using a cake decorator.

AIA

Directions for Decorating Easter Eggs

1. Fill a cake decorator; make a shell or zigzag border around middle of each egg.
2. A small portion of frosting may then be tinted green for stems and leaves.
3. Remaining frosting may be tinted any bright color for flowers. Flowers may be made directly on egg or made on wax paper and, when dry, peeled off and attached to egg with a dab of frosting.
4. The following alternate decorations should be added to chocolate on egg before it hardens.
   Tinted coconut
   Cake decorations
   Small colored marshmallows

Party Pleasers

Raggedy Annes

1. Diet bread, crackers or wafers
2. Celery, carrot sticks, carrot shavings

3. Peanut butter, cream cheese, meat spread, tuna, salmon
4. Hard-boiled eggs
5. Cherries, raisins, coconut

For the body, a circle of bread (or crackers or wafers) can be spread with margarine and any food from group 3. Use half a hard-boiled egg or more bread for a head. Legs and arms are made from celery or carrot sticks. Hair is made from carrot shavings or coconut. Eyes, nose, mouth and clothing decorations are made from Group 5 ingredients.

Raggedy Annes can be prepared ahead of time, or all ingredients can be put on a large platter and guests can make their own.

AIA

Party Platter or Shish Kabobs

Meatballs, cooked	Pickles
Cocktail sausages	Cheese cubes
Fish sticks	Shrimp
Vienna sausages	Cold meat, cut in cubes
Scallops	Mandarin oranges
Onion rings	Pineapple tidbits
Stuffed celery	Grapes
Carrot sticks	

Choose foods that suit your diet to make up a party platter. Guests help themselves. Several different sauces should be available. Many of these foods can be used to make shish kabobs. Give each guest a 6-inch wooden skewer to make his own favorite (or diet) treat.

AIA

Hamburger and Hot Dog Rolls

Use your diet bread recipe to make buns for allergic people.

For hamburger buns, grease 2½ inch aluminum foil baking cups. Put about ½ cup dough in each cup. Bake 15 minutes.

For hot dog buns, make your own baking cups out of heavy aluminum foil. Grease and fill with ½ cup dough. Place cups on cookie sheet and bake 15 minutes.

If the family goes to a restaurant for lunch, take one of these buns along and ask the waiter to just bring you the meat! Some restaurants will even warm your bun and bring it back all made up, along with the "normal" hamburgers. Be sure the meat used contains no allergens.

AIA

Raw Vegetables and Dips

  Carrots
  Cauliflower
  Celery
  Cucumbers
  Radishes
  Green onions
  Cherry tomatoes
  Green peppers

Arrange washed and trimmed vegetables on a tray. Serve with a variety of dunking sauces.

AIA

Milkfree, Glutenfree, Wheatfree

Dill Sauce

  4 egg yolks
  5 teaspoons prepared mustard
  1 teaspoon salt
  2 tablespoons dried dill
  ½ teaspoon pepper
  1 tablespoon sugar
  1 cup salad oil
  2 tablespoons vinegar

Beat egg yolks. Add next 5 ingredients and beat well. Add oil, one teaspoon at a time, beating constantly. Add vinegar and beat.

AIA

Glutenfree, Wheatfree

Curry Cream

  ½ cup mayonnaise
  ½ cup sour cream
  ½ teaspoon lemon juice
  1 teaspoon curry powder

Mix all ingredients well. Chill. Keep in refrigerator.

AIA

Chicken Livers

Boil chicken livers in salted water 20 minutes. Wrap each one in ½ slice bacon, fasten with toothpicks and broil till brown.

AIA

Meat Rolls

Add 1 teaspoon horseradish and 1 teaspoon minced onion to 3 ounces cream cheese. Spread on slices of dried beef, ham, salami or bologna. Fasten with toothpicks. Chill.

AIA

Bacon Rolls

Spread slices of bacon with peanut butter. Roll up, fasten with toothpicks and broil.

AIA

Garlic Buttered Popcorn or Puffed Cereal

Add sliced garlic clove to butter or margarine. Cook until garlic flavor is adequate. Add to freshly popped corn or puffed cereal. Heat 5 minutes in 350° oven.

AIA

Appendix A

Food Products and Where To Find Them

Much of the following information was supplied by the Allergy Information Association (Room 7, 25 Poynter Drive, Weston, Ontario, M9R 1K8), an exceedingly helpful organization for anyone allergic to anything.

Bread

a. Milkfree

Supermarket in-store bakeries usually have several kinds of milkfree breads. The baker is usually on the premises to check ingredients.

Kosher bakeries carry milkfree breads.

Most supermarkets carry specialty rye breads, most of which are milkfree; many are additive free and some are fatfree.

b. Wheatfree

Pumpernickel and other pure rye breads are often wheatfree but not glutenfree or chemical free.

Many bakeries specialize in additive-free breads.

For wheatfree diets, oat cakes and rye wafers make good substitutes.

For glutenfree diets, rice cakes and rice wafers make good substitutes.

Calcium or milkfree sources

a. Disodium phosphate
b. Calcium sandoz
c. Bone meal tablets
d. Dolomite tablets
e. Calcium gluconate

The following are also sodium-free forms of calcium which can be bought by the pound.

f. Calcium carbonate U.S.P. (It is inexpensive. Sprinkle ½ to 1 teaspoon per day in food, or put in clear gelatin capsule.)

g. Dicalcium phosphate (Ask your druggist to order it and put 7½ grains in capsule. Use 1 to 3 capsules daily.)

h. Powdered bone meal (Use ¼ teaspoon per day and increase to ½ teaspoon as tolerated. Sprinkle in food.)

Candy

Carob is a good substitute for chocolate. Look for many carob-based bars now available. Rice candy is also available in various places.

Cheese

Goat's milk cheese and sheep's milk cheese can be purchased in cheese specialty stores.

An excellent cheese substitute is "tofu," a substance made from soya. It is similar to yogurt and compares favorably with hamburger on a protein-cost basis. It is also called bean cake, bean curd, or dom foo yuen (Chinese). It can be served with meat or soya or scallions. It can be purchased in Oriental food stores, some health food stores and in supermarkets.

Coffee creamers

Watch for sodium caseinate or casein if you have milk allergy. Casein is a milk protein. One type of Coffee Rich is casein-free. Most creamers are basically coconut oil.

Cookies

Some macaroons are wheatfree.

There are many delicious eggfree and milkfree cookies. Read the labels.

Corn

Baking powder (Featherweight Brand, made by Cellu-Products has a potato starch base.)

Eggs

Jolly Joan Egg Replacer (A total substitute for eggs. Can be purchased from some health food, specialty and department stores.)

Yolkfree Egg Substitutes (for low cholesterol diets)

Egg-Beater made by Standard Foods. Warning: This product uses natural egg white and artificial egg yolk, and is not suitable for egg-free diets.

Flour

Cream of Rice. This product made by Grocery Store Products is excellent in many recipes as well as for a nutritious hot cereal, like its namesake Cream of Wheat.

Health food stores sell interesting and varied flours. Supermarkets sell a better range of flours now.

Ice Cream

If your community has any kosher food stores, inquire about milkfree ice cream.

Margarine

Mar-Parv is a milkfree margarine available in the U.S. It is made from partially hardened cottonseed oil, water, salt, mono and diglycerides, artificially colored (carotene) and flavored. 15,000 U.S.P. Vitamin A added. The Miami Margarine Co., Cincinnati, Ohio.

Diet Imperial Spread is a low-calorie product, consisting of 40 percent fat made from 100 percent vegetable oil and contains no milk products.

Fleischmann's Sweet Margarine is milkfree and sodium-free. It contains corn oil.

Soft Blue Bonnet Margarine is made with soya oil only. It contains milk.

As with any product, check labels before you purchase in case of formula changes.

Milk

Warning: Coffee creamers contain casein (milk protein). Those on lactose-free diets can usually use these creamers.

Coffee Rich (see page 83) is made from soybean and is free of sodium caseinate. It can be used in recipes.

a. Goat's Milk
   Some people can use goat's milk. Powdered goat's milk or condensed goat's milk can be purchased from some health food stores and drug stores. A few health food stores handle fresh goat's milk.
   Canned goat's milk can be purchased in any drug store and in many supermarkets.

b. Soy Milks
   Most milk substitutes are soybean based.
   Cho Free is a milkfree, sugar-free milk substitute. This is not a complete food product and should be supplemented with a suitable carbohydrate. It is designed for children with lactose intolerance and carbohydrate intolerance.
   Instant Soya Powder (Ener-G Foods)
   Nutramigen (Mead Johnson)
   Pro-Sobee (Mead Johnson)

Similac or Isomil (Ross Laboratories)
Soyalac (Loma Linda)
Soyamel (Worthington Foods)

c. Lactose Products

Lact-Aid (R) is for those with a lactose intolerance (not milk allergy). If you are not sure whether your problem is allergy or intolerance, consult your doctor. Lact-Aid (R) is an enzyme that is added to milk to make it digestible for those with lactose intolerance. Lact-Aid is available at drug stores, health food stores, etc., or write Sugar Lo Company, 600 Fire Road, P.O. Box 1100, Pleasantville, New Jersey 08232.

Natural Brand is a milk digestant tablet for those who are milk intolerant. It is taken just before a meal or ingesting of milk products. It is distributed by Natural Sales Co., P.O. Box 25, Pittsburgh, Pennsylvania 15230. It contains lactase (25 mg) and rennet (2 mg).

Mixes

Jolly Joan Products, now called Ener-G, are manufactured by Ener-G Cereal Inc., P.O. Box 24723, Seattle, Washington 98124.

Instant Soya Milk Powder	Barley Mix wheatfree
Egg Replacer	Oat Mix wheatfree
Potato Mix wheatfree, glutenfree	Rice Mix wheatfree, glutenfree, milkfree
Corn Mix wheatfree, glutenfree	Rice Bran (new product) wheatfree, glutenfree
Rice'n Rye Bread Mix wheatfree	Rice Polish (new product)

In addition to the above information, Fearn Natural Foods, a Division of Richard Foods Corp., of 4520 James Place, Melrose Park, Illinois 60160, manufactures the following products applicable for allergy diets:

Rice Baking Mix	free of wheat, corn, rye, oats and barley
Brown Rice Baking Mix	same as above
Natural soya powder	milkfree
Rice Flour	wheatfree, cornfree baking
Split Pea Soup Mix	wheatfree, cornfree
Blackbean Creole Mix	wheatfree
Bean Barley Stew Mix	wheatfree, cornfree

Loma Linda Foods of 11503 Pierce Street, Riverside, California 92515 provides a long list of food products available to the allergic:

Wheatfree:

Gravy Quik, Country Style	Gravy Quik, Mushroom

Nuteena
Sandwich Spread
Soyagens
Soyalac
i-Soyalac

Soybeans, Boston Style
Soybeans, Green
Spaghetti Sauce
Vita-Burger

Cornfree:
Dinner Cuts
Dinner Cuts NSA
Gravy Quik, Brown
Gravy Quik, Chicken
Gravy Quik, Country Style

Gravy Quik, Mushroom
Soyagen Carob
i-Soyalac
Vita-Burger

Milkfree:
All Loma Linda Products

Yeastfree:
Gravy Quik, Brown
Gravy Quik, Chicken
Gravy Quik, Country Style
Gravy Quik, Mushroom
Meatless Chili Beans
Ruskets, Biscuits
Ruskets, Bran
Ruskets, Crunchy
Ruskets, No Sugar

Soyagens
Soyalac
i-Soyalac
Soybeans, Boston Style
Soybeans, Green
Spaghetti Sauce
Vega-Scallops
Vita-Burger

With Yeast Extract Only:
Dinner Cuts
Griddle Steaks
Meatless Chicken Supreme
Nuteena
Ocean Platter

Patty Mix
Proteena
Sandwich Spread
Savory Dinner Loaf
Vege-Burger

Maltfree:
All Loma Linda Products

Eggfree:
Big Franks
Dinner Cuts
Dinner Cuts NSA
Gravy Quik, Brown
Gravy Quik, Chicken
Gravy Quik, Country Style
Gravy Quik, Mushroom
Gravy Quik, Onion
Little Links

Linketts
Meatless Chili Beans
Nuteena
Proteena
Ruskets, Biscuits
Ruskets, Bran
Ruskets, Crunchy
Ruskets, No Sugar Added
Sandwich Spread

Soyagens   Tastee Cuts
Soyalac   Tender Bits
i-Soyalac   Vege-Burger
Soybeans, Boston Style   Vege-Burger NSA
Soybeans, Green   Vegelona
Spaghetti Sauce   Vege-Scallops
Stew-Pac   Vita-Burger

Chicago Dietetic Supply, Inc., of 405 East Shawmut Avenue, La Grange, Illinois 60525, markets a line of special diet foods called Featherweight, many of which are suitable for allergy diets.

Featherweight Baking Powder   low sodium, cerealfree
Featherweight Barley Flour   wheatfree
Featherweight Corn Flour   wheatfree
Featherweight Oat Flour   wheatfree, cornfree
Featherweight Potato Starch   wheatfree, cornfree
Featherweight Rice Flour   wheatfree, cornfree
Featherweight Rye Flour   wheatfree, cornfree
Featherweight Soybean Flour   wheatfree, cornfree
Featherweight Tapioca Starch   wheatfree thickening agent
   Flour

Gerber Products Company, of 445 State Street, Fremont, Michigan 49412, has a long list of wheatfree, milkfree, eggfree, citrusfree, cornfree, glutenfree and milk-wheat-egg-citrus-free foods for allergic infants and young children.

General Foods, Inc., of 250 North Street, White Plains, New York 10625, also has lists of milkfree, corn-wheat-milk-egg-free, milk-egg-wheat-free, cornfree, milk-wheat-free, glutenfree, tartrazine-free foods among its many products.

These lists provide a valuable service to the allergic individual and are exceedingly helpful in avoiding foods that can cause their symptoms.

The Allergy Information Association in their booklet "Food Products and Where to Find Them" also discusses the following:

Oil

According to needs, look for:

Polyunsaturated vs. saturated.

Pure oils (e.g., soy, olive) vs. vegetable oils, which are a mixture of available oils.

Oils have preservatives (BHT, BHA) and additives such as anti-foamers, although some are additive-free.

Pasta

Health food stores carry soya flour noodles and macaroni.

Tacos are corn-based pasta-type products.

There are also sweet potato and potato pastas available at ethnic and health food stores.

Poi

Poi is used for helping people with allergies and digestive problems and is also good for babies who cannot tolerate grain cereals. Poi is available in grocery stores or supermarkets. If not available in your community, poi can be ordered, in a freeze-dried form, from Honolulu Poi Co., Ltd., 288 Libby Street, Honolulu, Hawaii 96819.

Soups

Most soups contain wheat/gluten. Many soups contain milk. The Featherweight groups, which are manufactured for salt-free diets, have a pea soup and stews that are cereal-free and milkfree. Look into special foods such as salt-free or sugar-free foods. While they are not specifically for your diet, they may be suitable.

Soya

Soyamel, made by Worthington Foods, a division of Miles Laboratories, Inc., produces more than forty vegetable protein foods which closely duplicate the nutrition, flavor, texture and appearance of many beef, pork and poultry products—from bacon and frankfurters to roast beef and fried chicken. These meat analogs or meatless "meats" are developed primarily from protein-rich soy and wheat, to which other proteins as well as important nutrients, flavorings and colorings are added.

Loma Linda has a line of canned, simulated meat loaf, weiners and other meatless products made of soya.

Sugar

Various sugars other than cane—beet, corn, grape or even artichoke—can usually be obtained at health food or specialty stores and perhaps among special diet products at supermarkets.

Artichoke sugar, available occasionally in Italian grocery stores, is a good sweetener. Artichoke juice to sweeten baking is more readily available.

Grape sugar, available at some health food stores, is very similar to powdered sugar in appearance.

Sugar Substitutes

Molasses or honey or maple syrup can be substituted in some diets for table sugar. Other diets require substitutes called sugar replacers such as sorbitol, mannitol or xylitol. These can be purchased at drug stores or health food outlets. Aspartame can be used to sweeten foods not requiring baking.

Vitamins

Be sure the vitamin is free of whatever you are avoiding. Your druggist may know or you may have to contact the manufacturer.

Appendix B

Sources for Allergy Diet Recipes and for Nutritional Information

"Baking for People with Food Allergies" (Home & Garden Bulletin #147)
U.S. Department of Agriculture
Superintendent of Documents
U.S. Government Printing Office
Washington, DC 20402

"Tasty Recipes, Mull Soy Liquid in Milk-free Diets"
Borden, Inc.
Pharmaceutical Products
350 Madison Avenue
New York, NY 10017

"Chemical Additives in Booze" and nutritional, additive and pesticide information
Center for Science in the Public Interest
1755 S Street
Washington, DC 20009

"Recipes for Featherweight Diet Foods" and nutritional information
Chicago Dietetic Supply, Inc.
405 East Shawmut Avenue
LaGrange, IL 60525

"Wheat-Gluten-Egg and Milk-free Recipes for Use at High Altitudes and at Sea level" by Ferne Rowman, Bulletin #5445
Colorado State University
Experiment Station
Fort Collins, CO 80523

"Soya Powder Recipes" and recipes for Rice Baking Mixes plus product nutritional fact sheets

Fearn Natural Foods
4520 James Place
Melrose Park, IL 60160

"Special Recipes and Allergy Aids"
 General Foods Consumer Center
 White Plains, NY 10625

Nutritional information
 General Mills, Inc.
 Consumer Service
 P.O. Box 1113
 Minneapolis, MN 55440

"125 Great Recipes for Allergy Diets"
 Good Housekeeping
 959 Eighth Avenue
 New York, NY 10019

"Meals Without Milk," "Creative Recipes Using Criticare HN" and
nutritional information
 Mead Johnson
 Evansville, IN 47721

"Wheat, Milk and Egg-free Recipes"
 The Quaker Oats Company
 Home Economics Department
 Merchandise Mart Plaza
 Chicago, IL 60611

"Allergy Diets"
 Ralston Purina Company
 Checkerboard Square
 St. Louis, MI 63199

Recipes using Rice Flour
 The Rice Council of America
 P.O. Box 22802
 3917 Richmond Avenue
 Houston, TX 77027

Sources

Allergy Information Association
Room 7, 25 Poynter Drive
Weston, Ontario M9R 1K8, Canada

American Allergy Association
P.O. Box 7253
Menlo Park, CA 94025

The American Dietetic Association
430 Michigan Avenue
Chicago, IL 60611

Asthma & Allergy Foundation of America
9604 Wisconsin Avenue, Suite 100
Bethesda, MD 20814

Appendix C

Additives and What They Do for Food

Glossary of Additive Classification

anti-caking agent: Keeps foods such as salt, baking powder, powdered sugar from lumping, caking or clustering by absorbing moisture.

antioxidant: Prevents oxidation, which causes foods such as butter to become rancid or fresh fruit to turn brown. Some are naturally found in foods that contain vitamin C and/or E (such as lemon juice).

color: Enhances food appeal and may be natural, but is often artificial.

emulsifier: Mixes liquids that normally separate, such as oil and vinegar. Many are derived from natural substances such as lecithin found in egg yolk or the mono and diglycerides derived from vegetables.

flavor enhancer: Magnifies or modifies food flavors, often by affecting certain nerves. MSG is a familiar example.

humectant: Retains moisture in such foods as shredded coconut, marshmallows, soft candies.

leavening agent: Makes such foods as bread and cake light and soft. Carbon dioxide is prime example.

maturing and bleaching agent: Employed mainly to whiten and mature flour to produce stable, elastic dough.

nutrient: Usually essential vitamins or minerals added to replace those lost in processing or to fortify foods to prevent diseases such as rickets or goiter.

pH control: Controls acidity and alkalinity to affect taste, texture and safety; the latter by increasing acidity of such low-acid foods as beets or by lowering acidity during the fermentation process of cocoa beans.

preservative: Preserves and extends the shelf life of many foods.

stabilizer & thickener: Absorbs water to improve texture and to prevent deterioration of volatile oils. Usually a natural substance such as gelatin or pectin.

sweetener: May be nutritive such as sucrose or non-nutritive such as saccharin.

Additives (from *FDA Consumer*, 1979 [HEW Publication #FDA 79-2115])

Acetic acid: pH control

Acetone peroxide: maturing and bleaching agent, dough conditioner

Adipic acid: pH control

Ammonium alginate: stabilizer, thickener, texturizer

Annatto extract: color

Arabinogalactan: stabilizer, thickener, texturizer

Ascorbic acid: nutrient, preservative, antioxidant

Azodicarbonamide: maturing and bleaching agent, dough conditioner

Benzoic acid: preservative

Benzoyl peroxide: maturing and bleaching agent, dough conditioner

Beta-apo-8 carotenal: color

Beta carotene: nutrient color

BHA (butylated hydroxyanisole): antioxidant

BHT (butylated hydroxytoluene): antioxidant

Butylparaben: preservative

Calcium alginate: stabilizer, thickener, texturizer

Calcium bromate: maturing and bleaching agent, dough conditioner

Calcium lactate: preservative

Calcium phosphate: leavening

Calcium propionate: preservative

Calcium silicate: anti-caking

Calcium sorbate: preservative

Canthaxanthin: color

Caramel: color

Carob bean gum: stabilizer, thickener, texturizer

Carrageenan: emulsifier, stabilizer, thickener, texturizer

Carrot oil: color

Cellulose: stabilizer, thickener, texturizer

Citric acid: preservative, antioxidant, pH control

Citrus Red #2: color

Cochineal extract: color

Corn endosperm: color

Corn syrup: sweetener

Dehydrated beets: color

Dextrose: sweetener

Diglycerides: emulsifier

Dioctyl sodium sulfosuccinate: emulsifier
Disodium guanylate: flavor enhancer
Disodium inosinate: flavor enhancer
Dried algae meal: color
EDTA (ethylenediaminetetraacetic acid): antioxidant
FD&C Blue #1: color
FD&C Red #3: color
FD&C Red #40: color
FD&C Yellow #5: color
Fructose: sweetener
Gelatin: stabilizer, thickener, texturizer
Glucose: sweetener
Glycerine: humectant
Glycerol monostearate: humectant
Grape skin extract: color
Guar gum: stabilizer, thickener, texturizer
Gum arabic: stabilizer, thickener, texturizer
Gum ghatti: stabilizer, thickener, texturizer
Heptylparaben: preservative
Hydrogen peroxide: maturing and bleaching agent, dough conditioner
Hydrolyzed vegetable protein: flavor enhancer
Invert sugar: sweetener
Iodine: nutrient
Iron: nutrient
Iron-ammonium citrate: anti-caking
Iron oxide: color
Karaya gum: stabilizer, thickener, texturizer
Lactic acid: pH control preservative
Larch gum: stabilizer, thickener, texturizer
Lecithin: emulsifier
Locust bean gum: stabilizer, thickener, texturizer
Mannitol: sweetener, anti-caking, stabilizer, thickener, texturizer
Methylparaben: preservative
Modified food starch: stabilizer, thickener, texturizer
Monoglycerides: emulsifier
MSG (monosodium glutamate): flavor enhancer
Niacinamide: nutrient
Paprika (and oleoresin): flavor, color
Pectin: stabilizer, thickener, texturizer
Phosphates: pH control
Phosphoric acid: pH control
Polysorbates: emulsifiers
Potassium alginate: stabilizer, thickener, texturizer
Potassium bromate: maturing and bleaching agent, dough conditioner
Potassium iodide: nutrient
Potassium propionate: preservative

Potassium sorbate: preservative
Propionic acid: preservative
Propyl gallate: antioxidant
Propylene glycol: stabilizer, thickener, texturizer, humectant
Propylparaben: preservative
Riboflavin: nutrient, color
Saccharin: sweetener
Saffron: color, flavor
Silicon dioxide: anti-caking
Sodium alginate: stabilizer, thickener, texturizer
Sodium aluminum sulfate: leavening
Sodium benzoate: preservative
Sodium bicarbonate: leavening
Sodium calcium alginate: stabilizer, thickener, texturizer
Sodium citrate: pH control
Sodium diacetate: preservative
Sodium erythorbate: preservative
Sodium nitrate: preservative
Sodium nitrite: preservative
Sodium propionate: preservative
Sodium sorbate: preservative
Sodium stearyl fumarate: maturing and bleaching agent, dough
  conditioner
Sorbic acid: preservative
Sorbitan monostearate: emulsifier
Sorbitol: humectant, sweetener
Spices: flavor
Sucrose (table sugar): sweetener
Tagetes: color
Tartaric acid: pH control
TBHQ (tertiary butyl hydroquinone): antioxidant
Thiamine: nutrient
Titanium dioxide: color
Toasted, partially defatted cooked cottonseed flour: color
Tocopherols (vitamin E): nutrient, antioxidant
Tragacanth gum: stabilizer, thickener, texturizer
Turmeric (oleoresin): flavor, color
Ultramarine blue: color
Vanilla, vanillin: flavor
Vitamin A: nutrient
Vitamin C (ascorbic acid): nutrient, preservative, antioxidant
Vitamin D (D_2, D_3): nutrient
Vitamin E (tocopherols): nutrient
Yeast-malt sprout extract: flavor enhancer
Yellow prussiate of soda: anti-caking

Appendix D

A Partial List of Where Sulfites Might Be Found

The following sulfiting agents can be found in some foods and medicines:

sodium bisulfite	sulfur dioxide
potassium sulfite	metabisulfite
sodium sulfite	

As an example, metabisulfite can be encountered in:

shrimp	beer
dried fruits	wine
French fries	restaurant salads and fresh fruits
potato chips	medicines

Appendix E

Allergenic Possibilities in Alcoholic Beverages

Beer

yeast	hops
malted barley	salt
corn	barley
rice	gelatin
dextrin	clarifiers: fish glue, egg white
ascorbic acid	metabisulfite

Wine

grapes	sugar
yeast	clarifiers: fish glue, egg white
other fruits	metabisulfite

Brandy (and distilled wine)

fruit (usually grapes)	yeast
sugar	flavorings
caramel	clarifiers

Whiskey

corn and other cereal grains	yeast
malt enzymes	flavorings
caramel	

(Canadian whiskey and bourbon have a good deal of corn; Irish whiskey a good deal of barley; Scotch whiskey sometimes corn.)

Gin
 English gin (usually wheat) juniper berries
 American gin (usually corn) sugar
 Dutch gin (usually malt wine) aromatic botanical substances

Vodka
 American vodka (usually corn) French vodka (usually potato)
 English vodka (usually wheat)

Rum
 sugar cane products (molasses) brandy (sometimes)
 yeast sake (usually rice)
 flavorings tequila (usually maguey,
 caramel a Mexican plant)
 liqueurs (usually whiskey or brandy or neutral spirits, fruit products, herbs and spices)

Appendix F

Dietary Suggestions in Migraine*

Avoid alcohol, particularly red wines and champagne.

Avoid aged or strong cheese, particulary Cheddar cheese.

Avoid chicken livers, pickled herring, canned figs, pods of broad beans.

Use monosodium glutamate sparingly.

Avoid cured meats, such as hot dogs, bacon, ham and salami, if these can be demonstrated to evoke vascular headache.

Eat three well-balanced meals a day. Avoid skipping meals, prolonged fasting or eating excessive amounts of carbohydrates at any single meal.

*Reprinted from the American Family Physician, *December, 1972; by Donald J. Dalessio, M.D., Head, Division of Neurology, Scripps Clinical and Research Foundation, La Jolla, Calif. 92037.*

Appendix G

Labels and What They Tell You

Ingredient Information:

The common or usual name of each ingredient in a food must be on the label in descending order by weight.

Example: Chicken soup (mythical)

chicken, water, noodles, salt, BHT, artificial colors and flavors

Artificial colors, with the exception of FD&C yellow #5 (tartrazine), need not be identified, but other additives must be named. In addition, certain foods, such as butter or ice cream, do not have to include artificial color on their labels and so-called "standardized" foods, such as catsup and mayonnaise, need not label their ingredients unless they employ optional ingredients other than the standard or mandatory ingredients set by the FDA. At least, at this writing, such a regulation covering optional ingredients is in the works.

Nutritional Information (necessary if a nutrient is added or a nutritional claim made):

This information is provided on a per-serving basis, with the serving defined.

Example: Nutrition Information
(Per Serving)
Serving Size = 1 oz.
Servings Per Container = 6
Calories 100 grams
Protein 3 grams
Carbohydrate 30 grams
Fat 1 gram
Percentage of U.S. Recommended Daily Allowances (US RDA's)
Protein 2
Thiamine 6
Niacin 1

Nutrition labels can be much more complete with a listing of vitamins and minerals, cholesterol, fatty acids and sodium (mandatory if claims are made as to amounts).

Appendix H

Foods to Avoid if You Are Allergic to Mold

Bread made with yeast
Bakery goods made with yeast
Melons, especially cantaloupe
Pastrami, pickled tongue, corned beef and other pickled meats
Smoked meats
Smoked salmon and other smoked fish
Beer, wine, yeast-containing cider
Buttermilk, sour cream, cottage cheese, hard and soft cheeses
Vinegar, mayonnaise, catsup and other products containing
    vinegar such as pickles, salad dressing, relish, sauerkraut

Appendix I

Foods to Avoid if You Are Allergic to Aspirin

Foods Containing Natural Salicylates:
    Prunes, peaches and plums
    Blueberries, raspberries, strawberries
    Apricots, cherries, currants
    Fresh grapes or raisins in wine or vinegar
    Nectarines

Foods with Added Salicylates:
    Bakery goods with the exception of bread
    Candy and chewing gum
    Ice cream
    Jell-O
    Soft drinks
    Jam
    Wintergreen
    Cake mixes

Appendix J

Books That Could Be Helpful

Allergy Information Association
The Allergy Cookbook (Diets Unlimited for Limited Diets, revised)
(Toronto, Ontario, Canada: Methuen Publications, 1983)

C. A. V. Barker
Recipes Containing Goat Products
(Toronto, Ontario, Canada: Coach House Press, 1972)

Claude A. Frazier
Parents' Guide to Allergy in Children
(Garden City, N.Y.: Doubleday, 1973)

Psychosomatic Aspects of Allergy
(New York: Van Nostrand Reinhold Co., 1977)

Coping & Living with Allergies
(Englewood Cliffs, N.J.: Prentice-Hall, Inc., 1980)

Becky Hamrick
The Eggfree, Milkfree, Wheatfree Cookbook
(Dallas: Cygnus Press, 1982)

Jacqueline E. Hostage
Living Without Milk
(New York: Betterway Publications, 1981)

Suzanne S. Lacey
The Allergic Person's Cookbook
(Springfield, Ill.: Charles C. Thomas, 1981)

Edith Piltz
Bland but Grand
(Garden City, N.Y.: Doubleday, 1970)

Doris J. Rapp
Allergies and the Hyperactive Child
(New York: Cornerstone Publications, 1980)

Phyllis Robb
Cooking for Hyperactive and Allergic Children
(Fort Wayne, Ind.: Cedar Creek Publishers, 1980)

Carol Rudoff
The Allergy Baker
Menlo Park, Calif.: Prologue Publications, 1980)

The Allergy Gourmet
(Menlo Park, Calif.: Prologue Publications, 1982)

Linda L. Thomas
  Caring and Cooking for the Allergic Child
  (New York: Sterling Publishing Company, 1980)

Marion Wood
  Delicious and Easy Rice Flour Recipes
  (Springfield, Ill.: Charles C. Thomas, 1972)

  Gourmet Food on a Wheat-free Diet
  (Springfield, Ill.: Charles C. Thomas, 1979)

  Good Housekeeping Special Diet Cookbook
  (Des Moines: Hearst Books, 1982)

Index